DEPRESSION DESPERADO

The Chronicle of Raymond Hamilton

By

Sid Underwood

EAKIN PRESS Fort Worth, Texas

For my wife, Teresa,
and in memory of my mother,
Pearl Alspaugh Bodine.

Copyright © 1995
By Sid Underwood
Published in the United States of America
By Eakin Press
An Imprint of Wild Horse Media Group
P.O. Box 331779
Fort Worth, Texas 76163
1-888-982-8270
www.EakinPress.com
ALL RIGHTS RESERVED
1 2 3 4 5 6 7 8 9
ISBN-10: 0890159661
ISBN-13: 978-0890159668

Library of Congress Cataloging-in-Publication Data
Underwood, Sid.
    Depression desperado : the chronicle of Raymond Hamilton / by Sid
Underwood — 1st ed.
      p.   cm.
    Includes bibliographical references (p.   ) and index.
    ISBN 0-89015-966-1
    1. Hamilton, Raymond, 1913–1935. 2. Thieves — Texas — Dallas —
Biography. 3. Bank robberies — Texas. 4. Depressions — 1929 — United
States. 5. United States — Social conditions — 1933–1945. I. Title.
HV6653.H36U53   1995
364.1'523'09764169 — dc20   95-30247
                                                                  CIP

Contents

Preface

"They's a lotta meanness back in them days."

Sitting around the Dearborn heater on a winter evening or on the front porch on a summer night, I have heard relatives and friends who lived during the Great Depression say the above many times. I had seen the movies, read the books. I knew there was "meanness" back then. John Dillinger, Bonnie and Clyde, Baby Face Nelson, Pretty Boy Floyd, Machine Gun Kelly, Al Capone. But invariably these conversations included another name: Raymond Hamilton. Ol' Raymond this and ol' Raymond that. My elders mentioned him for an obvious reason. For a time in his youth he lived in the same area of southwest Dallas County they lived in. They had seen him — some had known him.

Raymond Hamilton was one of the best-known desperadoes of the 1930s. His 1934 escape from the Texas state prison at Huntsville made the front page of *The New York Times*. This effort chronicles Hamilton's life from humble beginnings in Oklahoma to an early demise in the Texas death house. And finally, there is the matter of Raymond's ghost. He swore he would return to haunt those he felt had wronged him. So please do me a favor. If you are ever on a lonely Texas road at night and a 1934 Ford roars by, please wave it down. I want an interview.

Foreword

In the early 1930s, Raymond Hamilton, a diminutive Texas delinquent from the crime-ridden slums of West Dallas, went in just four years from being a runt bicycle thief to America's Public Enemy #1. Hamilton's amazing story, chock-full of a decade of carefully researched action-packed detail, has at last surfaced in this chronicle by Texas author Sid Underwood.

Jump-started by cronies Clyde Barrow and Bonnie Parker, Raymond Hamilton's meteoric career consisted of more robberies than anyone will ever know. His specialty was banks, his trademark to lock employees inside their own steel vaults — an M.O. that would be copy-catted by a plethora of wanna-be Hamiltons. He also pulled off four Houdini-like jailbreaks — one, the great Huntsville break, becoming the most spectacular and damaging to penal PR in the history of our federal and state joints to that time.

His territory was Texas and adjoining states, but after a heist he ranged as far as Michigan till the heat cooled down. While he was front page news in *The New York Times*, the hometown boy's Texas papers were only too happy to print his letters to the editor so that the public would "know his side of the story."

A charmer to strangers as well as friends, Underwood tells us, Hamilton was a dapper dresser, a ladies' man, and by the protocol of the day could be a real gentleman to his victims. He had so many friends and relatives in his pocket that forty people were indicted for hindering his capture. His biggest supporter, besides possibly his moll Mary O'Dare, was his older brother Floyd, so sucked in by Ray that he himself later went on to earn top spot on America's most wanted list.

Involved in one gun battle after another, Hamilton insisted to the end that he had never killed a person. It was a point of pride that his robberies be clean, cost-effective, and of high calibre; no low raps were pinned on Hamilton without the felon firing off a letter to his editors. By the time he was brought down at a callow twenty-one, he had been sentenced to several hundred years in prison. Embarrassing to the penal system, one main argument for Hamilton's death sentence was that no jail could hold him. A fuming prosecutor declared that giving the punk another life sentence would be like throwing a bucket of water in Lake Dallas.

Raymond Hamilton's story is in many ways more informative and fascinating than those of the cold-blooded killers of his times. This is why: he was relatable, even identifiable, to a huge number of beaten-down Americans who themselves were just a belt-notch away from taking up crime instead of more cold cornbread and salty gravy.

True crime writing has always enjoyed a large audience. We have a real craving to explore, one step removed, the netherworld of human nature. The best crime stories give us insight into the criminal mind and, by reflection, can help us understand ourselves and the mess our society is in. Writers in the genre have long known that if their main character is in some way sympathetic, their audience will more easily accept any inherent moral or message.

That is precisely what Sid Underwood has done with *Depression Desperado: The Chronicle of Raymond Hamilton*. Hamilton, though certainly notorious enough in his day, has not yet been appropriately celebrated in our modern media. He differed from his sidekicks Bonnie and Clyde in many ways, two especially notable: he was a better criminal and wasn't a mad-dog murderer. The simple-minded Clyde Barrow found lasting infamy partly because of Bonnie Parker, whose skill at writing newspaper poesy created such a romantic misconception of life on the run that their story finally was exploited by Hollywood. Mostly in passing, Underwood tells the real Bonnie and Clyde story, a service to anyone gullible enough to confuse the creepy duo with their slick Hollywood counterparts.

Contemporary of John Dillinger, Pretty Boy Floyd, and Machine Gun Kelly, Hamilton did more than his share to change the whole approach to law enforcement in this country. With fast cars bristling with automatic weapons, he and his pals forced law enforcement to upgrade their methods and learn to cooperate with one another. Effective communication between states was developed. Weak links in the prison system, such as guards on the take, were fixed. Swift justice and stiffer penalties were put in place; riding the lightning became a killer thug's greatest and very real fear. Also, a beleaguered citizenry became cooperative, reporting suspects and contributing large amounts of reward money.

Possibly the greatest change in federal law enforcement to halt the Depression desperadoes was active prosecution of friends and kin who harbored their blacksheep relatives. Family members by the droves, mothers included, were fined and jailed for impeding justice. Left to their own devices, miserably alone and on the run, life became brutally hard on criminals; their capture or surrender seldom long in coming. Raymond Hamilton's support from the private sector was the secret of his success; once it was taken away, it was his downfall.

Here is the essential social message that Underwood drives home: Though Hamilton may have come across as a regular guy, the sort who could make his way through life without robbing banks, he was different from the straight world in profound and fundamental ways. Hamilton was a classic case of arrested development, a child raised without discipline among people who themselves walked the line between right and wrong. Early on, he took to a life of crime and rebellion. He always was outside law-abiding society, just happening to want its adoration anyway. Every wrongful act he committed for personal gain had devastating consequences on his victims. Any sappy citizenry taken in by his media-enhanced boyish charm and plays for sympathy soon had to face that they were being robbed, kidnapped, locked in bank safes, and threatened with their lives. So in the end, it was public outcry and public support of the system that brought down the fair-haired boy.

Sid Underwood has written a non-sensational, dispassionate account of the life of Raymond Hamilton which is also a mirror of the time in which his candle briefly burned. Perhaps Underwood's return to an earlier era — when we still had the ability to recognize aberrancy if not control it — will give us a sharper focus on the incredible crime-ridden folly of our own hard times.

— WILLIAM ALLEN
Pulitzer Prize nominee
and author of bestselling
Starkweather: Portrait of a Mass Murderer

CHICKEN-FRIED CAGNEY — A Dallas Police Department mug shot of Raymond Hamilton could be a real-life southern version of the gangster parts played by Jimmy Cagney. — Photo courtesy Dallas Public Library

CHAPTER I

The Incubation of a Bad Egg

On May 21, 1913, a blond-haired, blue-eyed boy was born to John and Alice Hamilton in a tent on the banks of the Deep Fork River near Schulter, Oklahoma. They named him Raymond Elzie.

John and Alice had met in eastern Oklahoma, just across the line from Van Buren, Arkansas, and had married in 1904. Lillie, their first daughter, had been born in 1906. Their first son, Floyd, had arrived in 1908, and their second daughter, Lucy, three years later. At that time John was working at a lead smelting and mining company near Henryetta, Oklahoma.

John had quit the lead company in 1912 and bought some timberland along the Deep Fork River near Schulter. The family lived in two tents. John opened a sawmill and hired several millhands and loggers. A wife of one of the millhands served as midwife when Raymond Hamilton was born. John supplemented the sawmill income by doing custom farming during harvest. This work carried him from Texas to the Canadian border.

By 1915 John got the urge to try something different and moved his family to a farm north of Muskogee, Oklahoma. The farm was not in good shape, but the Hamiltons were glad to leave the mosquito-infested river bottoms. John continued to work the harvest trail when not working the Muskogee farm. Lillie, Floyd, and Lucy attended school at a one-room schoolhouse some three miles from the farm. Daughters Maggie and Audrey were born during this time.

The desire to open another sawmill caused John to gather his family and leave the Muskogee farm. He purchased land along the

1

Verdigris River, northwest of Wagoner, Oklahoma, and again set up a sawmill and hired several hands. The three oldest children attended a nearby school. Everything seemed to be going well with the sawmill operation and the Hamilton family until one day, when John and several sawmill workers went to Wagoner. John did not return.

The next morning a distraught Alice Hamilton got word from one of the millhands that John had run off with a local prostitute he had been seeing for some time. Also, he had mortgaged the sawmill and taken all the family's money. It was January 1919.

R. T. Paine, a friend of the Hamiltons during their Muskogee days, let Alice and the children move into a small, two-room shack on his farm. Alice, Lillie, and Floyd did odd jobs for Mr. Paine to earn their rent and to manage a subsistence living. Alice refused to divorce John, even though several local men had proposed to her.

Alice's faith that John would eventually contact her was rewarded in 1902. He was in Dallas and wanted the family to join him. Alice and the children, taking little more than the clothes on their back, boarded the first train to Dallas.

Dallas, like all cities, had rich areas and poor areas and among the latter was a poor stepchild of a neighborhood called West Dallas. Lean-to shacks and tents were more common than houses, and when the Hamilton family arrived in 1920 West Dallas was unincorporated. There were no city services such as water, sewage, and electricity. John Hamilton welcomed his family into a small frame rent house that had a kitchen, living room, and two bedrooms. John had a job at Wyatt Metal and Boiler Company on West Commerce Street.

It did not take the older Hamilton children long to realize West Dallas was far different from rural Oklahoma. Lillie, Floyd, Lucy, and Raymond enrolled at West Dallas High School, which included the primary grades. The three-story building was more than a little imposing after their experience in one-room schools in Oklahoma. Raymond had no desire to attend school, and his mother had to spank him to get him to go. The school was in an area even the hardened West Dallasites considered "rough." Floyd and Raymond were quickly introduced to a world of bullies and switchblades.

Even though West Dallas was culture shock for the Hamiltons, Alice tried to make the best of it. A devout Christian, she took the children to church every Sunday. John was no help because he would have nothing to do with church and was not overly concerned with education. Between 1920 and 1923, John moved his family several times and the children attended several different West Dallas and Oak Cliff schools.

Late in 1923 John Hamilton once again deserted his family. He left no message but did leave an almost new Oakland automobile. Alice and the older children were now faced with how to make a living. Floyd, now fourteen, worked seven days a week for a truck farmer and earned $1.50 a day — not enough to support the family. Floyd sought and found a higher paying job with the Trinity Portland Cement Company in West Dallas, earning thirty cents an hour. Alice worked odd jobs at a dairy and a laundry to help supplement Floyd's income. Floyd eventually decided to quit his cement company job and find his father. The search led him to Baytown, Texas, where John was working for the Kellogg Construction Company. The oldest Hamilton boy joined his father building oil refineries on the Gulf Coast. The pay was good but the work was dirty and hard. Floyd decided to return to Dallas.

When he returned, Floyd took a job with the V. C. Bilbo Truck Line and met a young man named Walter Siddall, who had an older in-law named Steve Davis. The friendship of Floyd and Walter led to the meeting of the now-divorced Alice Hamilton and Steve Davis. Following a brief courtship Steve and Alice married in 1927.

Davis was hardly a saint. One of his specialties was stealing chickens and turkeys. In one such incident that occurred in the Florence Hill community, south of Grand Prairie, Texas, a local farmer had some turkeys but he also had a bulldog that would bark at anything. The farmer was a very light sleeper, but Steve and his friends had a solution — a week before the turkey raid, they stole the bulldog. Local police soon discovered the thieves, and Steve found himself in court. During the trial the turkey farmer had a request of the judge.

"Now, Judge," the farmer said, "ask him how he steals them turkeys and don't let 'em holler. I know them turkeys didn't holler or I'd heard 'em."

The judge asked Steve how he accomplished the theft without having the turkeys alarm the farmer.

"Hell, Judge, didn't you ever steal no turkeys?" Steve asked, laughing.

"No, I never did — how did you steal them without making them holler?"

"You just put a 'tater over their bill, Judge, and they cain't holler," Steve said. "Then you just cross their wings and throw 'em out on the ground."

Steve and Alice lived in West Dallas and also lived briefly in Oklahoma. Raymond, Maggie, and Audrey were still with their mother but by now Floyd, Lucy, and Lillie had married and were living on their own. Alice's marriage to Steve Davis had a detrimental effect on Raymond's life. Steve and Raymond feuded, and the fourteen-year-old never again lived at home on a regular basis. Following these arguments Raymond would take to the streets, selling newspapers and doing odd jobs to feed himself. At times he would stay with relatives or friends, but often he would sleep in the back alleys or the river bottoms when the weather was nice.

Floyd Hamilton more and more was beginning to care for Raymond. The elder brother arranged for Raymond to get food on credit from a local grocery and for him to borrow money from a local man who ran a gas station. Floyd also made sure Raymond's debts were settled each Saturday after he received his paycheck.

Raymond hawked the *Dallas Dispatch* newspaper, the local scandal sheet that specialized in sensationalizing crime news. The newsboys had an easy time selling the paper on the streets of Dallas, even though many citizens derisively referred to the publication as the "Dallas Disgrace." While scrambling to make money, and to avoid Steve Davis and truant officers, Raymond mastered the ways of the streets. He made friends easily with the West Dallas crowd and early on learned how not to be an easy mark for the toughs and shysters. Raymond longed to have a truck-driving job like Floyd's, but was too young.

Steve and Alice tired of the West Dallas life and decided to move to the country in southwest Dallas County. They moved in with Steve's sister, Roxie Goldman, and her husband, Ben. The Goldman place was between Florence Hill and Cedar Hill. Because there was not enough room in the house, Alice, Steve, and the three children set up house in tents in the yard. Raymond and his sisters played with the children and stepchildren of the Goldmans in the pastures and creek bottoms of the area. The children now had a wholesome place to play along with a diet of fresh garden vegetables, milk, and eggs. On Sundays there was always the eagerly anticipated fried chicken dinner. Raymond was fond of his Aunt Roxie, and she treated him as one of her own. But this relationship was not enough to keep Raymond from returning to West Dallas when he fought with Steve Davis. Then, when things got tough in West Dallas, Raymond would return to the Goldmans.

Raymond attended the Florence Hill community school periodically while sisters Maggie and Audrey went regularly. Raymond played hooky as often as he could get away with it. He got along well enough with his schoolmates but made little effort to learn. Small for his age, Ray was always one of the last chosen to play ball at recess.

Alice and Steve decided to move to a house several miles east of the Goldman place, near Duncanville. The girls went to school in Duncanville, but Raymond refused to go. He would stay at home for a while and then a fight with Steve would send him back to West Dallas.

After some months in Duncanville, Steve got the moving urge again. He began to truck farm the Mountain Creek bottoms across the road from the Goldman place. Davis hooked an old Model T engine to a pipeline and drew water from Mountain Creek to water his vegetables, cotton, cantaloupes, and watermelons. This farm was home to the Davises from 1928 to 1932. Raymond spent some time at the farm but mostly stayed in West Dallas, making money by stealing bicycles. He would sell the bicycles at a shop in Dallas owned by R. A. "Smoot" Schmid. West Dallas youths knew the shop would buy the bicycles with no questions asked. Petty bicycle theft would soon be a thing of the past for Raymond Hamilton.

CHAPTER II

The Beginnings of Infamy

During the twenties Raymond Hamilton met and became friends with two people who would become a major part of his life: Clyde Barrow and Bonnie Parker. Barrow was born March 24, 1909, on a tenant farm near Telico, Texas, some thirty miles southeast of Dallas. He was named Clyde Chestnut Barrow, the middle name an indication of his hair color. During his criminal career his middle name was sometimes listed as "Champion" in crime records and newspapers. His parents, Henry and Cumie Barrow, had eight children.

In 1922 Henry Barrow decided to quit tenant farming and moved his family to West Dallas. For a time Clyde attended the Cedar Valley School, his only formal education. When Barrow became old enough to date, his crime career got started. He rented a car to make a trip to see his girlfriend Anne, who was visiting relatives in San Augustine, Texas. Barrow did not return the car to Dallas on time, and when the police came to claim it he panicked and ran. The police fired warning shots at Clyde, but he escaped and stole a car at Broaddus, Texas. Barrow, at seventeen, managed to get out of both situations without a fine or sentence.

Soon after the car incident Clyde and his older brother, Buck, were caught with a carload of stolen turkeys. Buck took the blame and received one week in jail. Not long after the turkey theft Clyde stole a car in Oklahoma. He brought it back to Dallas to remove the paint and identification numbers. His older sister, Nell, who was living with him, confronted him about the theft and a violent argument ensued. Nell left and went back to live with her mother. Clyde could not pay the rent when Nell moved, so he moved in with a friend who had an extensive criminal record — Frank Clause. Car theft and safecracking became Barrow's methods of making a living. In October 1929, Clyde, Buck, and a man named Sidney Moore robbed a safe in Denton, Texas. In the chase following the robbery Buck received a flesh wound. He was convicted and sent to state prison at Huntsville. Moore received a ten-year sentence, but Buck once again tried to take the blame to take heat off Clyde. Authorities were in no mood to go easy on the younger Barrow as they had evidence of crimes he had committed in Sherman and Waco, Texas. It was during this period that Clyde met a diminutive, blue-eyed blonde named Bonnie Parker.

Bonnie Parker was born October 1, 1910, at Rowena, Texas, between Ballinger and San Angelo. Bonnie was two years younger than her brother, Hubert (Buster) Parker, and three years older than her sister, Billie. Her father was a bricklayer, and the family led an average middle-class life. When Mr. Parker died in 1914, Mrs. Parker, whose first name was Emma, was faced with no way to make a living in Rowena. Her mother invited her to come live with her in Cement City, the part of West Dallas located near the cement plant. Emma accepted and moved her brood to Dallas, got a job, and left the baby-sitting to her mother.

In January of 1930 Bonnie, already married and divorced, went to live with a girlfriend in West Dallas. The girl had broken one of her arms, and the unemployed Bonnie agreed to help with house-work in exchange for room and board. This girl was a friend of a West Dallas ruffian named Clyde Barrow, and one evening he came calling while Bonnie was there. Clyde and Bonnie fell for each other after their chance meeting and soon were almost inseparable.

Raymond Hamilton's transient ways in Dallas County continued into the thirties. In 1931 the eighteen-year-old got a job building the levee on the Trinity River, a flood-control project providing jobs for many who had lost their employment due to the Depression. Raymond worked sixteen-hour days driving a Caterpillar tractor and a water truck. The long work days on the levee were keeping Hamilton out of trouble with the law. Then, one September Sunday in 1931, one of his West Dallas pals, Floyd Vincent, offered Ray a ride in a Buick he said he had bought. Vincent had actually stolen the vehicle in McKinney, Texas, and in the back of the car were four tires Vincent had stolen off a gravel truck. He told Raymond he had bought the

tires and wanted to resell them. Hamilton was suspicious about the
tires but believed Vincent's story about the car.

Raymond loved cars and readily accepted an invitation to drive
the Buick. While driving around West Dallas the car was spotted by
Dallas sheriff's officers who had been alerted by McKinney authorities to be on the lookout for such a car. Raymond's worst fears were
realized when the officers stopped the car, but he said nothing to the
officers to prove his innocence. He found himself in jail and was
assigned a court-appointed attorney. Since it was his first felony conviction, Hamilton received a three-year suspended sentence in a Dallas
court after agreeing to enter a guilty plea for theft of the tires.

Waiting outside the Dallas court were two McKinney officers
who arrested Raymond and took him to Collin County to stand
trial for theft of the Buick. He knew he couldn't prove his innocence
without breaking the West Dallas code of silence and squeal on
Vincent. Hamilton kept quiet, but this conviction landed him in the
McKinney jail.

While in jail, Ray bribed a trusty to get some hacksaw blades.
Earlier he had requested a radio, which he played as loudly as possible to mask the sawing sound. He and a larger cellmate sawed all
night long but could only make a hole large enough for Hamilton.
As the jailer made his rounds the following morning a prisoner several cells down from Raymond's said he was sick. While the jailer
checked the prisoner, Raymond slipped through the hole that had
been sawed and walked into the hallway that led out of the jail. As he
walked into the jail office one of the secretaries saw him and screamed.
Hamilton raced out the door to freedom on January 27, 1932. A
large manhunt failed to catch the West Dallas youth.

Raymond hitchhiked his way to Bay City, Michigan, where his
father was working with the Kellogg Construction Company. The
bitter winter weather in Michigan was too much for Hamilton, and
by March he had made his way back to West Dallas. Ray put out the
word on the West Dallas grapevine: he wanted to see Clyde Barrow.

Clyde had been out of prison only a month when he got word
Raymond Hamilton was looking for him. Barrow had been serving
time at the Eastham prison farm near Weldon, Texas, for various robbery convictions. The inmates at Eastham worked dawn to dusk in
the fields and in the timberlands as woodcutters. Those who failed
to keep up were sometimes beaten by the highriders and guards.
Barrow could not gut it out and took a way out used by others. While
cutting wood he convinced a fellow prisoner to chop off two of his
toes with an ax, knowing his injury would ensure removal from
Eastham.

Before Clyde's stunt, Buck Barrow shocked Texas prison authorities on December 27, 1931, when he voluntarily returned to Huntsville to serve time he still owed after escaping earlier. Buck explained to the incredulous officials that he had married following his escape and that his wife, Blanche, upon finding out he was an escapee, demanded he return to serve his time. The older Barrow brother swore he would keep his record clean after serving his time.

While rehabilitating from his foot injury, Clyde learned that Governor Ross Sterling had signed his parole papers. On February 2, 1932, he returned to his family and Bonnie. She was convinced he would go straight. Clyde's sister Nell had lined up a job for him with a construction company in Worcester, Massachusetts. By the end of February he was on the job, but he didn't like it. He was back in Dallas by mid-March. Over the protests of Bonnie, Clyde and a young man he had met in prison, Ralph Fults, planned a robbery in Kaufman, Texas, east of Dallas. The robbery attempt, made on March 22, 1932, was foiled by Kaufman County officers. Following a chase through pastures and down muddy roads, the lawmen managed to capture Bonnie but Barrow and Fults escaped.

When Clyde and Fults returned to West Dallas they made contact with Raymond Hamilton. A decision was made to rob the Sims Oil Company office in Dallas. Three days after the failed robbery attempt in Kaufman, the three West Dallas men entered the oil company offices brandishing pistols. Barrow and Fults ordered the safe opened, but there was almost no money in it. Barrow cursed their luck and they retreated from the office. Back in West Dallas, Clyde and Fults decided to lay low for a while, and Raymond decided to try to make another go of it in Michigan.

Once again Hamilton worked a little as he went, and arrived in Bay City on April 12, 1932, resuming his duties as a waterboy for the construction company. He soon tired of this and decided to head back to Texas.

With Raymond Hamilton hauling water in Michigan and Bonnie Parker in jail in Kaufman, Clyde Barrow was without his brain trust. He teamed up with two West Dallas men, Bud Russell and another man, and on April 30, 1932, they plotted a robbery. That Saturday was a beautiful spring day in North Central Texas. In Hillsboro, Texas, J. N. Bucher, sixty-one-year-old owner of a jewelry store, was preparing for another slow day of Depression-era business. Barrow had worked with Bucher's son at an auto top company in Dallas. He knew the old man had a jewelry store-pawnshop. The business and location seemed vulnerable; without Raymond and Bonnie, Clyde needed an easy job. He and his two partners made the sixty-mile trip to Hillsboro. They arrived early in the day to case the Bucher business, and while Barrow stayed in the car one of the other men went in, supposedly to buy guitar strings. Barrow waited outside because he was afraid he might be recognized by Mrs. Bucher, who had seen him on occasion with her son. Clyde's accomplice did not buy the strings, and the three drove out in the country to await nightfall.

Shortly before midnight, Barrow, Russell, and the other man returned to Hillsboro and drove in front of the Bucher business. Clyde was driving and remained in the car while the others got out and knocked on the door of the establishment, which also served as the Buchers' home. They shouted that they had returned to purchase the guitar strings. Bucher, aroused from his sleep, came downstairs and let the two in. He went to the back of the store to get the strings and was followed by Russell and the other man. After getting the strings and returning to the front of the store, one of the men pulled out a $10 bill. Bucher did not have change, so he called his wife downstairs to open the safe. The old man, already suspicious, was eyeing the men as his wife came downstairs. The men seemed nervous and Bucher thought he saw a pistol on one of them. He had a pistol under his housecoat and decided to show it. One of the men was much too quick, however, and drew his gun and shot Bucher through the heart. Mrs. Bucher screamed and fell over her dying husband, reaching for his pistol at the same time. Barrow's friends forced her to drop the gun and open the safe, from which they got $40. Clyde heard the shot and thought it an eternity before Russell and the other man came out of the store. The three sped off, leaving death and national headlines behind. Barrow now had blood on his hands.

The next day law enforcement officers combed North Texas for some young desperadoes who had killed one of Hillsboro's best known citizens. The killers seemed to vanish, and lawmen were stumped as to where they could have gone. A check with Dallas officers produced mug shots of two young West Dallas men: Raymond Hamilton and Clyde Barrow. Could they be involved? Dallas lawmen did not know their whereabouts, so they were considered suspects.

Raymond arrived in West Dallas from Michigan several days after the Bucher murder. When he found out through the grapevine he was wanted for questioning in connection with the slaying, he was shocked. He made connections with Barrow and got the lowdown. Raymond and Clyde decided to hide out in West Dallas and in the remote Mountain Creek bottoms south of town while the manhunt was on. Bonnie Parker was still in jail in Kaufman, wondering why she ever got mixed up with the likes of Clyde Barrow.

Finally, on June 17, 1932, the Kaufman County grand jury met and no-billed Bonnie. She returned to her mother and vowed she was through with Clyde.

Raymond and Clyde bided their time, living hand to mouth, hoping against hope the law would give up trying to catch them. Toward the end of June, they decided to leave the Dallas area and moved to Wichita Falls, Texas, where they rented a cottage. They had little money, but the small living quarters required only a small monthly rent. Bonnie could not stand life without Clyde and shortly she joined her lover and Raymond. The three lived a relatively normal life for several weeks, but finally Raymond and Clyde needed money. They decided not to commit any robberies in the Wichita Falls area.

On July 16, 1932, Raymond and Clyde pulled into Palestine, Texas. Roy Evans, a bookkeeper for the Palestine Ice Company, was in his office going over business when confronted by the pistol-wielding Hamilton and Barrow. They forced him to open the company safe, remove its contents, and then made him go with them as they drove out of town. They demanded Evans' money and beat him when he resisted. They then released Evans and headed back to Wichita Falls with nearly $1,000.

Flushed with success, Raymond and Clyde struck again eleven days later. Once again they hit southeast Texas, and this time Bonnie accompanied them and waited in the getaway car. On July 27 Raymond and Clyde walked into the First State Bank of Willis. With their firearms trained on the bank employees, they demanded money be placed in a sack. Then they did something that was to become Raymond's trademark: All employees and bystanders were herded into the bank vault and locked inside. Hamilton, Barrow, and Parker were miles away before local citizens freed the victims. Ray and Clyde had added several thousand dollars to their funds.

With money in their pockets, Raymond, Clyde, and Bonnie decided to return to Dallas. There they would have to stay on the move, but could still sneak visits with relatives and friends. They had a system to stay in touch, using code words in telephone conversations to indicate where and when they could be found. Friends and relatives also would receive letters that referred to numbers indicating locations and times of meetings.

Back on their home ground, Hamilton and Barrow wasted little time. On July 29, 1932, at about 10:00 A.M., C. H. Spears was sitting alone in the interurban rail station in Grand Prairie. The fifty-two-year-old station manager looked up from his desk and saw a young blond-haired man. While Ray held a pistol on Spears, Barrow opened the cash register and took out a small amount of bills. Fortunately for the Interurban line, Spears had earlier removed $700 from the register. Hamilton and Barrow ran to a fancy roadster they had recently stolen and sped away.

August approached, and as the Texas weather got hotter so did Hamilton and Barrow. Local law enforcement officers were not sure Hamilton and Barrow were in on all the recent problems, but they suspected the pair in many of the cases.

Raymond and Clyde picked the Neuhoff Packing Company payroll office in Dallas next. They had cased the area around the company and felt confident. Bonnie did not accompany Ray and Clyde on the Neuhoff job, but they were joined by a friend named Ross Dyer. When Clyde left Bonnie to join Hamilton and Dyer, he jokingly told her to listen for their names on the radio. It was August 1, 1932. The men drove up in front of the company shortly after noon. Barrow stayed with the car while Raymond and Dyer entered the offices, pistols drawn. Joe and Henry Neuhoff, company owners, were counting payroll money along with employee Elsie Weischlager when the desperadoes walked in.

"Where's the money?" Raymond demanded.

He then saw the woman with the money in a side office. Dyer kept his gun leveled on the Neuhoff employees while Ray grabbed the money. Dyer ripped the front telephone out of the wall and asked if there were any other phones. The Neuhoffs showed him another phone in the back and he ripped it out. By now Hamilton had the money and he and Dyer dashed out the front door to the sedan. Barrow drove a short distance to another vehicle they had stolen and they switched cars. By that time the Neuhoffs had reported the robbery, which netted $440.

Two Dallas officers were patrolling the area when they spotted three young men in a late-model sedan traveling fast. The officers gave chase, but Barrow easily outdistanced them and headed out Industrial Boulevard toward West Dallas. In West Dallas he picked up Bonnie and the group then fled to an abandoned farmhouse south of Grand Prairie, where they hid for four days. On August 5 Barrow and Hamilton took Bonnie back to West Dallas to her mother's and they rejoined Dyer. The men decided to head for Oklahoma, where they were not wanted for any crimes.

Hamilton and his confederates crossed the Red River north of

Sherman, Texas, and drove northeastward into Oklahoma. When the Texans came into Stringtown, Oklahoma, they noticed a dancehall on the left side of the road. It was Friday night and a dance was in progress. Dyer wanted to go in to dance and get a drink of whiskey or home-brewed beer. Raymond and Barrow agreed to let him go in for a short while, but they remained in the car. As Raymond kept watch out his window, a vehicle approached. An Atoka County sheriff's car pulled up a few yards from the desperadoes' vehicle. The officers inside stared at the car with the Texas plates and wondered why the young men were not with the rest of the crowd. Barrow's facial muscles flexed as he cocked the revolver that was lying in the seat. Sheriff C. G. Maxwell and Deputy E. C. Moore got out of their car and approached the Texas car, coming to Clyde's window. When the sheriff did not get the answers he wanted he asked the men to step out of their vehicle. Maxwell started to open the door on Barrow's side when Clyde drew his pistol and fired point blank, hitting the sheriff several times. Maxwell fell to the ground and Deputy Moore ran for cover, but Barrow was instantly out the door and fired one shot that struck Moore in the head. The deputy fell to the ground and began the death quiver.

The dancehall was bedlam as people screamed and ran out the doors of the building and dove to the ground. Raymond had the car started, and it sprayed dust and gravel as he pulled up beside Clyde. The wounded Maxwell valiantly fired at the vehicle. Raymond fired several shots into the fallen sheriff, and with each thud into his body Maxwell groaned. The sheriff had managed to hit one of the tires on the car. With Barrow now in the auto, Raymond floorboarded the accelerator. The car careened across a shallow borrow ditch as Raymond guided it onto the highway. The Texas men did not get far, as the flat tire caused their vehicle to flip in the ditch.

Neither Ray nor Clyde was seriously injured, and they managed to get a window open and crawl out. They ran up the hill into Stringtown, where they came to a house inhabited by a black family. Barrow barged in, told them he was Pretty Boy Floyd, and demanded a car. They said they had no car but that Walt Thacker down the street did. They ran hell-bent to Thacker's, but when they beat on the door no one answered. At that moment a man named Cleve Brady drove by and, seeing the commotion, stopped. Raymond and Clyde aimed their pistols at him and commandeered his car. They forced Brady to ride with them to give directions.

Barrow got behind the wheel and drove at breakneck speed until, some fifteen miles out of Stringtown, Brady's car threw a wheel. The auto spun violently and Hamilton was thrown out but escaped serious injury. Barrow and Brady got out of the car and, along with Raymond, headed for a nearby farmhouse. The desperadoes threatened Brady with death if he attempted to escape or yell out. The place was owned by John Redden, and his nephew Haskell Owens came to the door when Raymond knocked. Hamilton explained that they had had a wreck and needed assistance. The men and Owens loaded into his car. He hardly got out of the driveway when he felt the cold steel of Clyde's revolver pressed against his head. Once on the road to Clayton, Clyde drove. When they arrived in Clayton, Barrow noticed the car was nearly out of gas. He saw an unoccupied vehicle on the main street and pulled up behind it. The car belonged to Frank Smith of Seminole, Oklahoma.

As they left to get in the Smith car, they ordered the Oklahomans to stay put. Smith's vehicle was found the following Sunday near Grandview, Texas, some thirty miles south of Fort Worth. Hamilton and Barrow had actually made it to Grandview before dawn Saturday. They stole another car there and returned to Dallas.

Ross Dyer escaped from the dancehall after the shooting and caught a bus in Atoka bound for Texas. Lawmen, alerted to be on the lookout for travelers from that area, nabbed him in McKinney. He was willing to talk, and shortly after his arrest, Raymond and Clyde were wanted for the Atoka shootings. They were hot before, but now they were on fire.

CHAPTER III

Strikes and a Bird in Hand

After their return to Dallas, Raymond and Clyde parted. Clyde contacted Bonnie and they hid in the house south of Grand Prairie. Raymond hid in the back alleys of West Dallas and at times in the Mountain Creek bottoms. Floyd Hamilton acted as a go-between for Raymond and Clyde and their mothers, using the number system to determine what backroad to meet on. The meetings were short and Raymond and Clyde always came armed to the hilt. Following a few days of hiding, Raymond, Clyde, and Bonnie decided to visit Bonnie's aunt near Carlsbad, New Mexico. The aunt, Millie Stamps, lived a few miles from town and did not keep up with the news. She did not know her visitors were wanted in two states.

Carlsbad Sheriff Joe Johns was soon to get a welcome he would never forget. Johns had seen the auto with Texas plates and its three youthful passengers pass through town. On Sunday, August 16, Hamilton drove the car into Carlsbad to get some ice to freeze the ice cream Bonnie's aunt was preparing. Sheriff Johns jotted down the license plate number, and a check indicated the vehicle was stolen. Johns decided to pay Aunt Millie and her guests a visit.

When the sheriff arrived, everyone was in the house. Clyde and Raymond had left their guns in the auto because they did not want to alarm Mrs. Stamps. Fortunately for them, she kept a loaded shotgun. Bonnie answered the door, and when the sheriff asked the whereabouts of the men she told him they would be right out. While the officer was waiting, he decided he would check the car with Texas plates. Suddenly, Raymond and Clyde stepped out from behind the house; Hamilton was brandishing the shotgun. Johns went for his gun, but Hamilton fired a warning shot over his head. Johns soon found himself a captive speeding down the road into Texas. He sat in the back with Bonnie while Barrow and Hamilton alternated driving.

Raymond and Clyde drove through West and Southwest Texas, reaching San Antonio in thirteen hours. It was dark when they arrived, so they drove around town until just before dawn, releasing Johns unharmed some five miles out of town. Clyde floorboarded it, and they were gone. Within hours, kidnap charges in New Mexico would be added to charges in Texas and Oklahoma against the West Dallas criminals.

Wondering which way to go, Hamilton and Barrow decided to head southeast toward Victoria. They were exhausted from their journey but afraid to stop. In Victoria they ditched their car and stole a Ford V-8. They loved these autos because they were fast and their heavy-duty steel bodies provided some shielding from bullets. Barrow loved the Fords so much he wrote a letter to Henry Ford detailing why they were a good car for desperadoes to use.

By now word was out about the stolen Ford in Victoria, so law enforcement officers, in anticipation of the West Dallasites' next move, set up an ambush at the Colorado River bridge near Wharton, Texas. Indeed, Raymond and Clyde had decided to go to Houston, so they were on a collision course with the trap. They had already stolen another car — a Ford coupe — and Hamilton was driving it, following Bonnie and Clyde in the lead car. Bonnie was asleep as they approached the Colorado. Barrow was doing better than sixty when he noticed suspicious movement. He suddenly slammed on the brakes for all they were worth, and the car came to a fishtailing halt just short of the bridge. As he frantically began turning around, the officers jumped from cover and began firing. Bullets were hitting the car, but none hit Barrow or Parker or disabled their vehicle. They sped off back the way they had come.

Raymond slid his car all over the road to avoid colliding with Barrow and getting caught. By now all the officers were out and firing. The carnage shot out all the windows of Hamilton's car and flattened all four tires, but somehow he turned around and headed the other way without being injured. Clyde circled back and picked him up when his car would go no further. The astonished lawmen had only a bullet-riddled vehicle to show for their efforts.

After their dramatic escape at Wharton, Barrow and Hamilton once again decided to part. Raymond headed back to Michigan, and now he had to be extremely cautious when traveling. Authorities everywhere were alerted to be on the lookout for the desperadoes from West Dallas. Raymond made it to Michigan without a hitch, and Bonnie and Clyde went into hiding. Nothing would be heard from any of them for more than a month.

In early October, Raymond decided it would be relatively safe to return to Texas, so he bade farewell to his father and headed home. He was broke and his friends and relatives were being monitored too closely for him to contact them.

On October 8, 1932, cashier R. G. Brandenburg and assistant cashier Raburn Carrell were tending business at the First State Bank of Cedar Hill. It was a slow day at the bank as Carrell noticed a late-model sedan pull up out front. He saw the young blond man behind the wheel, but thought nothing of it and went back to his business. Suddenly, the bank door opened and in stepped the young man, holding a .45. Raymond held his jacket so that it partially concealed the weapon.

"I guess you know what this means?" Hamilton asked. "Is anybody else in here?"

Carrell replied that Brandenburg was in the back room. Raymond ordered Carrell to go to the room and followed him. Carrell called Brandenburg and he turned around. Raymond glared at him but said nothing, herding his victims into the teller's cage where the money and vault were. At this point the Tooley brothers, L. H. and E. H., entered the bank.

"Get over here with the others!" Raymond shouted. "If you don't, it'll be too bad!"

Hamilton ordered Brandenburg to give him the money; then he ordered the four men to get in the vault and locked them in. They would remain there for forty-five minutes before citizens outside finally worked the vault combination on instructions shouted by Brandenburg. It was a windy day, and as Hamilton ran from the bank to his car several of the bills flew out of his pockets and blew across the square. Ray raced off in his car, causing a cloud of dust.

When he was several miles out of town he decided to ditch his stolen car. He stopped, got out, and started walking up the road toward some men who were working. They were at the A. F. Day home, three miles south of Cedar Hill. The men were Day, his son-in-law, H. O. Felkner of Oak Cliff, Felkner's son, and a helper.

Raymond forced the men into Felkner's truck and ordered Felkner to drive toward the highway. Hamilton got in the back of the truck, but before reaching the highway Felkner stopped and protested that he could not drive with four sitting in the cab. Hamilton told the helper to get in the back with him. The helper hopped in the back with Raymond and they headed down the road. After they were on Highway 67 headed for Midlothian, Hamilton reached through the window of the cab and grabbed the hat Felkner's son was wearing and put it on. He laughingly asked Felkner if he looked like the same person. Felkner stopped in Midlothian to get gasoline and Raymond paid for it. When the group reached Waxahachie, Hamilton ordered Felkner to stop. Ray purchased sandwiches, cold drinks, and cigarettes for the men and himself. Following a hasty meal, they headed for Hillsboro. Felkner was trying to figure a way out of the predicament.

When they reached Abbott, Texas, on Highway 77, Felkner had his son turn off the gas while Hamilton wasn't looking. When the truck stopped, Felkner jumped out as if to see what was wrong. He lifted the hood and while Hamilton turned to watch the others, Felkner broke the distributor points. Raymond looked at the truck as best he could while holding the gun on his victims. After a few minutes of trying to get the truck started, he slammed the hood.

Hamilton ripped a piece of tarpaulin off the back of the truck, wrapped his $1,400 in it, and said goodbye to the men, warning them to stay put until he was out of sight. Ray started walking down the highway toward Waco and soon hailed a passing motorist, who stopped to give him a ride. The unfortunate man realized it would be a rather exciting journey when Hamilton brandished his pistol. Raymond forced the man to drive to Brenham, Texas, where he stole a car and headed to Houston.

Raymond's face wasn't yet that well-known in Houston, so he lived like a king for several weeks. The first thing he did was check into a motel and clean up. Then he went to a department store and bought a fancy suit. The salesperson doubtless wondered where a nineteen-year-old got that much cash. With a new suit and plenty of money, he was out on the streets to enjoy life. Things he never dreamed he would have were now his.

Three days after Raymond Hamilton robbed the Cedar Hill bank, Bonnie and Clyde surfaced in Sherman, Texas. It was late afternoon on October 11, and butcher Howard Hall was busy closing a small grocery. A store clerk, Homer Glaze, was the only other person in the store when a Ford with a young man and woman inside came to a stop in front. Clyde Barrow got out and went into the store while Bonnie eased over and got behind the wheel. Clyde ordered some bologna and cheese and as Hall was preparing to slice it, Barrow pulled a pistol on Glaze and demanded money. As Glaze was handing over some bills, Hall came at Barrow with a meat cleaver. The butcher took a swipe at him, and Barrow fired twice at point-blank range into the man's chest. Hall died en route to surgery at a hospital across the street from the store. Bonnie and Clyde escaped north into Oklahoma. The robbery netted less than $30.

The duo continued into the Midwest and lay low until late October. On Halloween they returned to Dallas because Bonnie was homesick to see her mother. This visit was brief; along with new partners Hollis Hale and Frank Hardy, both from Dallas, Bonnie and Clyde ventured back into the Midwest. They rented a tourist camp ten miles from Carthage, Missouri, and used it as their head-quarters for staging several small robberies in southern Missouri. The group parted in late November, and Bonnie and Clyde returned to Dallas. Raymond Hamilton had not been heard from.

Friday, November 25, 1932, dawned crisp and cool. On a lonely country road several miles out of Cedar Hill, Ray Hamilton and his new pal, Les Stewart, sat in their stolen car planning a robbery of the First State Bank. Head cashier Raburn Carrell opened the bank and worked on paperwork since no customers were in. The little red brick bank, the only one in town, was on the north side of the square. Carrell was distracted from his work when the Rev. L. B. Trone, Methodist minister, walked in. Trone had not come to bank. He had come to read the bank's copy of the *Dallas Morning News*, not having a spare nickel to buy one.

Hamilton and Stewart started toward town, with Stewart driving and Raymond nervously tapping the dash. Stewart wheeled into the square and drove slowly toward the bank. There was no traffic.

Raymond told Stewart he wanted to go into the Strauss Brothers Store first to look things over. Hamilton went into the store, which was just east of the bank, got a Coke out of the soft drink box, and paid the clerk. He went over by the door and leaned back against the wall and drank, eyeing the store employees and watching out the window. Finally he swigged the last of the drink and walked out.

Carrell and Trone were still engrossed in their bank activities when he walked in, gun drawn.

"Say, I know you — you were here before," Carrell blurted.

"Yeah, maybe so. Don't take so damned long this time to get the money. Both of you get behind the cage and get that money together."

As Trone looked on, Carrell quickly picked up a money sack

and began filling it with bills and silver. Soon Stewart entered, also with pistol drawn.

"All right, you two get in the vault," Raymond commanded.

With their victims locked in the vault, Hamilton and Stewart dashed out the front door of the bank to their car. Raymond whooped as the car's spinning tires threw pea gravel all over the square. The two men made away with $1,900.

The cashier and the preacher stood in the pitch blackness of the vault. Carrell managed to find the string to the small vault light and turned it on. The cashier peered into the vault cabinet and pulled out some bills.

"Well, at least he didn't get all of the money."

"I'm more interested in how we're gonna get out," Trone retorted.

Shortly after Hamilton left, the town drunk happened by the bank. Peering in the window, he saw no one. He staggered through the door and heard Hamilton's prisoners yelling.

"Why the hell should I let ya out? I didn't put ya in there."

He then stumbled over to Strauss Brothers. In minutes what seemed like the whole town was at the bank. Roy Fouts, one of the Strauss employees, was familiar with combination locks and turned the vault lock according to Carrell's shouted instructions. Within minutes, Carrell and Trone were freed and came out of the vault facing an excited crowd, including several Dallas County sheriff's officers. Meanwhile, Hamilton was driving across southern Dallas and Tarrant counties.

Just outside the small community of Lillian in southern Johnson County, Hamilton spotted a car at a small farmhouse. Raymond pulled in the driveway and got out. Henry Lile and his son came out of the house. Hamilton demanded the Liles' car at gunpoint. The shaken farmer raced into the house and returned momentarily with the keys, pleading with the men not to harm his son. Hamilton and Stewart leaped into their new vehicle and sped off down the road. Raymond and Stewart soon parted; Les lay low in the Dallas area and Hamilton retreated to his familiar haunts in Wichita Falls.

En route to Wichita Falls, Ray stopped at an out-of-the-way service station to gas up and use the restroom. When he went in to pay for the gas, a news bulletin interrupted the late afternoon radio program. "Just in from Austin—Governor Ross Sterling has revoked the parole he granted to West Dallas desperado Clyde Barrow in January. Since Barrow's release, he and a gang from the Dallas area have been charged with three murders, numerous robberies with firearms, felonious assaults and thefts. Texas law enforcement officials are combing the state looking for the band of hoodlums, who are to be considered armed and extremely dangerous. We now return you to your normal programming." The old station attendant took the money from Hamilton and stared out the window.

Hamilton had a plan when he got to Wichita Falls. He made contact with a friend, Gene O'Dare, and his wife, Mary. O'Dare and Raymond had robbed the Carmine State Bank on November 9, following Ray's trip to Houston. Hamilton convinced the couple that Mary should stay behind and that he and Gene should travel to Michigan to escape the heat being put on them by Texas authorities. On their way they could rob a large bank in the Midwest.

While Hamilton and O'Dare traveled north, Bonnie and Clyde were causing more headlines in Texas. On the evening of December 5, 1932, Barrow, Parker, and a new friend, W. D. (Deacon) Jones, shot and killed Doyle Johnson in Belton, Texas, during an attempt to steal the victim's auto.

The day following the Belton murder, Raymond Hamilton and Gene O'Dare were cooling their heels in Bay City, Michigan. The pair looked forward to going roller skating that evening with a friend of Ray's from the construction company where the latter had worked during his early retreats from Texas lawmen. The acquaintance knew his Texas pals were not in Bay City because they liked the winter weather and decided to relay his suspicions to authorities. That evening, while rolling around the rink, the trio was suddenly confronted by four members of the Michigan state police. When O'Dare made a move for his pocket, one of the officers decked him with a billy club. The officers informed Hamilton and O'Dare they were acting on information from Texas officials. Frisking Hamilton, the Michigan officers found a loaded revolver. One of the officers informed Ray and Gene that Texas officers were interested in talking to them.

Raymond and O'Dare soon learned their friend had done them in. He had related his suspicions to Sheriff W. A. Day of Midland City, Michigan. The sheriff in turn sent a telegram to Dallas officers on Monday, December 5, requesting photographs, fingerprints, and records of the West Dallas men. The information was airmailed to Day and detectives in Detroit. With the information in, the setup was made, and Hamilton and O'Dare were nailed. Deputy Sheriffs Denver Seale and Ed Caster of Dallas County, as well as P. F. Wilkerson and Kelly Rush of Hill County, were sent to Michigan to return Raymond and O'Dare, who had chosen not to fight extradition. Texas lawmen were gleeful; they had Hamilton and were hopeful his buddy Clyde Barrow would soon join him.

Hamilton and O'Dare, weary from the long trip and barrage of questions from the officers, arrived December 14 in Dallas, where they were placed in the county jail. The lawmen told reporters the desperadoes had given no trouble during the weeklong journey from Michigan. Recently elected Dallas County Sheriff R. A. (Smoot) Schmid, a giant of a man who was known as "Big Foot" because of his size fourteen feet, couldn't wait to get a look at Hamilton and O'Dare. Raymond recognized Schmid from the latter's days as owner of the downtown bicycle shop. Schmid was champing on a half-smoked cigar as he eyed Ray.

"Say, don't I know you?" Schmid asked Hamilton.

"You ought to, you big-footed son-of-a-bitch," Hamilton shot back. "You used to buy hot bicycles from all us boys from West Dallas."

CHAPTER IV

Trials and Tribulations

On Thursday, December 15, 1932, Raymond Hamilton was placed in a lineup at the Dallas jail. Raburn Carrell and the Rev. L. B. Trone of Cedar Hill identified him as the man who twice robbed the Cedar Hill bank. C. H. Spears, the interurban station attendant in Grand Prairie, shouted, "That's the man! That's the one who robbed me!" Joe Neuhoff of the Neuhoff Packing Company quickly identified Raymond in connection with the payroll robbery. O'Dare was not identified by any of the witnesses, but authorities were holding him for Fayette County officials in connection with the Carmine robbery.

The next Saturday, Sheriff J. W. Freeland of Hill County took Raymond to Hillsboro to be viewed by J. N. Bucher's wife. Freeland and a deputy took Hamilton into the Bucher business and asked the widow if he was the man who shot her husband. She shook her head and said he was not one of the men involved. The disgusted lawmen returned to the car with Hamilton. Freeland went back in the store and had a lengthy conversation with Mrs. Bucher. He then brought her out to the car to have another look at Ray. This time she decided that he was the man who killed her husband, and the officers took Hamilton to the county jail.

Not all was going against Raymond. As publicity and hysteria concerning the gang mounted, lawmen around the country wanted a crack at them. Dallas Deputy Sheriff Denver Seale received a telegram from City Attorney Homer Rinehart of West Plains, Missouri, asking for photographs and fingerprints of Hamilton and Gene O'Dare. The telegram said the two were wanted in connection with the kill-

23

ing of Sheriff C. R. Kelly of West Plains in December of 1931. Seale pointed out that Hamilton was in the McKinney jail at the time of the murder.

Already facing four felony charges in Dallas County and the murder charge in Hill County, Hamilton also was charged with the November 9 robbery of the Carmine State Bank in Fayette County. Bank president W. H. Sturmer and assistant cashier W. A. Plueckhahn identified Raymond and O'Dare as the robbers. In short order Ray was indicted for the two Cedar Hill robberies and the Neuhoff robbery. However, he was no-billed in connection with the Grand Prairie interurban station robbery.

Floyd Hamilton, taking his wife Mildred and son John, went to Tulsa to seek out a superintendent with the Kellogg Construction Company. Floyd felt this man could prove that Raymond had been in Michigan at the time of the Bucher murder. While Floyd was on his mission, Odell Chambless and Raymond's old buddy Les Stewart robbed the Home Bank of Grapevine, Texas, of $2,850. Stewart was captured shortly afterward in Fort Worth and admitted being an accomplice of Raymond Hamilton. After further persuasion, the twenty-year-old gave Chambless' name to officers. He hinted further that Chambless might try to get in touch with relatives of Hamilton or Clyde Barrow. Acting on this information, officers went to the home of Lillie McBride, Raymond's oldest sister, on Friday evening, January 6, 1933. Lillie was not at home but Maggie Fairris, next to youngest of the Hamilton girls, was there tending Lillie's son and Floyd Hamilton's daughter.

The officers were Fred Bradberry, Dallas County sheriff's deputy; Dusty Rhodes and Walter Evans, both with the Tarrant County district attorney's office; Malcolm Davis, Tarrant County sheriff's deputy; and J. F. Van Noy, Texas Ranger from Belton. The lawmen had parked their cars some distance from the West Dallas home at 507 County Avenue. Thinking Chambless might show, and wanting to know more about Hamilton and Barrow, Bradberry, Rhodes, and Van Noy stayed in the front room of the house to question Maggie while Davis and Evans stayed outside.

Maggie had just put the children to bed when a car suddenly pulled up in front. Could it be Chambless or Lillie? No, Chambless was not in the area and Lillie had not returned from visiting Raymond at Hillsboro. It was Bonnie and Clyde and W. D. Jones. They had been in town to visit Bonnie's mother and then had gone to Floyd's, which was only a few streets from Lillie's. Barrow had driven to Lillie's hoping to find Floyd. He got out of the car and started walking toward the house, leaving a very drunk Bonnie and a very nervous W. D. in the vehicle.

Barrow was toting a sawed-off shotgun as he walked up on the front porch and knocked on the door. As he did, Davis ran from the left side of the house, gun drawn. Clyde wheeled and fired, striking Davis and killing him instantly. Evans jumped from the other side of the house, but retreated when Barrow fired at him. By now, Deacon Jones was spraying the neighborhood with gunfire. The three officers in the house, startled by the wild scene outside, all hit the floor and crawled toward the back room. In a fashion that would have done the Three Stooges proud, the trio reached the door at the same time and became momentarily stuck. Bonnie had enough presence to start the car and drive around the block. Clyde, who had fled in the darkness, spotted her and waved her down. He jumped under the wheel and drove all night until they were far into eastern Oklahoma. They would hide in that area until March.

Lillie and a girlfriend, Lucille Hilburn, returned home about 3:00 A.M. and were arrested by officers. The following day five other relatives and neighbors, including Maggie and Steve Davis, had been jailed. Davis was arrested because police had found blood-stained clothing at his home in West Dallas. The officers roughed Steve up but released him when the blood in the clothing was found to be from a chicken.

Funeral services were held the following Sunday for Deputy Malcolm Davis in Fort Worth. The Rev. Frank P. Culver, Sr., presiding elder of the Fort Worth district of the Central Methodist Conference, told the hundreds in attendance:

> The tragedy of Deputy Davis' death should not be possible in this civilized age. No man or woman should be clothed with the power to turn loose upon the public those who murder and rob, but people get just what they demand. I am happy that the human heart is still filled with sympathy. I have the deepest respect for men who try to keep peace in this world and protect the public. We are too ready to criticize officers of the law. We do not always realize how much their protection means. They risk their lives and too often give their lives for our peace and security. No greater honor is due the soldier who dies on the field of battle than is due a peace officer who lays down his life for our protection. There may be born out of this tragedy a blessing which may come years after the grass is green on the grave of our friend.

Hysteria reigned in Dallas following the killing as police made more arrests and received numerous tips from people claiming to have seen Barrow and other gang members. Lawmen, armed with machine guns and riot equipment, combed the area looking for any clue. One police unit was even involved in a wreck as it was speeding to the scene where the desperadoes were allegedly seen.

When Floyd Hamilton returned from Oklahoma he was questioned but would not divulge any information. Meantime, Lillie McBride and Lucille Hilburn had been charged as accessories to the robbery at Grapevine. They were also scheduled to go before the Dallas County grand jury.

A week following the Davis murder, Lillie was charged as an accessory in connection with the Cedar Hill bank robbery. Les Stewart, who was in jail in Fort Worth, caused a stir when he led Tarrant County authorities to a spot near Grapevine where he and Chambless had buried $400. By now, Raymond Hamilton had been returned to Dallas from Hillsboro and was being grilled about the gang by local officers.

Is there a girl?

"Yeah, and she can shoot as good as the fellas. Holds a pistol in each hand."

What's her name?

"You'll have to ask her. I don't know her name or where she's from."

Saturday, January 14, Judge Noland G. Williams of Criminal District Court No. 2 announced the setting of Wednesday, January 25, for the trial of Raymond Hamilton on three indictments for robbery with firearms. While Ray was waiting for his day in court, Les Stewart was telling a Fort Worth jury that he and Odell Chambless had stayed four days at Lillie McBride's home prior to the Grapevine robbery. He added that he and Chambless smoked marijuana before the robbery.

One week before Hamilton's trial, Chambless surrendered to authorities in Pampa, Texas. He was cleared of the Davis killing when it was learned he had been arrested in Los Angeles that day. Chambless said he had gone to California after the Grapevine robbery, and while hitchhiking his way back to Texas he noticed a reward for him at the Santa Fe, New Mexico, city hall. He had therefore decided to go to Pampa, where his father lived, and turn himself in. Chambless was returned to Fort Worth to stand trial.

The *Dallas Morning News* couldn't resist poking fun at futile efforts of law enforcement personnel in connection with the Davis killer manhunt. In its edition of Friday, January 20, 1933, the *News* printed the headline "Pretty Boy is New Suspect in Killing: Jesse James Next?" with the subhead of "Dalton Brothers Also are Eligible for Chambless' Place on List." The story read in part:

With Jesse James dead, and therefore practically eliminated from the search for the slayer of Deputy Sheriff Malcolm Davis of Fort Worth, peace officers turned their detective ability Thursday on another vaunted Oklahoma outlaw and named Pretty Boy Floyd in connection with the Dallas County killing.

At the same time a report came that Floyd was wanted for a $1,200 bank robbery at Cleveland, Oklahoma on January 6, the day on which Deputy Sheriff Davis of Fort Worth was killed at a West Dallas house. Cleveland is 270 miles, or a good day's drive from Dallas, in Liberty County.

Sheriff J. R. (Red) Wright of Tarrant County was originator of the idea that the Sooner State bandit might be implicated in the Davis killing.

Sheriff Schmid was questioned Wednesday concerning Sheriff Wright's theory regarding Floyd.

"Aw, that's stuff," said Schmid.

"You mean, then, Sheriff, that you decline to concur with Sheriff Wright's theory?" he was asked.

"No, no, nothing like that," he protested.

Schmid really protested the Thursday before Raymond's trial, when Floyd Hamilton and attorney Frank Wilson showed up at the county jail wanting to speak in private with Ray. Floyd had approached Wilson about representing Raymond. The older brother had already tried to have an attorney speak with the nineteen-year-old but had failed. At first Schmid flatly denied the request. When Wilson asked the jailer to allow him to see Ray, he was told that he would have to get a personal okay from Sheriff Schmid.

Wilson and Floyd found the sheriff.

"What do you want to talk to Hamilton about?" Schmid asked.

"They want me to defend him," Wilson said.

"Well, you'll have to let me hear what you have to say to him," Schmid countered. "You can't talk to him alone."

As Wilson and Schmid entered the jail and stepped into the elevator, they were still arguing.

"I'll tell you," Schmid said, "you can talk to him through the screen."

"I guess I'll have to find a judge and do something about this," Wilson said. Schmid didn't realize the attorney was talking about securing a writ of mandamus.

"What's the judge got to do with it?" the sheriff roared. "I've got the keys to the jail!"

Schmid asked the attorney to remain upstairs while he checked with the district attorney to get legal advice. The decision of the

D.A., Robert Hurt, didn't please Schmid, but Wilson got his private audience with Ray.

On Saturday, January 21, Raymond appeared in court on three indictments of robbery with firearms. He strolled out three minutes later assured he would not receive the death penalty in connection with any of the charges. District Attorney Hurt told Hamilton's new attorney, Albert Baskett, that the state would waive the first count in each of the indictments, which meant the death penalty could not apply. The penalty Raymond faced on each of the counts was five years to life.

When Raymond first entered the courtroom, Baskett was not with him. Judge Noland Williams asked Hamilton if he wanted a special venire for his trial. Raymond pleaded ignorance and asked to speak with Baskett. The judge, growing impatient, asked Hamilton to call his attorney. Baskett wasn't in his office but was spotted on the street by a newspaper reporter. Hurt sent Special Investigator Denver Seale to get Baskett. Ray's lawyer pointed out that Hurt's decision to waive the first counts of the indictments precluded the defendant's right to a special venire. With that out of the way, Raymond was sent back to his cell.

The spectre of the death penalty still haunted Hamilton. His indictment on the Bucher murder at Hillsboro carried the death sentence. Hill County District Attorney Sam H. Allred had already written Hurt asking how much time would be used for the trials for the Dallas area cases. While these actions were pondered, Gene O'Dare was in the Fayette County jail, awaiting trial in connection with the Carmine robbery. Also, more and more, law enforcement officials were linking the pasts of Raymond and Clyde Barrow.

The Tuesday before Raymond's trial on Wednesday, his sister Lillie and her girlfriend Lucille Hilburn were returned to the Dallas County jail from the Tarrant County jail. It was the day before Ray's trial, but Baskett had yet to come up with any defense witnesses. District Attorney Hurt announced he would join Assistants Will Curtis and Dean Gauldin in the prosecution. The papers now labeled Hamilton, Barrow, and chums the "West Dallas Mob." After arriving at the Dallas jail, Lillie and Lucille asked Baskett to defend them against charges as accessories to several local robberies committed by the gang. Raymond's attorney arranged bond for the women's release.

January 25, 1933, saw some of the swiftest justice in Dallas County history. Before the day was over, Raymond Hamilton had been tried twice, convicted twice, and assessed penalties totaling fifty-five years. Hamilton pleaded not guilty to both indictments of robbery before Judge Williams. He was sentenced to thirty years in the first trial for robbery of the Cedar Hill bank in October and twenty-five years for the Neuhoff Brothers Packing Company robbery in August. The Cedar Hill case went to the jury at 4:00 P.M. and the verdict was returned at 5:30 P.M. The second jury began hearing testimony at 6:45 P.M., went to its quarters at 8:45 P.M. to consider a verdict, and returned the sentence of twenty-five years at 10:30 P.M. C. W. Coatney, butcher, foreman of the second jury, said nine were for ninety-nine years, one for five years, and two for fifteen years on the first ballot.

Raymond woke up Thursday morning facing not only fifty-five years at Huntsville but also a murder trial the following Monday in Hillsboro. During his trials Wednesday, Hill County D. A. Allred had conferred with Hurt and Baskett. Hurt informed him that Dallas would be through with Hamilton in time for the Monday date, and Baskett told him he would be ready to defend. In addition to the murder indictment against Raymond in the Bucher case, he was also under an indictment for robbery with firearms in the same incident.

On Sunday, January 29, 1933, six lawmen arrived at the Dallas County jail to transport Raymond Hamilton to the Hill County jail. The officers were heavily armed because of Hamilton's boasts that the law couldn't hold him and because they did not know the whereabouts of Clyde Barrow. Texas Ranger L. C. Sport, Hill County Sheriff J. W. Freeland, and four of his deputies delivered Raymond to Hillsboro.

The officers needn't have worried about Barrow. Bonnie and Clyde and Deacon Jones had left their hideout in eastern Oklahoma and were traveling through Springfield, Missouri. Clyde was driving — and speeding. Thomas Persell, a motorcycle cop, chased the speeding auto to the edge of town before it stopped. Persell gunned his machine and pulled alongside the car, but before the officer knew what was happening, Barrow and Jones were out of the auto and wrestled away his gun. They forced him into the back seat and threw a blanket over him. Jones sat beside Persell, holding a gun on him.

When the abandoned motorcycle was found, a frantic search ensued. Barrow took a tour of Missouri and stopped at Buffalo, Fairplay, Golden City, Carthage, and Oronogo, the latter where they stole a new battery for their car. Finally, Barrow released the embarrassed but unharmed Persell at Poundstone Corner. It was noon the following day before he was able to phone Springfield. He said that he had been with Bonnie and Clyde and an unidentified man. He said Bonnie (who was still not widely known) had dyed her hair red.

Officer Persell's odyssey received a great deal of newspaper attention. Barrow, Jones, and Parker vanished, it seemed, into the air.

With Bonnie and Clyde in hiding and Raymond Hamilton awaiting trial in Hillsboro, the month of February 1933 belonged to Gene
O'Dare and Les Stewart. On February 2 O'Dare was sentenced at
LaGrange to life imprisonment for his part in the Carmine robbery.
His lawyer said he would file a motion for a new trial and if that was
denied he would file an appeal. Gene was silent when the verdict was
read and was surrounded by seven deputies as he was led back to his
jail cell at the Fayette County courthouse. Hamilton was supposed
to have been tried with O'Dare, but was granted severance because
of his involvement in the Bucher murder case at Hillsboro. Stewart,
described as a "henchman of Raymond Hamilton," was indicted February 20 for robbery in connection with the second Cedar Hill bank
robbery. Raymond was still under indictment for that robbery.

On March 1, 1933, Odell Chambless was sentenced to thirty-
three years in prison for his part in the Grapevine bank robbery. He
took his chances before a jury and gained two years because the prosecution had offered a thirty-five-year term. Chambless had agreed
to plead guilty at his trial in Fort Worth Criminal District Court.

"What do you think you should get?" the defendant was asked
by Judge George E. Hosey.

"I don't know, Judge," Chambless replied. "I know I've done
wrong. I'll leave it up to you."

Present during the sentencing of Chambless was his sister, Mary
O'Dare, the wife of Gene O'Dare. Two days after Chambless was
sentenced in Fort Worth, Les Stewart saw twenty-five years in prison
added to the twenty-five he already had. In Dallas, Stewart pleaded
guilty before Judge Williams in connection with the second Cedar
Hill bank robbery. He had already been assessed twenty-five years
for the Grapevine robbery.

As the crackdown on the West Dallas gang continued, Raymond
Hamilton was getting restless in the Hill County jail. He sensed his
chances of avoiding a conviction were not good. Raymond knew Barrow was back in the area, and he also knew that his brother Floyd was
keeping Clyde informed. Raymond confronted Floyd during a visit.

"Tell Clyde it looks like I'm going to be convicted for this killing that he did," Ray said. "Why don't he come down here and break
me out?"

Raymond went on to tell Floyd that the jailer sat outside each
evening, unarmed and with the keys, and that all Barrow would have

to do would be to drive up, put a gun on him, and let Ray out. The elder Hamilton met with Barrow soon after and made the request.

"Well, okay, sure," Clyde agreed, "I'll go by the jail and see what our chances are."

The following day, Clyde said it was too risky. "We just can't pull this job off by ourselves," he explained to Floyd. "I've got a better plan. Let's you and me go to East Texas and rob the Mineola bank and give all the money to Ray's attorney to appeal his case."

Floyd was not keen on the idea, even though Barrow assured him he had cased the bank. Finally, Floyd agreed.

"Well, okay," Floyd relented. "But you go in the bank first. I'll wear a mask. It doesn't matter if you're recognized. In fact, it would probably make it easier for you."

Barrow and Floyd met at a predetermined spot outside Mineola, then drove in together. Hamilton went inside the bank to look things over. He didn't like what he saw: all four employees were there plus there were numerous customers. Clyde didn't like the report.

"Damn it, we just can't do it, then," Barrow said. "We'll have to get some help."

"If you don't want to rob it with just me, forget it!" Floyd snapped. The pair returned to Dallas without accomplishing anything.

By Wednesday, March 15, Raymond's trial in the Bucher case was well under way in Hillsboro. Hamilton was identified in court by Mrs. Bucher as one of the young men who had been in the store the night of the slaying. The defense attempted to establish an alibi. Testifying for Raymond were his nineteen-year-old stepmother and a J. W. Ringo. John Hamilton's second wife and Ringo both swore Raymond was in Midland, Michigan, during April and May of 1932. Ringo testified that Raymond was his roommate while they worked for Kellogg Construction Company and that they were together in Michigan the night of the Bucher murder. In attendance at the trial were Raymond's mother, Floyd, and Lillie. They all testified he had not been in Dallas during the time in question.

Also in attendance were Sheriff C. G. Maxwell, Deputy Sheriff Joe Shoemaker, and Deputy Sheriff Tom Stark, all of Atoka, Oklahoma. Raymond was wanted in Oklahoma in connection with the dancehall shooting. Maxwell said he expected to ask Governor Murray of Oklahoma for extradition of Hamilton so he could be returned to Atoka for trial.

By Friday, the jury had not reached a verdict after testimony and final arguments. Judge W. L. Wray said he would hold the panel until a decision was made or they became hopelessly deadlocked.

Saturday night the jury was still unable to agree on what to do with Raymond. Judge Wray asked the jury foreman if any progress was being made toward an agreement. The foreman said the panel was still deadlocked. The judge indicated he would dismiss the jury if it had not reached an agreement by the following morning. Finally, on Monday morning, March 20, after ninety-one hours of consideration, the jury reported to Judge Wray it was unable to agree on a penalty and was discharged. A poll of the jury showed that on the first ballot there was unanimity as to Hamilton's guilt, but disagreement as to penalty. On that ballot, five voted for ninety-nine years, one for the electric chair, three for fifty years, one for forty-five years, and two did not vote. On the final ballot there were nine for ninety-nine years, one for sixty-five years, and two not voting.

The same day Raymond Hamilton's Hillsboro jury was discharged, Texas Governor Miriam (Ma) Ferguson granted a full pardon to Buck Barrow. Clyde's older brother returned to Dallas and his family on March 22, pledging to start a new life and stay out of trouble.

Knowing another trial on the Bucher murder was forthcoming, Raymond decided it was time for action. He convinced two fellow prisoners, David Cates and J. B. Stephens, to join him in an escape attempt. By late afternoon Thursday, March 23, the men had sawed out of their cells. When two deputy sheriffs, Quill Pierce and Jim Hawkins, went to the jail to lock up a prisoner, Raymond and his friends jumped them from behind and forced them to turn over keys to an outer door. Raymond and his buddies grabbed a rifle and shotgun from the jail runaround. They ran across the street to a filling station, forced O. G. Freeman and Mrs. J. K. Hare from an automobile, and drove away to the northwest. They picked the right car because Mrs. Hare had just had the automobile drained and refilled with oil and the gas tank was full.

Raymond hit the country roads heading northwest, but a Hill County sheriff's car was right on his tail. Hamilton's old Hill County nemesis Kelly Rush was firing at the desperadoes' auto and managed to shoot the tires out. The vehicle careened wildly, and Ray was forced to stop. With two amateurs and two guns, and a limited supply of ammunition, Hamilton knew they were no match for the officers. He and his mates piled out of the car with hands up. As the deputies loaded the fugitives in the squad car, Rush couldn't resist booting Hamilton as he shoved him in.

"You son-of-a-bitch!" Hamilton screamed. "If I could get ahold of that pistol of yours I'd stick it up your ass and jerk the sights off!"

CHAPTER V

Blood in the Midwest:
A Trip Down the River

When Buck Barrow returned to Dallas he decided to get in touch with Clyde despite opposition from his wife and family. Soon he and Blanche met Bonnie and Clyde and W. D. Jones near Fort Smith, Arkansas. They traveled to Joplin, Missouri, where they rented a bungalow. For a while the group lived in the bungalow with no problems, but some of the locals in Joplin informed local law enforcement officers that the group from Texas did not act like typical tourists.

On the evening of April 13, 1933, Missouri State Highway Patrolmen G. B. Kahler and W. E. Grammer, along with Joplin Detectives Harry McGinnis and Tom DeFraff and Newton County Constable J. W. Harryman, drove up to the bungalow. Harryman approached the bungalow garage door and shouted "Officers!" Clyde Barrow and W. D. Jones opened the door slightly and fired sawed-off shotguns. Harryman fell, mortally wounded. Gunfire erupted everywhere as the other officers and Bonnie and Buck Barrow became involved. McGinnis made a move to retrieve Harryman, but the withering fire from the bungalow turned him back. As he ran for cover he was struck several times. One of the shots nearly severed one of his arms. He would die from his wounds.

Clyde and W. D. were wounded in the melee but managed to get in the car along with Bonnie and Buck. They drove out of the driveway and down the street to catch up with the frantic Blanche Barrow, who had panicked and started running when the gunfire erupted. She was hysterical, but Buck managed to wrestle her into the car.

Clyde headed west, and within eight hours the group reached Amarillo, Texas. They bought some bandages for a head wound sustained by Jones.

The group had left practically all of their belongings in Joplin. Included in the items left behind were Buck's pardon papers and undeveloped photo film. Following development of the film, authorities had additional names and faces of the Barrow gang.

Clyde and his confederates kept to remote rural areas and were not heard from until April 28. They were in Ruston, Louisiana, and needed another car, so they stole one belonging to D. Darby, an undertaker. Darby and his girlfriend, Sophie Stone, saw the desperadoes leaving and got in her car to pursue them. They gave up the chase some eighteen miles northwest of Ruston, but to their horror and surprise the criminals from Texas did a U-turn and began pursuing them. Barrow pulled alongside Darby and forced his auto off the road. Darby and Miss Stone were forced to ride with the gang but were released unharmed at Waldo, Arkansas, where Barrow gave them $5 to get home.

On Friday, May 5, 1933, Sheriff W. Loessin and Deputy Jim Flournoy of Fayette County picked up Raymond Hamilton at the Dallas County jail and took him to LaGrange to stand trial for the Carmine robbery. He had already been tried five times, convicted four times, and assessed sentences totaling sixty-five years. By the following Monday, eight jurors were selected for the Carmine trial. Attorneys were having a difficult time obtaining a jury due to opinions formed during the trial of Gene O'Dare. Twelve were selected, however, and testimony was concluded Tuesday. Hamilton's attorney presented no witnesses, and Raymond did not testify. His lawyer offered a motion for an instructed verdict, but Judge M. C. Jeffrey promptly overruled. Fred Blundell, district attorney for Fayette County, completed his presentation in two hours. H. Plunkum, assistant cashier, and H. L. Dore, cashier, along with three other witnesses, identified Hamilton as the companion of O'Dare. Ray was found guilty and given a life sentence to go with his other prison time.

With the manhunt for the Barrow gang intensifying, they headed north. On May 16 Clyde, Bonnie, W. D., and Buck robbed the First State Bank of Okabena, Minnesota, of $2,500. Blanche refused to participate in any holdups and was not with the group. Some of the citizens reacted quickly and opened fire on the fleeing gang, but Barrow and the others managed to get away unscathed.

Eight days after the Okabena robbery, there was more intrigue associated with Raymond Hamilton's LaGrange trial. On May 24,

Minnie Wolf, a beauty parlor operator from Wichita Falls, was indicted on perjury charges in LaGrange in connection with her testimony in the Carmine trial. She had appeared as a voluntary witness and testified that on the day of the robbery Hamilton was in her shop. Following his conviction at LaGrange, Raymond was returned to Hillsboro to stand trial again for the murder of John Bucher. Hamilton's return to the Hillsboro jail caused extra security precautions. All bunks were removed from white men's cells, and mattresses were placed on the floor, as Ray had used metal from bunks to pry bars open in previous escapes. On the morning of Monday, May 29, the task of selecting a jury for the second Bucher trial began. Eighty-eight of the 160 special jurymen examined for the case were in district court at the request of District Judge W. L. Wray. The judge asked them if they had any scruples about giving the death penalty in proper cases and whether through hearsay or otherwise they had an opinion about the guilt or innocence of Hamilton. Some were excused because of illness, but a majority had an opinion. When Wray finished questioning them, forty-four were excused.

Finally, both sides announced they were ready for trial. Raymond, appearing fit and showing interest in the case, wore a light brown suit. Albert Baskett was once again defending him, and A. L. Halford of Aquilla was the first juror chosen for questioning.

On Tuesday morning Hillsboro was startled at the news that a witness in the Hamilton trial, Mark Kitchen, had been kidnapped Monday evening by two men. The men bound and gagged Kitchen and threatened to harm him if he testified against Raymond. The kidnappers' identity was never learned. Tuesday afternoon testimony in the case began. The evidence in the second trial was basically the same as in the first. Mrs. Bucher once again claimed Raymond was one of the assailants who killed her husband. Kitchen testified that Hamilton came into Bucher's store the day of the murder. J. O. Gilbreath, Hillsboro architect, submitted a detailed sketch of the Bucher store. Among those in attendance at the trial Wednesday were members of the Hamilton family and Clyde Barrow's mother. That afternoon Baskett put one witness on the stand and read the testimony of two others who swore Raymond was in Michigan at the time of the slaying. Testimony from Hamilton's stepmother, Dorothy, and friend, J. W. Ringo, was read. Frank Holly, who had not testified at the first trial, took the stand and swore Hamilton was in Michigan when Bucher was murdered. Among those attending the trial was Ed Caster, Dallas County deputy who testified the Hamilton brothers had always been criminals and that Floyd had been arrested for stealing autos, motorcycles, and tires. In truth, the elder brother had never been arrested.

Testimony and final arguments in the case were concluded on Thursday. At 9:30 A.M. Friday, June 1, 1933, Raymond Hamilton was convicted for the murder of John Bucher. Raymond, showing no emotion, was given a life sentence as the jury was unanimous against the death penalty. Several ballots had to be taken before life was decided. Otto Hahn, a garage operator at Malone, was foreman of the jury. Hahn was foreman of a jury that had given David Cates, robber of a bank at Cotton, a seventy-five-year sentence. The first ballot to determine Raymond's guilt was three not guilty, nine guilty. The second through fifth ballots found eleven voting guilty and one not guilty. On the sixth ballot, all voted guilty but also voted against the death penalty. Following the sentencing, Sheriff Freeland said Hamilton would remain in the Hill County jail for a while. The life term was the second heaviest penalty meted out in Hill County. A black man had been hanged there some years before following a murder conviction.

With Ray in jail, Bonnie and Clyde and W. D. Jones met near-disaster in the Texas Panhandle. They were en route to meet Buck and Blanche at Erick, Oklahoma, when their car hurtled into a creek after Clyde missed a "bridge out" sign. Clyde and Jones were okay, but Bonnie was injured and burned when the vehicle caught fire. Barrow and Jones, with help from farmers who heard the crash, lifted the car off Bonnie. The Dallas desperadoes held the farm family captive and surprised and captured two lawmen who had been alerted. Clyde, Bonnie, and W. D. took the lawmen with them to Erick, where they met Buck and Blanche. The lawmen were tied to a tree and by the time they freed themselves, Barrow and his confederates were well on their way to Fort Smith, Arkansas. The Barrow gang rented a tourist cabin in Fort Smith, and Clyde hired a nurse to tend the ailing Bonnie. Clyde then returned to Dallas and brought Bonnie's sister Billie back to Fort Smith to look after her.

On June 22, 1933, Buck Barrow and W. D. Jones robbed a bank in Alma, Arkansas, of $3,600. The next day they robbed two Piggly-Wiggly stores in Fayetteville, Arkansas, of several hundred dollars. Buck and W. D. raced back toward Alma, where they encountered Marshal H. D. Humphrey, Deputy Salyers, and a citizen named Wilson. A shootout ensued, and Marshal Humphrey was killed. Buck and Jones managed to escape and returned to Fort Smith.

The West Dallas gang decided to get back on the road. They drove to Sherman, Texas, and put Billie on a train to Dallas. From

Sherman they drove to Great Bend, Kansas, and rented another tourist cabin. From their base at Great Bend, Buck and W. D. pulled off several small robberies. On July 18 the gang robbed three service stations in Fort Dodge, Iowa. Clyde then drove to Platte City, Missouri, and rented a cabin at the Red Crown Tourist Camp. On the evening of July 19, 1933, acting on tips, local, county, and state officers surrounded the tourist camp. A gun battle erupted and the gang managed to shoot their way to freedom, although Buck and Blanche were wounded. Blanche suffered facial wounds which were not life threatening. Buck was seriously wounded by bullets that struck him in the head.

Clyde next drove to Dexfield Park near Dexter, Iowa. The gang stayed in the park three days without incident until a local farmer spied the group and sensed they were not normal tourists. Before dawn on July 23, the park was surrounded by local and state officers and they were backed up by National Guard personnel. The battle that followed left Buck Barrow dying and Blanche Barrow captured. Clyde, Bonnie, and W. D. got away, but all suffered non-life-threatening wounds. Buck died July 29 in King's Daughters Hospital in Perry, Iowa, and Blanche was returned to Missouri authorities and received a ten-year prison sentence.

Ironically, on the Sunday morning when his friends were under siege in Iowa, Raymond Hamilton was attempting to escape the Dallas County jail. Some saws had been smuggled in to him, and he had tied some bed sheets together for rope. Raymond had managed to lower himself to the second story from his sixth-floor cell when he realized he needed more "rope." He returned to get more bedding, but much to his dismay, Deputy Charles Young was waiting for him. Ray, who was facing 263 years in the state prison, was in the county jail waiting to hear from appeal on his various convictions. Deputy Young searched Hamilton and found the saw blades secreted between the leather of his shoe soles.

Sheriff Schmid had seen enough. He ordered Hamilton to solitary confinement and placed an armed guard on him twenty-four hours a day. Raymond's escape attempt goaded Texas authorities into a plan of agreement with Oklahoma authorities to have the desperado extradited north to stand trial for the murder of Deputy Moore. The sheriffs of Dallas and Hill counties said they would love to see Hamilton have another murder conviction added to the two-centuries-plus time he had earned.

A footnote to the uproar concerning the escapades of Raymond Hamilton and Clyde Barrow was the burial of Buck Barrow. Buck, at the age of thirty, was buried July 31, 1933, in the West Dallas Cemetery. Numerous lawmen were in attendance in anticipation that Clyde might attempt to attend in disguise.

Three days after Buck Barrow was buried, District Attorney Hurt and Sheriff Schmid gave conditional approval to Oklahoma officials to obtain custody of Raymond Hamilton. Robert Burns, acting governor of Oklahoma, signed a requisition upon Texas Governor Miriam A. (Ma) Ferguson, asking that Hamilton be extradited to face trial in Atoka for the Moore murder.

"I will not oppose Hamilton's extradition if the Oklahoma officers will guarantee to return him to Texas in the event he does not receive the death penalty there," Hurt told reporters. "We have spent too much money convicting him in Texas to send him up there to serve a prison sentence."

On Monday, August 7, District Attorney Hurt received a message from Governor Ferguson asking his opinion on the Hamilton matter. The D.A. reiterated his willingness to send Ray to Oklahoma provided he was returned if he did not receive the death penalty. Sheriff Schmid was in full agreement. Monday evening, Oklahoma Governor William H. (Alfalfa Bill) Murray quashed the proceedings. Murray revoked the requisition that acting Governor Burns had instituted. Alfalfa Bill said he revoked the request because Hamilton already had a life sentence in Texas. Following Murray's action, Schmid declared he was ready to ask penitentiary agent (Uncle) Bud Russell to take Raymond to Huntsville as soon as commitment papers could be completed in cases that had not been appealed. Two of the Dallas County cases, totaling fifty-five years, had not been appealed, and 208 years of other cases were on appeal.

Raymond Hamilton began the trip to the state prison at Huntsville on August 8, 1933. He left Dallas chained to an automobile thief, W. W. (Goldie) Shepard. Ironically, Hamilton was sent to prison in connection with two automobile thefts in Fort Worth in which he received five years each. The other 253 years of his sentences were in appeal. Raymond flinched when the lead chain was placed around his neck, but when he noticed a photographer he straightened himself and gave a menacing look. Lillie was the only relative or friend present when Raymond was led from the jail.

"Don't worry, Sis, these guys can't hold me," Hamilton said defiantly. "I'll be home for Christmas."

Lillie, tears streaming, waved to Raymond as he left with Uncle Bud.

Russell, with sixteen other prisoners in addition to Raymond, stopped at the county jail in Corsicana to spend the night. Uncle Bud told Ray he knew he had a bad reputation but that he expected him to comport himself as a gentleman.

"Raymond, I know you've escaped several times and attempted it many times, but if you try that tonight you'll have me to deal with," Russell warned.

Hamilton and the other prisoners were sequestered over the jailer's apartment for the night after being admonished by Russell to stay quiet and not disturb the jailer's family. He needn't have worried. The other prisoners, in awe of Hamilton's record if not his physical stature, heeded his advice to stay quiet. Raymond knew he would get full blame if anything happened. The remainder of the trip to Huntsville was uneventful and Russell gave credit to Hamilton, stating he was "a model prisoner." When Raymond arrived at Huntsville, Warden W. W. Waid vowed he would reform him. Hamilton was assigned to Eastham prison farm near Weldon, where Clyde Barrow had been imprisoned. Raymond distinguished himself as one of the best cotton pickers pound-for-pound Eastham had seen. But cotton was not the six-letter word on his mind: *escape* was the word.

During the summer of 1933 other desperadoes were competing with Raymond and friends for headlines. There was the Kansas City Union Station Massacre, in which four officers and outlaw Frank Nash were killed. Pretty Boy Floyd, Harvey Bailey, and George (Machine Gun) Kelly were attempting to prevent Nash from returning to prison. Nash, caught in the crossfire, was killed. Bailey and Kelly later gained further notoriety in connection with the kidnapping of Oklahoma City oil millionaire Charles Urschel. Urschel was later found alive near Paradise, Texas, where the outlaws had imprisoned him. Bailey and Kelly were subsequently apprehended and convicted. At their sentencing the judge asked if they had anything to say. Kelly remained silent but the defiant Bailey replied, "Yeah, Judge, I got somethin' to say. You can kiss my ass and Kelly's too."

Bonnie and Clyde returned to Dallas September 7, 1933. They lived off meager handouts from relatives and friends until November 8. That day they robbed the McMurray Oil Refinery office in Arp, Texas, getting away with several thousand dollars.

A week after the raid at Arp, W. D. Jones was captured in Houston. The Dallas officers who had tracked him down returned him to Dallas for questioning. Jones sang like a bird for the lawmen, but he interspersed facts with preposterous tales of how he was in fact a prisoner of Barrow. Jones' ramblings were not of use, but the intensive manhunt for Barrow was beginning to bear fruit.

The link lawmen needed was Clyde's brother-in-law, Joe Bill Francis. Francis was married to Marie Barrow but had little use for his notorious in-law. Acting on tips from Francis and information from a dairy farmer who lived near the Sowers community northwest of Dallas, county officers set up an ambush of Clyde and Bonnie on the evening of November 22, 1933. The farmer had noticed meetings between a young couple and others near his place. This information, along with Francis' knowledge of Barrow's movements, led to the ambush. The mothers of Barrow and Parker had planned to meet them that evening. But this evening there were others waiting in the darkness. Sheriff Schmid and Deputies Bob Alcorn, Ed Caster, and Ted Hinton were hidden in bushes nearby. They were packing machine guns and high-powered rifles. The sheriff insisted on issuing a formal halt warning if Bonnie and Clyde showed. With Raymond Hamilton in prison, the sheriff wanted nothing more than to parade Barrow and Parker down Main Street.

Soon the crisp night was interrupted by the sound of an auto slowly approaching the area. The lights from the vehicle illuminated the car the mothers were in. Alcorn and Hinton could see well enough to identify the driver as Barrow. They signaled to the sheriff that it was Clyde. Schmid stood up from his vantage point and bellowed, "Halt!"

Barrow floorboarded the accelerator and began firing out his window. The officers returned the fire, inflicting heavy damage on the vehicle and wounding Clyde and Bonnie in the legs. None of this was enough to prevent the desperado pair from escaping.

Clyde drove to Grand Prairie, where he commandeered another vehicle, and he and Bonnie headed to Oklahoma and safety.

CHAPTER VI

The Eastham Break

Although Raymond Hamilton gave every appearance of being a model prisoner at Eastham, in truth he was plotting escape. Floyd Hamilton visited his brother every two weeks, but there was no way to discuss escape strategy as their conversations were monitored by an assistant warden. Finally, during one of the visits, the warden was called away for a few minutes. The second he was out of sight, Raymond pulled out of his pocket a ring he had made in prison.

"A man wearing this ring will come to see you soon with my escape plan," Raymond told Floyd. That man would be James Mullen, an eight-time loser Ray promised $1,000 for his part in the escape. Mullen was released from prison shortly after Christmas 1933. On January 11, 1934, he showed up at the West Dallas home of Raymond's sister, Lillie McBride, looking for Floyd. Lillie told Mullen where Floyd lived, and groundwork for a possible prison break was laid. On January 12 Mullen met Floyd Hamilton at the latter's home and produced the ring Raymond had shown Floyd.

Mullen told Floyd that Raymond wanted them to plant some guns under a drainage ditch bridge near the prisoners' cellhouse. The elder Hamilton brother wondered aloud how Raymond would be able to get the weapons once they had been stashed. Mullen said Fred Yost, a trusty at Eastham and acquaintance of Raymond and Clyde Barrow, would take care of that. Mullen said a getaway car could be parked about a mile away in the riverbottoms and that whoever commandeered it would need some automatic weapons.

The authorities were keeping steady vigilance on Floyd and his car, and he certainly had no automatic weapons. In the back of his mind, Floyd knew what Raymond had in mind. Persuading Mullen to spend the night, Floyd used the West Dallas grapevine to get in touch with Bonnie and Clyde and set up a meeting. The following day Floyd and Mullen bought .45-caliber pistol ammunition from two Dallas pawn shops and drove to a secluded area between Lancaster and Ferris, where they met with Barrow and Bonnie. Barrow didn't like what he was hearing.

"You're nuts if you think you can plant guns that close to Eastham," Clyde said. "They've got high-riders with Winchesters and they've got dogs to trail you down if they don't kill you first."

Bonnie had no such reservations as she assured Barrow he could bring it off and cackled over the thought of springing Raymond. Her desire to see Ray back bruised Clyde's ego and doubtless made him jealous.

"Don't forget that area is a damned forest and there ain't but one road leadin' in and out of it," Barrow protested.

"Yeah, but don't forget he's servin' time for murderin' ol' man Bucher and never squealed on you," Floyd told Clyde.

Barrow finally relented. The next day he and Bonnie, accompanied by Floyd and Mullen, drove to the prison farm area near Weldon and checked out the escape route. After much bickering about how the guns would be planted and who would do it, it was agreed Mullen and Floyd would do it after darkness set in. Clyde dropped the pair off about a quarter mile from the farm. They had to cross a freshly plowed field. It was muddy and cold as they made their way, carrying two .45-automatic pistols with extra magazines of ammo. They had wrapped the weaponry in an old innertube. Floyd and Mullen circled the back of the prison by the mule barn. Finally, they worked their way to a point where they were cut off by a guard tower. They summoned enough courage to run in view of the tower and fortunately for them it was momentarily unoccupied. They worked their way around the cellhouse area to the bridge and stashed the guns. About that time the bloodhounds started howling in their pens, and Mullen and Floyd wasted no time getting back to Barrow.

"Hell, man, where have you been?" he whispered. "I was fixin' to leave!"

Sunday, January 14, 1934, was a joyous day for Raymond Hamilton. In a visit from Floyd he received precious information. The guns were planted and Clyde and Bonnie, along with Mullen, would be with the getaway car. Tuesday, January 16, would be the day.

On Monday, the day before the escape, the trusty named Yost

smuggled the pistols to Raymond. Hiding the weapons presented a problem, but Hamilton had it figured. Raymond had persuaded a cell chum, Joe Palmer, to act out a ruse in return for his freedom. Palmer, an asthmatic who hated the Eastham authorities because they beat him when he could not keep up with the work, was more than happy to participate. Raymond gave Joe the pistols to hide in his bunk. Palmer feigned a furious asthma attack and was allowed to remain in bed throughout that Monday. In the wee hours of Tuesday morning, January 16, Hamilton eased his way to Joe's bunk and Ray took one of the pistols. Their plan was set.

At 7:00 A.M. the work details set out for the timberland. The morning was cool and foggy as guard Ollin Bozeman led his work detail, which included Joe Palmer, away from the cellhouse area. When Bozeman reached his work area he noticed Hamilton in his group. Although not unduly alarmed, because Raymond had given no trouble to date, Bozeman summoned highrider Major Crowson. When Crowson reached the scene Ray and Joe pulled their weapons and yelled "Hands up!" Crowson fired immediately, inflicting a scalp wound on Palmer. Joe returned the fire point-blank, hitting Crowson twice, once in the abdomen and once in the head. The highrider gasped and fell mortally wounded, blood pouring from his wounds. Hamilton fired at Bozeman, hitting him in the hip. The guard clutched at the wound and fell to the ground. Pandemonium reigned as prisoners and authorities dodged for cover, and Raymond and Palmer started their dash to freedom. Three other convicts, Henry Methvin, Hilton Bybee, and Joe French, followed them on a mile run to the getaway car.

When Barrow and Mullen heard Hamilton and the others getting near, they started spraying the treetops with machine-gun fire to deter pursuing officers. French fled in an opposite direction from the other four and did not make it to the getaway vehicle. Upon arrival at the auto the winded Hamilton and nervous Barrow quickly decided to let Bybee and Methvin ride out too. Palmer leaped in the front seat with the rescuers while Hamilton, Bybee, and Methvin crawled in the luggage compartment.

With every law enforcement officer in the Southwest on the lookout, the desperadoes stayed on the backroads toward Rhome, Texas, where they planned to meet with Floyd Hamilton and L. C. Barrow, Clyde's brother. The group stopped late that afternoon for gas at Hillsboro. The station attendant, not realizing his customers' identity, told a wild tale of how Bonnie and Clyde shot their way right in to the Eastham cellhouse and freed Raymond Hamilton. Barrow acted amazed at the story as he paid the attendant. Clyde drove to the predesignated meeting spot near Rhome, where Floyd and L. C. were waiting with a change of clothes for the fugitives. The group decided to break up to make it more difficult for lawmen.

Following the raid, Bozeman and Crowson were rushed to a Huntsville hospital. Bozeman was treated and released, but physicians expressed little hope for Crowson. Prison Director Lee Simmons said no special precautions had been taken to guard Hamilton despite his constant declarations that he would escape. Simmons predicted that the escapees would hide in East Texas. That night Simmons visited Crowson in his hospital room. Crowson whispered an apology for leaving his assigned area and riding too close to the inmates. Simmons told him not to worry — he (Simmons) would deal with the escapees. The next day Major Crowson, twenty-four, was dead.

The day following the escape, Joe French was captured in the Trinity River bottoms near Eastham. Saying he knew nothing of the escape plan, he said he was just trying to take advantage. Following the escape, Sheriff Smoot Schmid crowed to anyone who would listen that he had warned Texas prison officials to watch Raymond Hamilton carefully because he would without question attempt to escape. The sheriff recalled when he warned the prison authorities about Hamilton that one had said, "Hamilton is as gentle as a male manicurist. He's just like any other prisoner."

"Raymond Hamilton boasted repeatedly that he would escape," Schmid said. "He even said he would come to Dallas when he got out and kill Deputy Will Moore."

Lt. Will Fritz of the Dallas Police had also warned penitentiary officials not to send Raymond out on work crews, but rather to hold him behind the Walls at Huntsville. Prison leaders could only curse themselves for not heeding the advice of Dallas area lawmen concerning the West Dallas desperado.

Local and state authorities were now receiving the aid of the federal government in their battle with the West Dallas gang. Frank Blake, chief investigator for the Dallas Bureau of the Department of Justice, said the outlaws had violated the Dyer Act by driving stolen vehicles across state lines, and all federal agents were empowered to search for them. The alarm over the outlaw band from Texas was now national.

Three days after the escape, a filling station robbery in Hugo, Oklahoma, was credited to Raymond and Clyde, but in truth they were not together at that time. Rains in East and Central Texas were hampering efforts of lawmen in their search for the escapees and their rescuers. Reports were coming in from all over the Southwest from well-meaning but overzealous citizens saying they had seen members of the gang.

Three prison guards lost their jobs in the aftermath of the break. Lee Simmons fired B. S. Mathis, J. R. McCaffitty, and Doc Robertson because they failed to stand at their posts with the convict squads when the shooting erupted.

"I am not firing you because you got out of the line of fire but because you ran off and left your squads of men," Simmons said to the men. "I don't blame any man for seeking shelter when he is fired upon, but I do blame you for running off and leaving the men you have sworn to guard."

Tom Small, assistant farm manager, told Simmons he found the three guards 500 yards behind the line of fire and away from the convicts they had taken into the woods that fateful Tuesday morning.

On January 22 the name of W. D. Jones resurfaced. The "Deacon," still held in the Dallas County jail, was indicted by the Bell County grand jury on a charge of murder for the shooting of Doyle Johnson. Jones told Dallas officers he had participated in the murder.

The month of January 1934 was filled with an intensive manhunt for Raymond Hamilton and Clyde Barrow. Deputy Sheriff H. W. Keller of Dexter, Iowa, sent to Sheriff Smoot Schmid a sawed-off shotgun confiscated after the shootout at Dexfield Park. Deacon Jones identified the shotgun as Clyde Barrow's, and lawmen determined it was the gun used to kill Deputy Sheriff Malcolm Davis.

A possum hunt was added to the wild goose chases Dallas officers conducted. A former deputy sheriff said he had seen people in the bottomlands between Garland and Rose Hill that he believed to be the West Dallas gang. A check by authorities revealed a group of possum hunters. The combination of hysteria and reprehension over the West Dallas band's activities generated reactions that must have caused a chuckle or two in the outlaw camp.

The story continued of how members of the gang held target practice daily. Actually, the majority of the time they did no practice shooting for fear of arousing attention. The police did have a confiscated photo showing Barrow thrusting his fist through a hole in a road sign. W. D. Jones told officers that Barrow had made the hole with less than a dozen shots. Authorities reported that Raymond Hamilton and Bonnie Parker were also excellent shots.

Lawmen described Barrow as one who would "kill without compunction anyone who gets in his way."

"Why, he'll just shoot a man to see him kick as he dies," said one

officer. "He doesn't care whether his victim is an officer or an innocent citizen who just accidentally happened to be present."

One grizzled deputy assured reporters, "We'll get 'em if they
keep comin' to Dallas."

On Tuesday, January 30, Hilton Bybee was arrested in Amarillo.
Bybee had spent his brief freedom in Oklahoma and the Texas
Panhandle.

With February came a bum rap for the West Dallas gang. They
were accused of robbing a bank in Independence, Kansas. It may
have been Pretty Boy Floyd and some of his confederates, but Barrow and Hamilton were still in hiding.

Though not active in early February of 1934, the desperadoes
were in the news. An Allred-for-Governor Club, with Gerald C.
Mann as chairman, was formed in Dallas. James V. Allred, attorney
general of Texas and aspirant for the Democratic nomination for the
governorship, had been in North Texas for several days conferring
with supporters and visiting his brother, Raymond Allred of
Longview, who was at Baylor Hospital in Dallas recovering from injuries received in an auto accident. A campaign plank advocating a
reorganization of the Texas state police system to combat vicious,
violent lawlessness was announced by Allred.

"Our very government is challenged," Allred declared. "The
Barrows and Pretty Boy Floyds have been unloosed upon a helpless
public. Some time ago I declared for a reformation of the pardon
system, but that alone will not be enough. We need to modernize. A
central bureau of identification to cooperate with local police officers
should be established within such a state police organization as the
Highway Patrol. Machine gun bandits and kidnappers have gotten
ahead of our officers because of our present antiquated machinery.
The only way to put them out of business is to speed up ourselves."

Several days after the Allred speech in Dallas, a Highway Patrol
officer reported seeing Bonnie and Clyde and Raymond Hamilton
in an auto near Terrell. The trio escaped the pursuit of the officer. It
could have been Barrow and Parker, but Raymond was in hiding in
Wichita Falls. Perhaps the third person was Joe Palmer or Henry
Methvin.

The furor over Hamilton and Barrow carried over into the treasure hunt field. A south Dallas County resident filed an application
with the sheriff's department to dig for money he believed the pair
had buried in the Mountain Creek bottoms. The applicant told
Deputy W. D. Walker that he had already received permission from
the landowner to dig.

"He said I could dig there all I want to," the man said. "I've already found some brickbats and other things."

Without bothering to get the man's identity, Walker gave his permission.

"We've never heard of that bunch having any money," said the deputy as he walked away with a broad grin. "In fact, we know they're broke most of the time and never have anything but chili money.

"But," he added, "I know a little more now about how these stories about old-time bad men and their buried treasure got spread so far."

On February 12 the gang was once again falsely accused. A group of bandits had a shootout with officers near Springfield, Missouri, and escaped. They were last seen entering Oklahoma. Again the chances were good that officers had encountered the Pretty Boy Floyd gang, whose habit it was to always retreat to the Cookson hills of northeastern Oklahoma when pursued. (Barrow usually hid in southeastern Oklahoma.)

With Valentine's Day came the news that the state legislature was bequeathing something other than candy or good wishes on Raymond and his cronies. As part of an appropriations bill, the lawmakers provided for a reward of $1,000 for Barrow and $500 each for Hamilton and Parker, dead or alive.

By mid-February the gang's resources were depleted and they had had time to visit relatives and friends at out-of-the-way places in North Texas. Raymond Hamilton had been in hiding in Wichita Falls, where he had linked up with Mary O'Dare, Gene's wife. The short brunette had always liked the fast-talking Hamilton, and with Gene in prison, Ray now had Mary to be his moll.

With Mary in tow, Hamilton met with members of the gang near Vernon. Hamilton and Barrow discussed where and when to strike. On February 19 the group, now comprising Henry Methvin, Joe Palmer, Raymond Hamilton, Clyde Barrow, Bonnie Parker, and Mary O'Dare, left Vernon to meet near Greenville with members of the Barrow and Parker families. Following the get-together the gang loaded up and headed for Ranger, where they burglarized a National Guard armory, arming themselves with Browning automatic rifles, automatic pistols, and plenty of ammunition. The next day the gang met Floyd Hamilton south of Dallas on the Lancaster Highway. Floyd said he would hide some of the weapons for them, and it was agreed they would meet a week later near Cedar Hill.

On February 26 Floyd and his wife, Mildred, took Bonnie's mother, Clyde's mother, L. C. Barrow, and Billie Mace to meet with

Hamilton and Barrow on a deserted country road in the Trinity River bottoms near Rockwall. Raymond introduced Mary O'Dare to the family. Unmentioned during the frivolity was the fact that Raymond and Clyde had cased the Henry Bank in Lancaster.

The following day Raymond, Clyde, and Joe Palmer drove into Lancaster and parked on a side street near the R. P. Henry Bank. With Palmer remaining in the car, Hamilton and Barrow got out and walked briskly into the bank, surprising L. L. Henry, cashier, and customer Olin Worley. Clyde brandished a sawed-off shotgun and Raymond had a tow sack tied to his belt to gather the money. Hamilton pushed Worley aside and Barrow rushed to the back of the bank, where he found another customer, Bud Brooks, who had been reading a newspaper when the robbers entered. The bandits made Brooks and Worley sit on the floor and forced Henry to open the safe drawer. While Clyde maintained order with the shotgun, Raymond gathered $4,138.50 in his sack. They then forced their victims to follow them to the back door. From there they beat a hasty retreat to the getaway car. Palmer had the engine running, and before anyone had time to react the three were gone.

"They just walked in and quietly told us what to do," Henry related later. "Evidently the whole thing had been planned, for there was no discussion between the two."

Worley said the shotgun held by Barrow did not waver a fraction of an inch and was obviously held by steady hands.

"You could tell by looking at him that he would shoot in an instant if he thought it was necessary," Worley said.

After leaving Lancaster the trio headed for a rendezvous with Bonnie, Henry Methvin, and Mary O'Dare at the Bluebird Farm on the Wilmer Road. The holdup car, which had been stolen from G. Jeff Waggoner of Wichita Falls, was abandoned at that point. The crew of desperadoes then fled the area in an auto they had stolen from the Earle Johnson Motor Company of Temple. While the group motored toward one of their old hideaways in southeastern Oklahoma, Clyde, who was driving, noticed in the rearview mirror that Raymond, in the back seat, was cutting Mary in on a share of the Lancaster money.

"Ray, she don't get none of that," Barrow complained. "It's split between Bonnie and me and you. She didn't do a damned thing."

"Hell, neither did Bonnie," Raymond challenged. "She's my girl ---she gets a cut."

Mary ended up getting part of the money, but it was less than a fourth.

Fearing possible capture in Oklahoma, where lawmen were constantly combing the hills for Pretty Boy Floyd, the Texas desperadoes headed into the Midwest. They ended up in the Terre Haute, Indiana, area, where they spent several days. During this period (Two Gun) John Dillinger, using a wooden "gun," escaped from prison. Midwestern authorities, already alerted to be on the watch for the West Dallas gang, now had to begin a manhunt for Dillinger. In Terre Haute, Raymond and Clyde bought new suits for themselves and dresses and jewelry for Bonnie and Mary. But all was not well. Barrow did not trust the O'Dare girl and barely concealed this feeling. Hamilton had nothing but contempt for Methvin and feared Henry's hair-trigger mentality would eventually cause more problems. Bickering among the gang members continued for several days, culminated by a violent argument between Bonnie and Clyde.

Raymond had seen enough. He promptly stole a car, and told Mary to get in and wait for him. Hamilton said his goodbyes to Clyde and Bonnie and left. It was March 6, 1934.

CHAPTER VII

Money and Mayhem

Hamilton, already plotting his strategy, set a course for Texas. He and Mary ended up in Beaumont, and, while he hid out, Mary went to Dallas to meet with Floyd Hamilton. Floyd had cached some of the firearms from the Ranger burglary, and Ray sent word through Mary to bring them to Beaumont. The elder Hamilton and a friend, S. J. (Baldy) Whatley, took the guns to Raymond.

Raymond returned to Dallas in mid-March and during one of his meetings with Floyd was introduced to John Basden, a truck driver from West Dallas who was down on his luck and in need of some fast money. Ray told the men of his intention to rob the Grand Prairie State Bank. Basden wanted to go along, but Raymond did not like the idea. Floyd volunteered to come along too and sit in one of the getaway cars. Finally Ray agreed, and on the morning of Monday, March 19, they drove into Grand Prairie. Floyd was driving Basden's auto and Raymond and Basden were in Ray's sedan. Floyd parked outside the bank and went in to get change for a $20 bill. He came out, gave Raymond a signal that the bank was right for a robbery, and got back in Basden's car. At that time the only people in the bank were J. E. Waggoner, bank president; J. T. Yeager, cashier; and Maude Crawford, bookkeeper. There wasn't much business because it was cold and there was ice on the roads.

Raymond and Basden burst into the bank, with .45s drawn. Miss Crawford was warming herself by the stove in the back of the bank by the vault. Raymond walked up to her.

"Lady," he said, "you just stand right where you are and we won't bother you."

Hamilton then pulled out a white mail bag from under his coat and started gathering money. Waggoner, who couldn't hear well, at first wasn't exactly aware of what was happening. He approached Basden, who was nervously holding the gun.

"Sit down, old man!" Basden ordered. "Damn, I'm not used to this business."

"Is this all the money?" Raymond asked.

Yes, that was all of it.

"What about the vault?"

No answer.

Ray went inside the vault and gathered up some roll money. That was all they had in there, as they had been expecting the blond bandit to strike sooner or later.

"Okay, everybody in the vault. And hurry," Raymond said.

Just then, Frank Gracey of the Dallas Production Credit Association came into the bank. He was greeted by Raymond, who waved him into the vault with the rest. Unbeknownst to Ray, the bank had installed a device on the vault door that wouldn't let it completely be closed without a special combination. It would partially lock and would not close or open completely. Ray shoved and shoved, trying to close the door.

"Why in the hell won't this door close?" he yelled. "No wonder you don't keep any more money in there than that."

He then motioned to Basden, who was about to drop dead from heart failure, and the pair dashed out the back door. Raymond threw the money bag in Basden's car and told Floyd to meet them that night at a hiding place near Henrietta, Texas. He jumped under the wheel of his sedan and Basden, still nervous, was having trouble getting in. Ray backed out and shot off down the road before Basden even got his door closed.

That evening Floyd drove to Henrietta in Basden's car and handed the sack of money to Raymond. Ray divided the $1,543.74 equally among Basden, Floyd, and himself.

Raymond found Mary in Wichita Falls, and they set out to have as good and inconspicuous time as possible. They went to southeast Texas, where Raymond abandoned his Chevrolet sedan and stole a new V-8 near Lufkin. In the abandoned vehicle authorities found a deposit slip from the Grand Prairie bank and several cartridges from a German Luger automatic pistol, but Hamilton was miles away.

Shortly after the Grand Prairie robbery the Texas Rangers officially became involved in the search for Raymond Hamilton and Clyde Barrow. Two Rangers from Capt. H. D. Odneal's company in

Fort Worth were assigned full-time to the hunt. It was also about this time that retired Ranger Frank Hamer was secretly assigned to join forces with Ted Hinton and Bob Alcorn of the Dallas sheriff's office to track down Barrow.

On Friday, March 23, Hilton Bybee escaped from the Houston County jail in Crockett. He had been returned from Amarillo to stand trial in connection with the murder of Major Crowson. However, two days before his escape, the charge had been dismissed when Warden W. W. Waid said Crowson told him he had been shot by Joe Palmer. While Bybee was escaping jail in southeast Texas, Raymond Hamilton was also in the area. Hamilton once again visited Lufkin and stole an automobile. Authorities found the auto he ditched and in it they found torn deposit slips from the Grand Prairie State Bank, a machine gun, rifle, and pistol bullets. Hamilton stole the vehicle from Mrs. R. C. Musselwhite, wife of the Lufkin city attorney, as she sat on her front porch and screamed for help. Three other witnesses identified the thief as Hamilton. Officers still were under the mistaken impression that Clyde Barrow and Raymond were together. Soon after this, Hilton Bybee was captured by officers near Woodson in West Texas and jailed in Breckenridge.

As March ended and April began, a chain of events would bring about one of the greatest manhunts in U.S. history. Raymond Hamilton was running low on funds, and with Mary O'Dare as his mate in bed and on the road, he planned a strike. Raymond's target was the bank in West, Texas. His reward was $1,865.75. Ray entered the bank at 10:30 A.M. Saturday, March 31, 1934. He waved his automatic pistol at bank officials and employees. Raymond forced the five men to lie on the floor and the two women employees to sit in nearby chairs. He scooped up some money from a teller's cage.

"I want more money and I want it now!" he demanded.

One of the bankers timidly told Hamilton other funds were in the vault under a time lock.

"This is the first place I've been where money was under a time lock at this time of day," Raymond said.

He then herded everyone into the vault and slammed the door. Ray gathered up the rest of the money in the outer bank and dashed out the door to the car. Mary drove as Raymond looked for any pursuit. They headed out the old Waco highway and cut off toward the east at Katy Lake. They made it fine until they got to Leroy, where their vehicle stuck on a muddy country lane. Two local boys and a farmer, Charley Uptmor, offered to get a team of mules and pull Raymond and his moll out. Ray pulled a pistol on the startled locals. Hamilton then demanded Uptmor pull the getaway car out with his car. Raymond held a gun on the men as Mary guided their auto out of the hole behind Uptmor's car. Raymond leaped in on the passenger side and waved a pistol-drawn farewell to Uptmor and the boys.

The robbers were now headed toward Mexia, and every time Mary would let off the accelerator Hamilton would implore her to drive all out. And she did — right off the road, over a ditch, and into an embankment. The impact propelled Ray's head through the windshield. He suffered multiple lacerations and a broken nose. Mary hit the steering wheel so hard it broke, injuring her chest and knocking her unconscious. Raymond, a frightful sight with his bleeding face and smashed nose, finally gathered his senses and shook Mary. She came to but nearly fainted again when she saw him. They were near the Horne Hill community outside Mexia, and just when it appeared they would have to flee on foot they heard an auto approaching. Mrs. Cam Gunter of Thelma and her son Jolly, four, saw the car in the ditch and the pitiful-looking couple beside it. Mrs. Gunter, using a tow rope she had, gunned her auto in an attempt to pull out the desperadoes' car but the rope broke.

A. P. Mattox, a farmer who had been watching from the distance, went to a nearby farmhouse to borrow a chain. About the same time a local citizen, James Bennett, passed the scene but did not stop. The injured man standing at the scene looked all too familiar. Bennett wheeled up the farmhouse lane to intercept Mattox and warn him there might be more to the situation than it appeared. Raymond did not like what he was seeing. He told Mary to gather everything she could from their car and put it in Mrs. Gunter's vehicle. Lest the woman question his sincerity, Hamilton pulled a pistol out of his car. Mrs. Gunter screamed and ran for her son. By now, Bennett, who had borrowed Mattox's shotgun, was charging. Ray fired once over his head and Bennett stopped. At that, Ray forced Mrs. Gunter to get in her car with Mary, and he set the screaming Jolly out of the car. Raymond raced off down the road toward Mexia.

The nearest telephone was four miles from the wreck scene, so Bennett and Mattox were delayed in contacting lawmen. Meanwhile, as news of the robbery and kidnapping spread, groups of farmers formed posses to search the area. Sheriff W. B. Mobley arrived at the wreck scene and searched the abandoned car. He found $4.45, a money wrapper, empty cartridges, and pistol clips. Mobley and his deputies also found a check made out to the Grand Prairie State Bank.

"If some of these farm boys catch this fella before we do, he could be in for some trouble," the sheriff said. "But if it's who I think it is, he's long gone by now."

Will Buchanan, a detective from Waco, notified area physicians to be on the lookout for the robber and his female companion. The doctors needn't have worried—Hamilton wasn't about to stop again until he felt safe. Mrs. Claude Rogers, who lived near the wreck scene, took charge of the Gunter child. Bank officials and the farmer, Uptmor, were shown photographs of Raymond Hamilton and identified him as the man they had encountered. Authorities couldn't be sure his moll was Mary O'Dare, but they knew the wife of Ray's former partner had not been seen for some time.

By nightfall, Raymond, Mary, and Mrs. Gunter were in Houston. Hamilton got cleaned up and rented a hotel room, and the trio settled in for the evening. Ray promised to release their hostage the following morning in return for a promise that she would not attempt escape. True to his word, the following morning Hamilton released Mrs. Gunter after stealing a new Ford sedan. He apologized to his victim for the inconvenience and gave her money to get home. Mary was excited about the new car and especially its yellow wheels. Feeling cocky after his latest success, Ray headed for Dallas. It was Easter Sunday, April 1, 1934.

Clyde Barrow, Bonnie Parker, and Henry Methvin were back in Texas on that sunny Sunday. Bonnie had a white rabbit she wanted to give her mother for Easter. They planned to meet family members at a predetermined spot that morning some four miles west of Grapevine near Highway 114. Barrow and Raymond Hamilton used the area frequently as a rendezvous point in particular and a hiding place in general. The thick postoak timber and backroads made the area ideal for "cooling off."

While waiting for family members, Bonnie and Henry whiled away the time drinking whiskey. Clyde was not drinking. He had heard Hamilton had robbed the West bank and knew lawmen might be in the area searching for him. About 2:45 that afternoon his suspicions were confirmed. Three Texas State Highway Patrol motorcycle officers appeared on the scene. The officers, Polk Ivy, E. B. Wheeler, and H. D. Murphy, were on routine patrol. They were aware of Raymond's robbery the day before, but they were not actively searching for him since the robbery had occurred some sixty miles south.

The lawmen noticed a black sedan with yellow wheels parked off a gravel side road. There were three occupants in the auto. It could be anyone out enjoying the beautiful spring day, Ivy thought as he passed by the vehicle and continued up the road. Wheeler and Murphy were more curious and brought their machines to a halt a few yards from the car.

Clyde knew he had the drop on them and decided to capture them for a joy ride. But his orders "Let's take 'em" were misunderstood by the drunk and trigger-happy Methvin. Henry quickly stepped out of the car and fired a shotgun blast into Wheeler. The officer fell dead off his motorcycle. Before Murphy could react, Methvin and Barrow shot him dead. Clyde was mad enough at Henry to kill him too for his foolhardy action and roundly cursed him. Before Ivy knew what had befallen his fellow officers, Barrow was speeding toward eastern Oklahoma.

With Raymond Hamilton and Clyde Barrow scourging the Southwest and John Dillinger running wild in the Midwest, the pressure on law enforcement authorities at every level was intensifying. Governor Ma Ferguson was expected to announce new and larger rewards for the apprehension of Hamilton and Barrow. It was learned that the murder of Murphy, twenty-three, had come twelve days before he was to marry twenty-year-old Marie Tullis from his hometown of Alto. The couple had already rented an apartment in Fort Worth, where the lawman headquartered.

Raymond Hamilton's new car had no radio, so he knew nothing of the tragedy at Grapevine as he cruised into West Dallas late that Sunday afternoon. Ray let Mary out about a block from Floyd Hamilton's house and told her to tell Floyd he would meet him near Grapevine. When Mary told Floyd where Raymond planned to meet him, and when she bragged about the yellow wheels on the car, the elder brother nearly fainted. The meeting place was only about a mile from where the shootings occurred, and Barrow's car also had yellow tires. Driving the backroads like a demon, Floyd reached his brother before the law could. Floyd told Raymond about the murders, and quickly the brothers changed out the wheels on their autos so Ray would not be driving with the telltale yellow ones.

By nightfall, Ray, with Mary in tow, was en route to New Orleans, where he ditched his car, stole another one, and then registered at the Lafayette Hotel. His name was well known in New Orleans but his face was not, so he wined and dined Mary, buying her jewelry and clothes. Staying at the hotel under an alias, Hamilton and his moll were doing their best to prove that crime does indeed sometimes pay.

Conclusive evidence linking Barrow to the Grapevine murders came Monday, April 2, when Barney Finn, veteran identification expert with the Fort Worth Police Department, identified Clyde's fingerprints on a whiskey bottle found near the scene of the shootings. Shortly thereafter, murder charges against Barrow and Bonnie Parker were filed in Justice of the Peace J. H. Faulkner's court in Fort Worth. Once again, reports of the West Dallas desperadoes were received and had to be checked by carloads of officers who were heavily armed. Hysteria was real.

"We don't know where he is," said one officer. "I've driven, walked, and hunted until I'm about to drop. We've gone everywhere and done everything we can and we don't know where he is. He might be in Dallas or within ten miles of it and he might be one thousand miles away."

Clyde Clayton, the man Raymond Hamilton stole a car from in Houston prior to returning Mrs. Gunter's to her, announced he was offering a $45 reward for the return of his auto. Lawmen, meanwhile, were under the delusion that Ray and Clyde were planning to reunite. This misconception doubtless hindered the authorities, as they concentrated their search efforts in areas the two had been known to frequent.

The identity of Raymond's female companion was still a mystery. A check of female acquaintances of Ray's from West Dallas revealed they were in the area and had no interest in robbing banks and fleeing for their lives. In addition to Hamilton's old flames, numerous friends and relatives of Bonnie and Clyde and Raymond were now being questioned by officers for any shred of evidence that could lead to their capture. The officers were amazed at how little the relatives and friends knew when questioned.

Federal officers were now in the chase to stay, according to Frank J. Blake, chief of the Dallas bureau of the Department of Justice. Capt. R. W. Aldrich of Headquarters Company in Austin announced that Capt. Harry D. Odneal and three members of his company of Texas Rangers were assigned to the case. Local officers everywhere were involved in their jurisdictions trying to help stamp out the reign of terror fomented by the West Dallas criminals. At least at this point Barrow could rest assured he had a place to stay if and when the hated "laws" snuffed him out. Hugh Moore, an undertaker in Arlington, said he would furnish the desperado a grave and a $44 tombstone.

"Not only that," said Moore, "but I'll guarantee the care of his grave for ninety-nine years."

Following the Easter killings, Bonnie and Clyde and Henry Methvin laid a patchwork trail between eastern Oklahoma, East Texas, and Louisiana, the latter where Henry's parents lived. Shortly after the murders of Wheeler and Murphy, the Barrow gang would add to their list a victim from the other side of the law. Once again, Methvin was the catalyst. Through the underworld grapevine Henry had caught wind that Wade McNabb, former trusty at the Eastham prison farm, had bragged that Clyde Barrow had been his "wife" at Eastham. Methvin had chided Barrow with the story before, and now he really turned it on, hoping this would assuage Clyde's contempt for him over the Grapevine killings.

Clyde demanded to know where McNabb lived. Methvin said he lived in Greenville, and away they went. A query here and a query there turned up McNabb's whereabouts. Spotted walking down the street, he was ordered to get in the car. The trio drove him to near Waskom, Texas, near the Louisiana border. Clyde and Henry marched McNabb into the woods, and ordered him to get on his knees and say his prayers. After McNabb, twenty-two, blubbered a few words, Methvin clubbed him on the head with a shotgun butt. Barrow then shot the unconscious victim twice in the forehead at point-blank range. Bonnie asked no questions when the two returned to the car.

McNabb's body was discovered Tuesday, April 3, by Dick Vaughn of the *Houston Press*. He had been sent to make the search after the newspaper received an anonymous letter in printed scrawl. The letter stated that if the directions of an enclosed map were followed the carcass of one of "Lee Simmons' chief rats" would be found. Vaughn went to Shreveport and enlisted the aid of Sheriff T. R. Hughes, who added Deputy Sheriff R. A. Shaw to the search party. After several hours of searching, the trio located the body. Barrow and Methvin did not rob their victim, for the searchers found sixteen dollar bills and a pair of crooked dice on him. Officials in Panola County, Texas, were alerted, and Sheriff John Sanders of Marhsall began an investigation.

Although authorities did not suspect Barrow of McNabb's death, they were still after him in connection with the Grapevine murders. More than half of the 100 members of the Highway Patrol were concentrated at strategic points in North Texas in a comprehensive search for Barrow and Raymond Hamilton. Patrolmen were arriving in Dallas and other North Texas locales from as far as Brownsville and Corpus Christi. Capt. O. S. Hamm of Dallas was in general command, with Lt. Lee Miller second in command. Third in order was Lt. W. J. Roberts, who was stationed at Waxahachie.

While part of the Highway Patrol attended funeral services for Patrolmen Wheeler and Murphy, the remainder were searching the homes of relatives of Clyde Barrow, Bonnie Parker, and Raymond Hamilton in and near Dallas. At least fifteen such places were visited, according to Lieutenant Miller. Relatives of the three were more or less indifferent to the search, Miller said, saying, "Help yourself," but declining to assist. The Texas Rangers started congregating in Dallas with Captains D. E. Hamer, H. D. Odneal, E. H. Hammon, and Privates J. J. Shown, J. O. Brannon, and W. R. Todd on the scene to aid in the search for the West Dallas desperadoes. Numerous officers from various cities were represented in crowds that gathered to pay final tributes to Wheeler and Murphy in Fort Worth. Wheeler was buried at Cleburne and Murphy at Alto. The reward for the capture of the killers was raised to $1,694 when members of the Dallas Police Department pitched in $79 for that purpose within a few minutes after a petition was posted.

"We cannot accept rewards but we can contribute to a fund to help catch Clyde Barrow," was one statement in the preface of the petition explaining the purpose of the collection.

At Lufkin, near Alto where Murphy grew up, employees of the Highway Department raised $100 as a "Texas Rat Extermination Fund" and offered it as a reward for the capture, dead or alive, of Barrow or Hamilton. Citizens attending the meeting added to the fund. At Sherman, County Judge Jake L. Loy asked the commissioners' court to buy additional firearms for the sheriff's department.

Barrow was still on the prowl Wednesday night, April 4. Along with Bonnie and Methvin, he kidnapped and robbed John Hall, a filling station operator at DeKalb in northeast Texas. The trio, who were riding in a new sedan, robbed Hall of $40 and four gallons of gasoline and forced him and a customer into their vehicle about 9:00 P.M. Hall and the customer were released eight miles out of DeKalb. Hall identified Barrow from newspaper photos. The station operator noted the license number on the bandits' car, and it was broadcast to all patrolmen.

Reports that Barrow had been seen in Dallas brought lawmen on the run, but no trace of the criminals could be found. Though denying he was assuming charge of the case, Capt. L. G. Phares, head of the Texas Highway Patrol, spent Wednesday afternoon in conferences with federal and local investigators in connection with the search.

"Members of the patrol are bending every effort toward the capture of Barrow and will continue to do so until the chase is ended," Phares said. "But they will work in cooperation with local authorities in all districts in which it is believed he might be found. In Dallas Captain O. S. Hamm will be left in charge of the patrol's part of the search."

Phares spent much time in the afternoon in conference with Frank J. Blake, chief investigator of the Dallas Bureau of the Department of Justice, but declined to make any statement concerning the meeting. Blake said federal officers had joined the search several days before. Working with city and county officers, Hamm made his headquarters at the Dallas city detective office, where he was offered access to the identification bureau facilities and use of any equipment and men that might be needed.

Meanwhile, reports of the desperadoes being here, there, and everywhere were rampant. Texas Rangers, headed by Capt. D. E. Hamer, Gainesville officers, and a group of Oklahoma officers joined forces in an effort to attend what was expected to be a reunion of Barrow and Raymond Hamilton in Love County, Oklahoma, near a toll bridge on the Red River north of Gainesville. The supposed reunion never occurred, as the outlaws were hundreds of miles apart and had no intention of getting together.

Subscriptions toward a reward for the capture, dead or alive, of Barrow, were reported in many sections. The fund raised by the Dallas police reached $237. A $100 reward was raised by the Tarrant County Sheriff's Department in Fort Worth. Checks were received at the headquarters office of the Highway Patrol at Austin, raising the entire fund to more than $2,000. A $500 reward was posted by the state, and $1,000 was guaranteed by Captain Phares.

The body of Wade McNabb was positively identified by his father, S. T. McNabb, a brother, S. M. McNabb of Greenville, and a sister, Mrs. Cleo Kirkland of Tyler. After a statement by the relatives, the body was turned over to his father and was taken to Greenville for burial in the family plot.

With Raymond Hamilton and Clyde Barrow out of sight, one of the Eastham Five was again in the news. Of forty-five special veniremen examined, only two were selected for the trial of Hilton Bybee in Throckmorton. Bybee, charged in connection with the armed robbery of the filling station near Woodson, was awaiting trial on the Thursday following the weekend crime spree of his more notorious pals. The court had overruled a state motion for change of venue before selection of the jury started. John Lee Smith, defense attorney, said he would base his case on Bybee's alleged insanity. He told the court he believed his client was insane because of the way he answered the attorney's questions.

In the Friday, April 6, 1934, edition of the *Dallas Morning News*, a story ran that summed up the situation pertaining to the desperadoes. The article was accompanied by photographs of Raymond

Hamilton, Clyde Barrow, and Bonnie Parker. The headline read "BAR-
ROW GANGSTERS MAINTAIN HOLD ON SLIPPERY FREEDOM" and was
subheaded "OFFICERS CONFIDENT END NEAR AS HUNT GROWS IN IN-
TENSITY IN STATE." It read in part:

> In headlong flight from one of the greatest manhunts in the
> history of the Southwest, Clyde Barrow, Bonnie Parker and
> Raymond Hamilton Thursday night still maintained a slippery
> hold on their perilous freedom.
>
> Though having received no clues on which they might hope
> for a speedy capture of the outlaws, investigators are almost
> unanimous in the belief that the gangsters are nearing the end of
> their sorry trail.
>
> With the public becoming acquainted with the appearance of
> the outlaws through published pictures and descriptions, the out-
> laws should find it increasingly difficult to avoid recognition by
> persons who will immediately notify officers and set them on
> their trail. Only a few reports were received by officers Thursday
> of persons believed to be Barrow or Hamilton and investigators
> were of the opinion they may have found temporary protection in
> a hideout . . .

CHAPTER VIII

The Long Arm Gets Longer

On Friday, April 6, 1934, the Barrow gang was confronted by officers near Miami, Oklahoma. They tried to flee but their vehicle became stuck on a muddy road. Constable Cal Campbell and Police Chief Percy Boyd pulled up to the Barrow car and got out with guns drawn. Barrow and Methvin opened fire on the officers immediately with Browning automatic rifles. Campbell fell dead with a wound to the heart. Boyd, wounded in the head and shoulder, surrendered and was forced into the car. They drove around northeastern Oklahoma and southeastern Kansas before releasing Boyd near Fort Scott, Kansas. Boyd was treated for his wounds at a Fort Scott hospital. He identified Clyde and Bonnie as two of his captors but was unsure of the third person's identity.

Federal, state, and local authorities mounted a manhunt in Oklahoma, Kansas, and Arkansas. Roadblocks were set up along roads crossing the Red River into Texas. Sympathy wishes poured in to the family of Constable Campbell, sixty-three. Five daughters and two sons began making funeral arrangements for their father.

Upon learning of the events in Oklahoma and Kansas, law enforcement personnel in the Dallas area girded for what they felt would be the imminent return of Barrow and/or Raymond Hamilton. The license number of Clyde's car was broadcast repeatedly from both police and general radio stations, including WFAA, KRLD, and WRR in Dallas. The number was given as 231-047, Oklahoma, 1934, and the car was described as a new Ford sedan.

The ability of Hamilton, Barrow, and the like to evade the

clutches of the law brought about some interesting theories. One such was advanced by Deputy Sheriff Richard Rogan of Victoria. He said he believed that one way the outlaws were avoiding capture was to pull up into a truck van and then drive to a safe area, back out, and go on their merry way. It was an interesting hypothesis, but a method never used by the West Dallas gang. When a car was getting too "hot," there was a simple remedy: get another one.

From Washington, D.C., came word that the Department of Justice was prepared to use its every resource in helping to bring about the apprehension of Clyde Barrow and Raymond Hamilton. An announcement was made:

> The attorney general instructed the director of the division of investigation of the Department of Justice to utilize every resource of that division in order to bring about an early apprehension of Clyde Barrow and associates.
>
> All field officers of the division of investigation in the section of the country in which Barrow is at present located are cooperating with local authorities and rendering every assistance to bring about the early apprehension of this desperado.
>
> The activities of Barrow and his associates constitute an open defiance of the power of law enforcement agencies and illustrate the manifest need of federal assistance in a cooperative effort to suppress this type of crime. Such acts as these have caused the attorney general to recommend to the Congress of the United States the passage of additional and necessary legislation to enable the government to do its full part in meeting the emergency caused by the repeated crimes of violence having interstate character.

The heat at the state as well as federal level was being turned up on Clyde and Raymond. The Junior Chamber of Commerce of - Graham, Texas, offered a reward of $100 for the capture, dead or alive, of Clyde Barrow and Raymond Hamilton. Speaking for the group, which had only been organized three days before, President MacWilliams said members hoped that those who killed E. B. Wheeler and H. D. Murphy would be brought to speedy justice. Citizens of Graham were outraged over the killing of Wheeler, who had lived there for two years and had many friends. The Texas Highway Commission issued a statement asking that contributions to a fund for the apprehension of the murderer of the highway patrolmen be sent to the Austin National Bank in the capital, where T. H. Davis, vice-president, was custodian of funds being contributed. The request, signed by John Wood, chairman, W. R. Ely, and D. K. Martin, said:

Two young members of the state highway patrol, H. D. Murphy and E. B. Wheeler, have been ruthlessly murdered in the discharge of their duties. The highway commission is determined that their murderers be brought to justice. In the interest of humanity and for the future welfare and protection of this fine body of men this must be done. Financial assistance, not available to the commission, is, of course, needed.

Funds for the apprehension of the slayers are being voluntarily raised by the employees of the highway department, of which the highway patrol is a unit. Many organizations and citizens of Texas have expressed a desire to contribute to the fund for the apprehension of the slayers.

The commission appreciates these offers of help and appeals to those wishing to see the murderers brought to the bar of justice to send their contributions to the Austin National Bank, Austin.

After being treated for his wounds at the Fort Scott hospital, Police Chief Boyd of Miami gave details about his kidnapping. He said Barrow acted arrogant and said he was too smart to get caught. Boyd said Bonnie had a white rabbit that she fed a carrot during the trip. The chief also ruled out Raymond Hamilton as the third party after viewing photos.

The money being put up to get Barrow, Raymond, and the rest kept adding up. Every employee of the Highway Department had contributed to a $350 reward for the capture of the outlaws. State employees throughout the state were called on to contribute less than a week following the Grapevine massacre. The murder of the patrolmen even ended up causing a row within the Dallas Bar Association. The statement of L. P. DeLee, Dallas attorney, that Clyde Barrow and his cohorts were justified in killing the lawmen because the officers were "meddling where they had no business," was severely taken to task by the association. Over the signature of President R. G. Storey, a statement was issued condemning the words attributed to DeLee:

> The bar association does not in any way or manner approve of any of the purported statements regarding this ruthless murder. Mr. DeLee, who is not a member of our association, has a right to his own individual opinion, but I feel certain that his interview does not reflect the opinion of the members of the Dallas Bar Association or the bar at large.
>
> The executive committee of the Dallas Bar Association held a special meeting today to consider this matter. If Mr. DeLee was correctly quoted the executive committee most emphatically and unqualifiedly condemns each and all of the statements of Mr. DeLee in which he sought to justify the murders.

DeLee had obtained the pardon on which Barrow was released from the state penitentiary.

During the first week of April 1934, Raymond Hamilton read with interest newspaper accounts about himself and Clyde Barrow. With plenty of money and the sexual relationship with Mary O'Dare, Raymond felt quite proud. The only problem was his broken nose, which at times allowed him to breathe only through his mouth and at others caused him to become nauseated and pass out. Raymond remembered a doctor in St. Louis who had the reputation in the under-world of "asking no questions." He and Mary decided to leave their comfortable setup at the Lafayette and journey to St. Louis by train. When they got there, the doctor did not want to operate on Ray unless the desperado undressed. When Raymond refused to do so, the doctor gave in and operated on Hamilton, who was dressed in an immaculate suit and held a .45 revolver. Hamilton and his moll boarded the next train to New Orleans.

Back in New Orleans, Ray began to wonder about his relation-ship with the Barrow gang. He loved Bonnie and respected Clyde but had no patience with their $50 robbery mentality or their inabil-ity to avoid shootouts. Hamilton wrote a letter to his attorney, Albert Baskett of Dallas, declaring the Lancaster robbery the last he and Clyde were in together. Raymond wrote the letter on stationery from the Lafayette Hotel and sent a $100-bill retainer fee and a Lafayette Hotel statement not receipted, for $3.30. Hamilton addressed it to Baskett in care of Sheriff Smoot Schmid. He placed a fingerprint made with ordinary ink on the hotel statement to prove his identity. The print was identified as that of Ray's right thumb by Bertillon experts at the Dallas Police Department and by the identification bureau at the sheriff's office. The hotel statement showed that Hamilton and a woman companion had registered at the New Orleans hotel as F. A. Murphy and wife of Lake Charles, Louisiana. It bore the date 5-5-45, an obvious error with reference to the month, and showed that Raymond and Mary occupied Room 526, for which $3 a day was charged. They made two telephone calls, one for ten cents and one for twenty cents. Baskett told reporters he had represented Raymond Hamilton in several cases and that he felt the desperado had written the letter to prove he had nothing to do with the murder of Constable Campbell.

"Raymond is wanted in Oklahoma for the killing of a man at Atoka," Baskett said. "He is afraid of that state now, believing that he would be sentenced to death if he was ever tried for the Atoka killing. He is anxious that he not be connected with the Commerce killing for that would result in his being taken to Oklahoma if he is ever captured."

Baskett expressed the opinion that Hamilton was a bank robber, not a killer.

"He could not have stayed with Clyde Barrow long, and I am sure it was this which caused their separation," the lawyer said. "Hamilton might kill if he was in a tight place, but he told me just before he went to the penitentiary that he had never killed a man and I believe him. He was present at the Atoka killing, however, and his part in the Huntsville killing when he escaped through a hail of machine gun bullets fired by Barrow's gang would brand him as an accessory."

Hamilton said in his letter that he was leaving another letter for Baskett at the Lafayette Hotel, and the attorney wrote for it. Both Chief Deputy Sheriff Bill Decker and Police Lt. Roy Richburg expressed the opinion that Barrow and Hamilton had been traveling separate roads since the Lancaster robbery when shown Ray's letter. Both believed the letter genuine.

"The fingerprints check, the handwriting checks," Richburg said, "but the best proof that the letter is from Hamilton is the fact that he enclosed a one-hundred-dollar-bill. Cranks who write letters like that do not enclose money."

The possibility that Raymond might be planning to give himself up through Baskett was discouraged by the attorney.

"Hamilton would not like to face a jury in the Huntsville killing," he said. "His reference to a letter written to Governor Ferguson may indicate, however, that he is asking for clemency."

A reference that Hamilton made in his letter about being in Houston early the preceding week confirmed officers' belief that he conducted the bank robbery at West and that it was he who kidnapped Mrs. Gunter. Raymond's letter, postmarked April 7, 1934, stated:

Dear Mr. Baskett:

I am sending you a bill from a hotel I was staying at, at the time of the killing in Commerce, Okla. I haven't been with Clyde Barrow since the Lancaster Bank Robbery. I'm sending you one hundred dollars and want this put before the public and proved right away.

I am sending you more money just as soon as I find out you are doing as I ask. I'm enclosing also my finger prints on this bill. I'm also leaving a letter at this hotel for you. You can call for it. my finger print will be there when you call for it. You know I try and do keep my promise.

I want you to let the public and the whole world to know I am not with Clyde Barrow and don't go his speed. I'm a lone man and intend to stay that way. I wrote Mrs. M. A. Ferguson but I guess it was in vain.

I was in houston Wednesday night April 4 and have been here since Thur, even. April 5. Yours Truly

RAYMOND HAMILTON

Along with his letter to Baskett, Raymond also penned a note to Governor Ferguson. James E. Ferguson, the governor's husband and himself a former governor, refused to disclose the contents of Hamilton's letter. However, it was learned the outlaw pleaded that he not be blamed for the murder of the highway patrolmen. Hamilton was quoted as saying he had not been in the company of Clyde Barrow for several weeks. The letter had been mailed from Houston. Austin lawmen interpreted the letter as a plea for sympathy and an attempt by Raymond to keep as many crimes off his already crowded dossier as possible. In the letter Hamilton renewed his contention he had never killed anyone, and in an obvious jibe at Barrow he added that he had never held up a filling station.

"Please don't put such a low rap as that on me," Hamilton said.

While Barrow was playing cottontail with officers in the Southwest and Raymond was becoming one of Texas' great men of letters, their old buddy Hilton Bybee was getting his comeuppance in Throckmorton. Bybee was sentenced to twenty-five years' imprisonment on Sunday, April 8, 1934, by a district court jury. He was convicted of robbery with firearms and kidnapping in connection with the filling station holdup in March.

On the same day that Hilton Bybee was sentenced, Clyde Barrow's name was once again in the news. Word came from Topeka, Kansas, that a car believed to have been abandoned by Bonnie and Clyde was found. Topeka officials notified Dallas authorities that another auto nearby had been stolen, and they believed the desperadoes were headed for Texas.

Officers in the Southwest now had another worry to go with Barrow and Raymond Hamilton. Federal and state officials in Texas and other southwestern states were alerted that John Dillinger might be in the region. They were advised to be on the lookout for a car with Minnesota license No. B-420-213.

Highway Patrol Chief Phares of Texas said he was preparing hundreds of photostatic copies of pictures of Clyde Barrow, Bonnie Parker, and Raymond Hamilton for blanket distribution throughout Texas. Phares said he planned a campaign to educate filling station operators and others who came in contact with motorists so that the desperadoes could be positively identified and their movements traced. He said he would mail the pictures of the outlaw trio to anyone on request.

"I don't see how Barrow and his companions can run around all over the Southwest like they do without being detected," Phares said. "Perhaps if we can get enough persons familiar with their appearance it will reduce the number of false clues and enable us to concentrate on accurate tips."

Sheriff Smoot Schmid agreed with Phares and prepared his own group of photographic prints of the West Dallas gang. The lawman turned his efforts over to the Department of Justice for distribution to federal officers nationwide.

"We know practically all the places in which Barrow has hidden since things got so hot for him," Ranger Capt. D. E. Hamer said. "Through the cooperation of officers in Texas, Oklahoma, Colorado, Kansas, Missouri, Arkansas, Louisiana, Nebraska and Ohio and other states, we have an organization which will make sure that he will not remain in one place for long."

County officers arrested a man they believed to be one of Barrow's contact men in South Dallas on Sunday, April 8. They recovered an army .45 automatic pistol that had been stolen from an armory at Ranger more than a year before. The man was taken to the place of his arrest Monday in an attempt to recover three more pistols of the same kind. They were not found, however, and he was returned to the county jail, where he was held for further investigation.

Considerable excitement was caused on April 9 by reports that both Hamilton and Barrow had been seen in Dallas. One rumor was squelched when officers discovered that the supposed Hamilton, riding in a large coupe, was S. M. Merrick, a local businessman, who recently bought an automobile of the same type Hamilton was supposed to be using.

A reward of $100 for the arrest of Clyde Barrow, Bonnie Parker, and Raymond Hamilton was offered by the Dallas district attorney's office. The fund was contributed by District Attorney Robert L. Hurt and his staff and was to remain in effect during their tenure in office. Officials, perplexed and angered over their inability to capture or kill Raymond Hamilton and Clyde Barrow, began to fix their sights on easier targets. A subpoena was issued for the appearance of a J. Frank Norris of Fort Worth before the Dallas County grand jury to give information concerning alleged shielding of Clyde Barrow and his comrades by Dallas County officials. Norris was reported to have said in a radio broadcast from Fort Worth that certain officials were communicating to Barrow information concerning plans of the officers to capture him. The subpoena was issued to require Norris on his appearance before the grand jury to have with him any records concerning his claims, and to produce for the grand jury a copy of the speech he made over the radio.

On Friday, April 13, Floyd Hamilton and Steve Davis were mentioned in connection with the manhunt for Raymond Hamilton. A hearing on application for a writ of habeas corpus for the two men was passed by Judge Noland G. Williams because Capt. D. E. Hamer of the Texas Rangers had not been served notice to appear with the two men, allegedly prisoners of the Ranger force. The hearing was reset. The pair were arrested a week before, attorneys claimed, and were hidden by officers. The arrest of Raymond's brother and stepfather was directly related to the previous arrests of James Mullen and John Basden. Before Mullen was arrested, he came to see Floyd. Mullen was driving a new Studebaker that Ray had stolen and given to him. He expressed to Floyd his desire to see Raymond, and the elder Hamilton brother explained to Mullen that he would have to get permission from Raymond for the meeting to take place. Mullen complained that Raymond had paid him only $750 of the $1,000 he had been promised for his part in the Eastham break. Floyd went ahead and gave the $250, unaware that Mullen was a dope addict who would soon blow the money.

It wasn't long after Mullen and Floyd parted that the former was recognized and arrested by the Dallas sheriff's department. Suffering from withdrawal pains, he was promised a shot of dope and the possibility of having addict charges dropped if he would sign a statement. Mullen signed a statement for Sheriff Schmid that implicated Floyd along with Raymond and Bonnie and Clyde with the Eastham break. Mullen went on to say that Floyd was involved in the Grand Prairie bank robbery and that he had money and several stolen army guns hidden between the walls of his house.

Schmid knew the description of the two men who robbed the Grand Prairie bank did not fit Floyd, and he also was aware it would be difficult to get a search warrant to tear out the walls of his house based on testimony of Mullen, who had a lengthy criminal record. Schmid chewed on his cigar and schemed. He would need the help of the Texas Rangers.

The sheriff's plan was simple: keep Floyd Hamilton long enough to trump up a charge. Justification was easy, as the possible capture of Raymond Hamilton and Bonnie and Clyde was at stake. At Schmid's request, four Rangers went to West Dallas and arrested Floyd and Steve Davis. The Rangers took their captives to Floresville in South Texas and jailed them. None of the men's relatives were told where they were being taken. The pair would be held some three weeks without explanation. They were not allowed to contact their families or attorneys.

About ten days following their incarceration, Winter King, Dallas County assistant district attorney, and Denver Seale, special investigator for the district attorney's office, came to see Floyd and Davis. King told Floyd that he had been charged with the Grand Prairie robbery and with aiding in the Eastham escape, which made him an accessory to the murder of Major Crowson. But King had an option for Floyd. If he would help capture Bonnie and Clyde, they would drop all charges and pay him $5,000.

Floyd questioned the men's sincerity and reasoning. They admitted that Seale had designs on someday becoming sheriff, and King's wish list included a judgeship. Credit for doing in Barrow and Parker would surely help them achieve their goals. Hamilton declined the offer and then offered his own deal. He said he was sure Raymond and Bonnie and Clyde would consider turning themselves in if the state would assure them a life sentence instead of the death penalty. King vetoed the idea, saying too much had transpired for the desperadoes to expect anything but the worst if they were captured. Floyd reiterated his stand against having anything to do with the lawmen's efforts to nab his brother and friends. King and Seale then grilled Steve Davis, but Raymond's stepfather was not privy to the gang's movements and so provided little if any helpful information. It is doubtful the old turkey thief would have squealed no matter what he knew.

On April 13, 1934, the manhunt for Clyde Barrow centered in Louisiana. Federal authorities and lawmen from Louisiana and Texas converged on a hideout near Ringgold, some thirty miles southeast of Shreveport. Their attempt to capture Barrow was unsuccessful, but their suspicions that he was frequenting the area were accurate.

On the same day authorities were attempting to capture or kill Barrow in Louisiana, attorneys in Dallas were attempting to gain freedom for Floyd Hamilton and Steve Davis. The sheriff's office informed Judge Noland Williams that it had not been able to serve Ranger Capt. D. E. Hamer with notice to appear in court. Alice Davis had applied for the release of her husband and son on a writ of habeas corpus. But there was no luck but bad on Friday the thirteenth for Steve and Floyd.

John Basden learned on Monday, April 16, that the state would ask for the death penalty for his part in the Grand Prairie robbery. Judge Williams set Basden's trial for the following Thursday and ordered a special venire of 200 drawn immediately after his indictment. Basden was identified by three bank officials in a hearing before Judge Grover Adams in which his release was sought on a writ of habeas corpus, but Adams refused to grant bond. Basden had been arrested by Denver Seale and Deputy Sheriff Ed Caster at a grocery warehouse in North Dallas. He was identified as one of the robbers by J. E. Waggoner, president; J. T. Yeager, cashier; and Maude Crawford, bookkeeper.

On April 17, the day after legal proceedings began against Basden, Bonnie and Clyde met with relatives near Mount Pleasant. Bonnie finally was able to give her mother the white rabbit. The relatives urged the fugitives to flee the country, but instead Barrow had a scheme to move their kin to a home on Henry Methvin's father's place. Neither side accepted the other's suggestions, and following some hugs and good wishes Clyde and his moll were on the road.

The following day in Dallas, John Basden got a reprieve of sorts. His trial was passed when it was called by Judge Williams. Failure of the court to obtain a waiver of personal service on the members of the special venire was assigned as a reason for the continuance. The judge said he would set the case for the following week, and officials stated they were sure Basden's accomplice in the Grand Prairie heist was Raymond Hamilton.

On Thursday, April 19, applications for a writ of habeas corpus for the release of Floyd Hamilton and Steve Davis were filed in Austin by Alice Davis and Mildred Hamilton. Adjutant General Henry H. Hutchings was ordered to produce Hamilton and Davis before Judge J. D. Moore at 9:00 A.M. the following Saturday. The application alleged accurately that the men had been arrested in Dallas April 5 and had been held in custody although no complaint had been filed. Hutchings assured the women that their men would be in court Saturday, but professed ignorance as to their whereabouts. He said only that he knew they were in the charge of a Texas Ranger and were being held in "some county jail for safekeeping."

While Alice and Mildred were waiting for Steve and Floyd in Austin, John Basden was "singing" for Smoot Schmid in Dallas. Basden admitted to the sheriff that he had participated in the Grand Prairie holdup and implicated Raymond Hamilton and Floyd

Hamilton as well. The statement, which described the robbery and escape in detail, was written out by Assistant District Attorney J. J. Muleady and signed by Basden in the presence of witnesses. Following the Basden admission, an indictment of Floyd Hamilton was returned to Judge Williams. This had the effect of rendering fruitless the habeas corpus writ on the elder Hamilton brother. A capias was forwarded immediately to Austin for presentation to Judge Moore for the holding of Hamilton for Dallas County.

Following Basden's revelations, Sheriff Schmid recovered $182 of the $1,500 taken in the Grand Prairie robbery. Basden admitted to the sheriff that the money was at his home in West Dallas. The money, buried in a tin can in Basden's garage, was part of the $500 he received from Raymond for his part in the crime. Lawmen reiterated that bank officials identified Raymond Hamilton from mug shots as the other man who entered the bank. Basden told Schmid that he and the Hamilton brothers had driven to Oklahoma following the robbery, stopping en route at Paradise, Texas, to buy gasoline. Floyd, according to Basden, returned to Dallas, got his car, and met with Raymond and Basden near Henrietta, Texas. From there Raymond went his way and Floyd and Basden returned to Dallas.

Also on April 19, word came from two gas station attendants at Atlanta, Texas, that Bonnie and Clyde had been at their station. The attendants based their identification on newspaper photographs. They said there was another man in the back seat (no doubt Henry Methvin) and that the suspects drove off in the direction of Texarkana.

On Sunday, April 22, Texas Ranger Sgt. Joe Osaba loaded Floyd Hamilton and Steve Davis in his V-8 sedan and transported them to Dallas from Austin. In Dallas the men were allowed to confer with their attorneys. The lawyers informed Davis and Hamilton they had changed their minds and demanded the men be returned to the capital. Osaba loaded Floyd and Steve in the sedan and headed back to Austin.

Floyd was in Dallas long enough to learn that Basden's trial was set for May 7. Assistant District Attorney King said he would insist Floyd be held without bond on the robbery indictment, and that he would make strenuous efforts to keep Davis confined. When Floyd and Steve arrived in Dallas, they were met by a battery of newspaper photographers who were anxious to get photos of the brother and stepfather of the notorious Raymond Hamilton. Floyd ducked his head and Davis held a magazine in front of his face to avoid being photographed. Officers now admitted to the press that they had taken into custody for questioning Alice Hamilton Davis, Mildred

Hamilton, Maggie Fairris, and Lucy Brown. Raymond's mother, sister-in-law, and sisters were said to have made statements which would be "a material aid to the investigation." The women were released following their grilling by authorities.

Floyd Hamilton was returned to Dallas on Monday, April 23, to stand trial for the Grand Prairie robbery. Sheriff Schmid and Deputy Fred Bradberry went to Austin to retrieve the elder Hamilton brother. When they returned him to Dallas he was taken to police headquarters, where Bertillon records were made. Steve Davis was ordered released in Austin by Judge Moore after a hearing on a writ of habeas corpus. Judge Noland Williams ordered a special venire of 200 for Floyd's trial. On the way to Dallas from Austin, Schmid aimed a barrage of questions at Floyd Hamilton. The giant lawman admitted to Hamilton that it was he who had ordered the arrest and secret trip to Floresville. Floyd refused to answer the sheriff's questions or denied his accusations each time. Smoot became so enraged he began to pound the car seat and threatened to have Bradberry stop the auto so he could beat Hamilton. When Floyd arrived in Dallas, Schmid allowed Mildred Hamilton to see her husband for the first time in weeks. The sheriff had requested she bring Floyd a suit to wear for his mug shots, but Floyd told her to bring overalls instead. He knew he would look like his brash brother Raymond in a suit, and that was the last thing he wanted. Floyd and John Basden were in the same lineup, and bank officials from Grand Prairie immediately identified Basden as one of the robbers. Despite every effort on the part of Schmid to coerce the officials into fingering Floyd, they refused to do so. He did bear a resemblance to Raymond, but not enough to fool the bank employees.

Floyd Hamilton had dodged the Grand Prairie problem, but his troubles were just beginning. On Tuesday, April 24, word came out of Crockett, Texas, that Hamilton would be tried there in connection with the Eastham escape. This announcement was the result of a ten-page statement taken from James Mullen. Mullen's statement also implicated Raymond Hamilton in the shooting death of Major Crowson. The statement went on to include Bonnie and Clyde as conspirators in the Eastham break. Mullen had given his statement to Sheriff Schmid, Texas Ranger Jim Shown, Assistant D.A. Winter King, and other officers, and it was made public by District Attorney T. B. Greenwood of Anderson County. One of the more interesting facets of Mullen's statement was his contention that one of the reasons for the Raymond–Clyde split was Hamilton's dismay about Bonnie being Barrow's lover when she was still married to

Roy Thornton. Hamilton and Thornton had been chums in West Dallas, but it is laughable that Clyde and Bonnie's lovelife bothered Raymond's moral sensitivity. He certainly had no qualms about his relationship with Gene O'Dare's wife, Mary.

With Raymond and Bonnie and Clyde still on the prowl, authorities braced for more lawlessness. Funds were running low for Hamilton, and he had a plan. He sequestered Mary O'Dare in Amarillo and made plans to knock off a bank. Raymond figured once he had made his escape he could pick Mary up and they could head to California to cool off and enjoy some different scenery. Raymond had another running buddy now, T. R. Brooks of Wichita Falls. Due to lack of cash, and to avoid the constant surveillance of highways in North Texas, the pair hoboed their way back to Dallas. Hamilton wanted to strike away from Amarillo so that after he made his way back to Mary they would have smooth sailing on their westward voyage. Once on his home ground, Raymond wasted little time in stealing a car and mapping his strategy. The date was set: Wednesday, April 25, 1934.

The quiet routine of the First National Bank of Lewisville was shattered on that day when Raymond Hamilton calmly walked in, produced an automatic pistol, and demanded money. The bank officials and customers were paralyzed by the sight of the blond bandit whom they readily recognized.

Approximately $1,000 was hurriedly gathered, and Hamilton was out the door with his booty. As Raymond ran out the door, local resident Tom Bullock Hyder, a state legislator, was trying to walk in. Ray shoved him aside and sprinted for the getaway vehicle. Ironically, it was Hyder who had pushed for a $25,000 reward fund for the apprehension of Hamilton, Clyde Barrow, and associates. But the representative had never dreamed of meeting one of the desperadoes face to face, much less during the commission of a crime.

Shocked at first, Hyder gathered his senses and jumped in his vehicle to pursue Raymond and Brooks. As Hyder prepared to speed after the robbers, he saw Lewisville Constable D. H. Street coming on the run. He opened the passenger door and Street dove in, ready for the chase. Raymond took a northerly course, and as his pursuers passed through each little town they slowed enough to yell out the window for reinforcements. In a matter of minutes all of North Texas seemed to be joining the chase or coming out to watch the show. Wet roads slowed Hamilton some, but he kept it floorboarded and did not hesitate to drive across fields and pastures he felt were dry enough to travel. The excitement of the robbery and wildness of the chase had the rookie Brooks petrified.

By now there was more pursuit, and even though Raymond did not see it he could feel it. He left Gunter, Texas, headed for Sherman. Authorities were notified and a roadblock was set up at Howe, ten miles south of Sherman. Manning the roadblock were Grayson County Deputy Sheriff Collier Yuery, Deputy D. S. McDaniel, and Dr. John T. Nall, arms instructor of the Sherman police force. The men had plenty of firepower and had it prominently displayed. Local citizenry had cleared the streets as if William S. Hart was going to ride in with guns ablaze. Raymond topped the rise coming into Howe going far too fast to stop and escape the roadblock.

Ray's car careened wildly and came to a halt only feet from the barricade. Hamilton bailed out with his hands up and a sheepish grin on his face.

"Don't shoot, boys," he said. "I'm fresh out of guns, ammo, whiskey and women."

The officers saw no whiskey or women but they knew better about the other. By now, Brooks, shaking all over, was out with hands held high. Money from the robbery was protruding from the robbers' pockets. Dr. Nall searched the pair, finding two .45 automatic pistols on Raymond. By now a crowd had gathered and Hamilton was not without words.

"Do you know who you got?" Ray asked Nall.

"I think I do, Raymond."

"You're damned right—I'm Raymond Hamilton."

Nall asked Raymond his partner's identity.

"I don't know. I picked him up and he's just another bum like myself."

Hamilton's cross-country flight had consumed two hours and mobilized lawmen and citizens at every level in North Texas. Raymond and Brooks were loaded into McDaniel's car and taken under heavy guard to Sherman. At 1:50 A.M. Thursday, Ray was brought back to Dallas by a small army of officers. Brooks was locked in the county jail at Denton. Incarcerating Hamilton in Dallas was agreed to by county, state, and federal officers at Sherman after prison manager Lee Simmons was assured by District Attorney Robert Hurt of Dallas that a speedy trial would be given. Judge Noland Williams announced that a special venire would be drawn and that Raymond would be tried the following Monday for the Grand Prairie bank robbery. Hurt said the state would ask for the death penalty, explaining that Texas laws provided a maximum of the electric chair for robbery with firearms.

Tragedy was a sidelight of Raymond Hamilton's latest escapade. Howard Gunter, a Collin County deputy sheriff who had been involved in the chase, was killed in an auto accident near Sherman while driving Hamilton's car from Howe.

Along with the news about Hamilton in North Texas came word from the Texas Panhandle that Mary O'Dare had been captured in Amarillo. She had been apprehended Monday, April 23, by Special Investigator M. L. Miller of D.A Hurt's staff. Miller and other officers held Mary under house arrest at the Cadillac Hotel in Amarillo, hoping Raymond would show so they could capture or kill him. They promised to go light on her if she agreed to testify against Ray. District Attorney Hurt added that

> Hamilton already has two-hundred-sixty-three years of prison sentences against him. We believe he deserves the death penalty and that a Dallas County jury will give it to him.
>
> He was in the Lancaster robbery and the Grand Prairie robbery, and in either case a jury should give him death as punishment.
>
> With so many years of imprisonment assessed against him, Hamilton didn't stay in prison long, and we don't think it would do any good to give him any more prison terms.
>
> He deserves the death penalty and if Denton County will let us try him first, we will do all in our power to see that he gets it.

Assistant District Attorney Winter King left for Denton immediately to request the Denton County prosecutors to permit trial of Hamilton in Dallas first.

CHAPTER IX

Flirting With Ol' Sparky

Smoot Schmid now had both Hamilton brothers in his jail. It was better than Christmas. The sheriff was so elated he even decided to let Raymond and Floyd visit. Newspaper photographers were allowed to record the meeting, but Smoot finally had enough of the photographers and shooed them out.

"See if you can talk some sense into Floyd, Ray," Schmid said as he departed.

"What the hell did he mean by that?" Floyd asked Raymond.

"The sheriff told me they had enough evidence to convict you on the Grand Prairie robbery," Ray said. "He told me you'd get a break if you plead guilty — maybe as little as five years. But if you demand a jury they're gonna try for the chair."

Raymond told his older brother that Schmid wanted him to convince Floyd to plead guilty.

"That's a joke," Floyd countered. "Nobody from the bank saw me. All they've got is Basden's statement, and my lawyers said it'll take more than that. Why should I beg for five years?"

After awhile the sheriff came to return Ray to his cell.

"Well, Ray, did you talk some sense into your brother?"

"Naw, I guess he's just too damned hard-headed," Ray deadpanned as he gave Floyd a sly wink.

After Schmid turned the key on Raymond, he summoned Hurt and the pair returned to visit Floyd. Hurt was carrying enough legal paper to start a bonfire. The sheriff told Floyd the papers represented only part of the criminal charges the authorities planned to press against him. The lawman was still looking for that guilty plea. Floyd called his bluff and said he would plead guilty to nothing. The elder Hamilton's attorneys later told him the only way Schmid could have gotten an indictment was to promise the grand jury he would be identified as soon as he was returned to Dallas.

The sheriff was desperate to get something concrete on Floyd. He even went so far as to tell him that his mother had had a nervous breakdown and that he could visit her. Floyd agreed, and Schmid and Deputy Ed Caster drove him to the Davis home. Steve Davis let them in the back door and they went into Alice's bedroom. When Floyd's mother saw the handcuffs on him, she started crying. Floyd asked why she was so distraught, and she said Schmid had told her that he and Raymond were going to the electric chair for the Grand Prairie robbery.

Floyd flew into a frenzy and said Schmid's contention was a lie — that the law had no evidence to convict him. He knew the same did not hold true for Raymond, but he was still incensed. His mother repeated the sheriff's offer of a five-year sentence if he would plead guilty and she urged her son to do so. Knowing that his mother had been misled, Floyd stormed out of the house. Schmid accused Floyd of having some of the Grand Prairie money buried on the property. Hamilton told the sheriff to dig up the place and he could have half of everything he found. Smoot ranted and raved about Floyd's "smart mouth" all the way back to jail.

On Thursday, April 26, Mary O'Dare was returned to Dallas from Amarillo. The twenty-year-old was placed in the Dallas County jail, but not allowed to visit Raymond. Mary was questioned for three hours by Winter King and then taken to Waco by Texas Rangers. A complaint charging her with robbery in connection with the West job was filed, and one had already been filed against Ray. For her interview with King, Mary was "dressed tastefully in black and had an inexpensive fur about her neck. She bore little resemblance to what would be expected as the woman companion of an outlaw like Hamilton. She spoke courteously in a soft, well modulated voice to all who addressed her and readily admitted she had been Hamilton's almost constant companion for nearly two months. She admitted she knew he was robbing banks but insisted that she knew nothing of the details of any of the holdups and denied that she took part in any of them."

Mary bragged about her cooking, and officers who stayed with her while she was being held at the apartment in Amarillo agreed she served excellent meals. She said Raymond left her at the Amarillo apartment after running low on money and planned to return for her following the Lewisville robbery. Mary stated that she had planned to leave Hamilton after the next robbery and that she intended to try to talk him into surrendering.

While Mary was entertaining the district attorney's office with her tales about life with Hamilton, Raymond seemed to enjoy the security of jail and regular meals. He was laughing even though Hurt was busy going through his records in an effort to speed his trip to the electric chair.

"It's hell, and don't let anybody tell you it ain't," Raymond told reporters in describing the fugitive life.

Hamilton told of frequently being without money and not having enough to eat. He said when he robbed the Lewisville bank he did not even have enough money to buy gasoline for his stolen car. Raymond also told of sleepless nights. He said two nights before he struck in Lewisville he slept briefly in a boxcar at Denison, but a special agent for the railroad awakened him and ordered him out of the yards.

"And I was glad to get out," he said with a laugh. "For I wasn't ready yet to be caught."

Raymond said he seriously considered giving himself up to officers following his escape from Eastham, but changed his mind. He said he had lost twenty pounds since his escape. Ray was willing to talk freely about his crimes as long as the reporters confined the conversation to generalities. He refused to give any detailed information about holdups except those in which the evidence against him was overwhelming. Hamilton admitted robbing one bank that had already gone defunct, but refused to divulge its location. He said it was not true that the employees at that bank had tried to borrow fifty cents from him after he lined them up against a wall at pistol point, only to find the bank was broke too.

"If they'd asked me for that small a loan I might have let 'em have it," he joked.

The desperado said he spent money faster than he could rob it. He said he stayed broke from his constant effort to evade the law and live the good life. Ray stated that after he and Clyde Barrow parted ways at Terre Haute, Indiana, he mainly rode trains and buses because they "were safer." Hamilton repeated his contention that he had never killed anyone, and even maintained that he had never wounded anyone. The former statement was probably technically true, but the second was an outright lie. When told authorities were preparing a death penalty against him under habitual criminal statutes, Raymond's expression changed from a smirk to a glower. Hamilton lied through his teeth, saying he knew nothing about the plot to free him from Eastham and that he joined the break at the last minute. This directly contradicted testimony of those who had been recaptured following the break. They had correctly fingered Ray as the ringleader.

Raymond claimed authorship of the New Orleans letter, but said he dictated it and another person wrote it. He then went on to describe how he slipped through a highway blockade of Harris County officers near Houston following the West bank robbery: "I knew the Houston officers would be watching for me and that they knew there would be a man and woman in the car. We came across four hitchhikers on the road, picked them up, piled their luggage all around and told them to act like friends of ours. We were stopped just outside Houston by some officers. They saw a car full of people, knew it couldn't be Raymond Hamilton, talked to us a minute and drove on."

On Thursday, April 26, when Mary O'Dare was moved from Dallas to Waco, she admitted that she had had enough of the wild life associated with Raymond Hamilton.

"It's probably best that I don't see him anymore," Mary said. "He's a swell guy and I like him. But I've found out I don't love him. I saw my husband, Barney Pitts, today while we were at Wichita Falls. He says he has forgiven me and will take me back. Just as soon as I get out of this trouble I'm going back to him and I'm going to make him the kind of wife he wants."

Mary quickly added that Barney, a tailor in Wichita Falls, had never been in any trouble with the law. Of course she could not say the same for her first spouse, Gene O'Dare, who was serving several sentences concurrently for robberies, some of which were committed with Raymond Hamilton.

"I didn't love Gene, but I married him," Mary said. "It was just one of those things."

She divorced O'Dare shortly after he was arrested and later married Pitts, she said. It was later brought out that Mary was the sister of Odell Chambless, another convicted felon who was serving time.

Living with Raymond during part of his crime spree was no fun, according to Mary. She said there were few places they felt safe and frequently they were without money. Mary admitted she had met Clyde Barrow and Bonnie Parker while running with Hamilton, but said she knew little about them.

"They seemed like swell people," she said when asked about Raymond's infamous friends.

While Mary O'Dare was gabbing about life with a desperado, a more sober activity was occurring in Sherman. A $100 cashier's check was presented to the sheriff's department in recognition of services in capturing Raymond Hamilton and Ted Brooks. It was endorsed to Mrs. Howard Gunter, wife of the officer who was killed while driving Hamilton's car from Howe. The check was given by the Merchants and Planters National Bank of Sherman. Grayson County Sheriff J. Benton Davis said that he had not learned definitely what rewards would be paid for the capture of Hamilton. Later, Governor Miriam (Ma) Ferguson was requested by State Representative Hyder to give part of the $500 reward she offered for Hamilton's capture to the widow of Gunter. Since Gunter had assisted in the capture of Raymond before he was killed in the auto crash, Hyder argued his widow should receive part of the reward.

On April 27, invoking a seldom used section of the Penal Code dealing with habitual criminals, District Attorney Robert L. Hurt demanded the death penalty for Raymond Hamilton and said he would resist all efforts by Hamilton to plead guilty and add another prison sentence to the 263 years he already had. Hurt announced his decision as Mary O'Dare was brought back to Dallas by Denver Seale, special investigator. Having made $5,000 bond at Waco on charges of being an accomplice in the West bank robbery, which was allowed following failure of bank officials to identify her, she was released upon the promise to remain in Dallas and reappear Saturday, April 28, for further questioning. There were no charges against her in Dallas County.

"We don't want any prison term for Hamilton," Hurt said. "We wouldn't take it if it was two thousand years. He deserves the chair, and we will try and see that he gets it."

Under Article 64 of the Penal Code, prosecutors were certain that nothing less than life imprisonment would be meted out to the desperado when he faced trial again. The article read: "A person convicted a second time of any offense to which the penalty of death is affixed as an alternative punishment shall not receive on such second conviction a less punishment than imprisonment for life in the penitentiary."

Meanwhile, officers continued to piece together the puzzle they hoped would end the criminal career of Hamilton and his gang. Hurt and Assistant District Attorney Dean Gauldin returned from LaGrange Friday, where they had gone to obtain certified copies of conviction of Hamilton there on highway robbery charges. Their purpose in obtaining the record of his conviction was to be able to include the fact that he was convicted in preparation of the indictment in Dallas County.

By Saturday, April 28, Dallas officers were softening slightly in their handling of their charge from West Dallas. They allowed Raymond to meet briefly with Mary O'Dare. After Mary and Ray talked for a few minutes, she decided he was not so bad after all. Meanwhile, District Attorney Hurt was busy laying the groundwork for his attempt to see Hamilton receive the death penalty. Hurt's argument would be that Raymond's record showed he was a dangerous criminal "that should be exterminated."

The indictment under the habitual criminal statute had been drawn and plans were made for it to be returned by the grand jury the following Monday. In the indictment Raymond Hamilton was charged with robbing the Grand Prairie State Bank, and J. E. Waggoner, president, was named as his victim. Hurt requested the trial date to be May 7, 1934. Judge Williams of Criminal District Court No. 2 was once again to preside. The trial of Floyd Hamilton in connection with the same robbery would be postponed until a later date. As if Raymond didn't have enough heat on him in Dallas County, word came from Denton County that an indictment charging him with robbing the Lewisville bank had been returned. No action had been taken yet against Brooks.

Mary O'Dare, who had enjoyed the spoils of victims during her tenure with Raymond Hamilton, was herself a victim during her term in Waco. A suitcase of her clothes, valued at $200, was stolen from an automobile at the McLennan County jail. She had bigger worries, though, because the sheriff of Limestone County wanted to question her concerning the kidnapping of Mrs. Cam Gunter near Mexia.

District Attorney Hurt spent Sunday, April 29, mapping his campaign to send Raymond Hamilton to the electric chair. Hurt was quick to point out that if Raymond didn't receive death for his part in the Grand Prairie robbery there would still be other opportunities to do him in. In particular, Hurt cited the Eastham break as another instance where Hamilton might receive the death sentence.

From Austin it was announced by L. G. Phares, chief of the Highway Patrol, that $3,615 was in the bank waiting to be turned over to the person who captured the slayers of the patrolmen on Easter. The money had been received in small contributions from all parts of Texas. Phares reiterated his belief that Clyde Barrow and Bonnie Parker were responsible for the lawmen's death. The chief said he expected the reward fund to grow beyond $5,000. This fund was being offered in addition to the reward posted by Governor Ferguson. Phares said he believed the slayers would be apprehended shortly.

On Monday, April 30, the legal machinery of Dallas and Denton counties began to accelerate efforts to send Raymond Hamilton to the electric chair. Judge Williams set Hamilton's trial for the following Monday. The Denton County grand jury indicted him for the Lewisville robbery and announced that an early trial would be sought. Raymond's buddy Brooks was still in the Denton County jail, as his case had not been considered.

As soon as Judge Williams received the indictment for the Grand Prairie State Bank robbery, with a second count under the habitual criminal act, he ordered Hamilton brought from jail. The desperado, who was still a minor under Texas law since he had not reached twenty-one, was brought to the courtroom through a little used steel door in the second floor hallway of the Criminal Courts Building. He was guarded by Chief Deputy Bill Decker and Deputy John Chiess. Decker walked with a hand on Raymond's shoulder and sat at his side in court. The grand jury remained in court when Williams called Ray before him.

"I'm setting your trial for next Monday, Raymond," the judge said. "Have you got a lawyer?"

"No sir," Raymond said.

"I'll appoint counsel for you," the judge continued. "I'll appoint two — M. E. Kramer and J. H. Martin."

"If I can get a lawyer before then, will it be all right for me to hire him?" Hamilton asked. The judge assured him that would be fine.

Raymond was then escorted from the courtroom where a year before he had received a major portion of the 263 years of prison sentences he had begun serving prior to the Eastham break. Hamilton was returned to his cell in solitary confinement.

The Tuesday following Raymond's arraignment, he once again made an effort to clear himself of the Bucher murder. Hamilton had convinced Smoot Schmid to get Sheriff Freeland and District Attorney Allred of Hill County to come to Dallas to confer with him. Neither official would discuss their talk with Ray, but it was learned that he denied again his guilt in the Bucher slaying. Raymond told a half-truth when he told the Hill County officials that Clyde Barrow was not at the murder scene. Word was circulating that Ray had told one of his attorneys that Barrow was present. Hamilton's attorneys told the press that he would plead guilty to the Grand Prairie charge and ask for mercy. A venire of 400, an unusually large number for a robbery case, was drawn Wednesday, May 2, for Raymond's trial. With the large venire scheduled and with Hurt and his staff champing at the bit for the death penalty, the selection of the jury was arduous. Hamilton's attorneys, with practically no hope of avoiding a conviction, were realistically planning for a penalty of life imprisonment.

"We will demand that Hamilton be sent to the electric chair," Hurt said. "To send him back to prison would be like throwing a bucket of water into Lake Dallas. He already has two-hundred-sixty-three years against him and he was running around the country with that on his back and robbing banks at Lancaster, Grand Prairie and Lewisville."

In connection with the state's continued investigation of Hamilton's exploits, members of the family of Clyde Barrow were brought before the grand jury at the insistence of Assistant District Attorney Winter King, who had taken a leading role in the Hamilton investigation. The members, including Henry and Cumie Barrow, were questioned.

On Friday, May 4, while federal agents were in a dither over reports that John Dillinger was on an ocean liner bound for Great Britain, local lawmen were jolted when Raymond Hamilton announced from his cell that he and Mary O'Dare planned to get married. Mary confirmed the plan when she filed for divorce in Wichita Falls against her tailor husband, Barney Pitts. Ray said Mary had agreed to marry him if officers would allow it.

Raymond's lawyers announced on Saturday, May 3, that they would file at least five motions in an effort to save Hamilton from immediate trial in Dallas County. Word also came that Albert Baskett, Hamilton's regular attorney, might join the proceedings, particularly if a death sentence was handed down. In a complete reversal of strategy, on the Sunday before his trial, Raymond's attorneys announced he would plead not guilty if forced to go to trial immediately. Martin and Kramer said they would seek a change of venue on the grounds that an impartial and unprejudiced jury could not be found in Dallas County due to the great publicity surrounding the native son's transgressions. Attempts to delay Raymond's trial failed Monday afternoon when Judge Williams overruled a motion for change of venue. The judge earlier had overruled motions to void the indictment, to quash the indictment, and to put Floyd Hamilton on trial first for the same offense. The defense effort to have Raymond's trial moved to another county included the presentation of thirty witnesses, among them the circulation managers of Dallas newspapers, and the introduction into the record of complete files of each daily newspaper since Hamilton's capture at Howe.

With the motions that sought to delay trial out of the way, the venire was called in and the court started receiving excuses. The motion to void the indictment alleged that the sentence given Hamilton for the robbery of the Carmine State Bank was void since it was for life, rather than a term of years, as provided by statute. Claiming the language of the second count of the indictment was inflammatory and tending to prejudice the jury against the defendant, the second motion sought to quash the indictment. To avoid the certain granting of the third motion, which sought trial of Floyd Hamilton first, the state moved to dismiss the case against Floyd.

"Rather than see this notorious criminal, Raymond Hamilton, given a delay in his trial, we will dismiss the case against his brother," District Attorney Hurt said. "Floyd Hamilton is as guilty as Raymond, but we are willing to dismiss the case against him in order to try Raymond now."

Raymond sat as an interested spectator throughout the day, watching the proceedings closely. When all the motions had been overruled and the veniremen from among whom the jury would be selected filed into the room, Hamilton turned half around in his seat and looked closely as each one passed along the rail just back of his chair. The veniremen filed steadily by, and a number of them, apparently knowing by Hamilton's position in the courtroom that he was the defendant, looked closely at him. Several of them grinned. The majority of the veniremen, however, only glared at Hamilton as they passed, and looked ahead for seats. Although the day was occupied with the hearing of legal details and technicalities, the courtroom seats were occupied throughout the day, and many people were standing in the open spaces around the room. Raymond was closely guarded in court. With his escape record, officers were taking no chances. In addition to the regular bailiff, Frank Bennett, Deputy Sheriffs John Chiess and Ed Caster sat close to Hamilton and at least two other deputies were in the courtroom throughout the day.

Twelve men who said they could give Raymond Hamilton the death penalty, if the circumstances and facts in the Grand Prairie bank robbery deserved it, took places Tuesday, May 8, in the jury room. The twelfth juror, W. A. Thompson, was selected at 1:45 A.M. Thompson, though seventy-nine and therefore exempt from jury service by law, remained on the venire. He had served on the last jury that tried Noah Roark, a lawyer, for murder, the case resulting in a forty-year sentence.

As each member of the venire took his place in the witness chair for examination as to his qualifications to serve as a juror in the case, Hamilton looked at him closely and attended the questioning carefully. Attorneys put question after question as to the beliefs of each venireman concerning death as a punishment for crime. During the day several veniremen said they could not assess the death penalty for robbery unless someone had been killed in the holdup and they were promptly excused by the prosecution. Albert Baskett, along with Martin and Kramer, pressed each prospect as to any stories he might have read in the newspapers and as to any opinions he might have formed as a result.

Members of the jury were M. P. Crowder, unemployed former streetcar company employee and former abstractor; Green Reynolds, meter tester for Dallas Power and Light; J. H. Brown, plumber; J. P. Shrader, former Collin County official; H. G. Foster, farmer; Clarence Henry, proprietor of a produce company; Augustus E. Buffington, unemployed; Charles F. O'Connor, unemployed former shoe salesman; Clayton C. Lary, substation operator for Dallas Power and Light; W. K. Williams, electrical engineer for Dallas Power and Light; W. L. Leifeste, cotton and grain dealer; and Thompson, retired well driller.

Three of Raymond's sisters, Lillie McBride, Maggie, and Audrey, were in the courtroom during the Tuesday proceedings. Tuesday evening at about 10:00 P.M. Baskett was stricken suddenly with hemorrhage of the nose and was forced to leave the courtroom. Baskett's daughter administered first aid and his physician was phoned. The doctor demanded the attorney come to his office immediately so he could be treated.

With two alternatives before them, the jury Wednesday night considered for several hours before retiring whether to cut short Raymond Hamilton's criminal career by sending him to death, or to extend him the mercy of a life term in the state penitentiary. Charged by Judge Williams to find Hamilton guilty and assess his punishment at death or life imprisonment, or to acquit him of the robbery and the habitual criminal count, the jury began deliberating at 5:30 P.M. Raymond had already eliminated the last possibility, conceding immediately after the jury left the courtroom that he expected to be found guilty.

After deliberating for half an hour, the jury was taken to dinner and returned at 7:00 P.M. to renew its study of the case. Judge Williams returned to his chambers at 8:00 P.M. and remained waiting to accept a verdict until 9:25. Then he sent word by the bailiff that he was going home, and advised the jury to retire for the night and hold no further deliberations until morning.

The taking of testimony on which Hurt and assistants Gauldin and Curtis based their demand for a death verdict occupied only two hours. With the charge prepared and read to the jury at 2:30 P.M., an hour of argument was allotted each side. Brief recesses were taken between addresses to the jury, and Hurt closed his appeal for the state at 5:30 P.M. Defense arguments were presented by Martin, Kramer, and Baskett.

As Hurt closed his argument, he turned to Hamilton and pointed an accusing finger, addressing him as Texas' public enemy number two. Hamilton's beady eyes returned Hurt's glare. After the jury left the room, however, Raymond straightened in his chair, sighed, and wiped the moisture of nervousness from the palms of his hands. The white handkerchief with which he had begun the day was sodden and soiled. Hurt repeated again and again that the state was not interested in a life sentence for the West Dallas desperado. He referred at intervals to the fact that Hamilton was already under life sentence for the Carmine robbery, but that had not prevented him from escaping and robbing again.

Raymond was identified as one of the robbers by J. E. Waggoner, J. T. Yeager, and Maude Crawford. In addition, he was identified in connection with the Carmine holdup by Sheriff William Loessin and Roy H. Giese, district clerk, both of Fayette County. The defense attorneys did not attempt to break down the stories of the prosecution witnesses, but made each one go over his story again in detail in order to detect any flaw in the state's case. The defense offered no testimony to controvert the accusations that Hamilton was guilty not only of the Grand Prairie heist but also of the Carmine robbery.

During presentation of testimony the courtroom was so crowded it seemed not another person could enter. However, at the afternoon session, when arguments were offered, spectators moved closer together and the number was increased considerably. The usual inner circle crowd occupied most of the space within the railing in front of the judge's bench.

While the Dallas County jury remained undecided after thirty-six hours as to whether to sentence Raymond to death or life imprisonment, other counties, confident their juries would act quickly in sending him to the chair, sought Thursday to be given custody following the Dallas trial. The jury remained deadlocked Thursday night and retired at 9:25. They were reported standing ten to two. It was understood the vote was in reference to the penalty, that ten jurors favored death and two favored life imprisonment.

Two other Texas counties in which Raymond was charged in death sentence cases sent representatives to Dallas and asked for the right to try him. Sheriff W. B. Mobley of Waco (McLennan County) and his chief criminal investigator, J. S. Stanfield, conferred with Judge Williams and Sheriff Smoot Schmid about taking Hamilton for trial on the West bank robbery charge, on the assumption that the local jury would not reach a verdict after deliberating so long. When Williams told Mobley that he believed Denton County had a prior claim, the sheriff quickly agreed that Denton should take Hamilton first. Mobley said, however, that if Denton failed to assess death he would take Hamilton to Waco for trial. Judge Gambill, county attorney for Denton County, had preceded the Waco officers to Dallas with a bench warrant for Raymond to be used in the event of a hung jury or life sentence in Dallas. Gambill said the case for the robbery of the Lewisville bank was set for the following Wednesday and that he would see that Hamilton got a quick trial.

The deadlocked jury communicated with Judge Williams at 2:30 P.M. and reported the ten-to-two vote.

"Do you think you could reach a verdict?" the judge asked Foreman Shrader.

"Well, I can't say," Shrader replied. "It's a pretty hard case and I'm not able to tell right now whether we'll be able to get together."

On Friday, May 11, 1934, Raymond Hamilton once again escaped the electric chair. The jury refused to assess the death penalty against the arch criminal and were discharged at 4:30 P.M. by Judge Williams. Only two of the jurors, O'Connor and Foster, were against the death penalty.

Immediately after the jury was released, District Attorney Hurt delivered to Sheriff Schmid a warrant for Hamilton's arrest for the murder of Major Crowson. The charge had been filed six days earlier, but had not been made public until after the Dallas trial. Although Raymond had temporarily escaped a death sentence, it was announced he would go to trial the following Wednesday in Denton on the Lewisville robbery charge. County Attorney Gambill reiterated his pledge to seek the death penalty.

None of this was enough to appease Hurt. He explained his disappointment:

> As district attorney, aided by two of my able assistants, Will
> Curtis and Dean Gauldin, we prosecuted Hamilton vigorously

and relentlessly. Each venireman examined by the state was asked this question:

"If the state proves that the defendant robbed the Grand Prairie bank and during the robbery no shot was fired, no person was injured or killed, and proved that Hamilton was the man who was convicted and given a life sentence at La Grange for robbery with firearms, where the death penalty was sought, would you as a juror give the defendant, Raymond Hamilton, the death penalty in this case?" To which each juror answered he would.

Each of these facts was proved to the jury beyond reasonable doubt, and not a single witness appeared to controvert these facts by the defendant.

The ten following jurors voted in accordance with their oath and in accordance with the answers they gave in the above question: Green Reynolds, J. H. Brown, M. P. Crowder, J. P. Shrader, Clarence Henry, Augustus E. Buffington, Clayton C. Lary, W. K. Williams, W. L. Leifeste and W. A. Thompson.

The following two jurors, having been asked the same question and answered it in the affirmative, failed miserably to carry out their oath as jurors and voted against the death penalty: H. G. Foster and Charles F. O'Connor.

I congratulate those ten fearless jurors who believed in the enforcement of the criminal laws of this state and who stand ready and willing, as has been shown in this case, to return a verdict carrying the death penalty against a defendant who most deserves that penalty. They were fearless and stand on the side of the good citizenship of Texas, and if every time a criminal whose guilt was established was tried by such men as these ten, law enforcement in Dallas County and Texas would be an easy matter and that kind of criminal, such as Raymond Hamilton, Clyde Barrow and those other desperadoes would soon be swept from the face of the earth.

The State of Texas met the burden placed upon it in the trial and it then became the duty of the jurors to assume full responsibility for the verdict or failure to reach a verdict.

They must answer to the good people of Dallas County why a desperado like Raymond Hamilton should be permitted again to escape the electric chair for his innumerable deeds of violence in this country.

Raymond was smiling when taken into the courtroom to hear the jury dismissed.

"I knew from the start I wouldn't get the death penalty in this case," Hamilton joyfully lied.

Sheriff Schmid did not share Ray's pleasure.

"It may not be this year, but that boy is going to end up in the electric chair where he belongs!" the lawman roared.

CHAPTER X

A Bloody End
and a Date With Death

As Raymond was hearing the good news on Friday, May 11, in Dallas, more charges were being assessed against him in Fort Worth. Charges of robbing the National Guard Armory at Ranger were filed with United States Commissioner Newan against Hamilton, Clyde Barrow, Bonnie Parker, Henry Methvin, and Hilton Bybee. Fred S. Dunn, Department of Justice agent, announced that they had been accused of stealing four Browning automatic rifles and thirteen Colt .45 pistols from the armory on February 19.

While Raymond Hamilton was once again dodging the electric chair, Clyde Barrow's mother was being interrogated by law enforcement agents. Speculation was that Mrs. Barrow was arrested in the hopes that news of the event would provoke her notorious son to make a rash move that would result in his death or capture. Word spread about Mrs. Barrow's arrest despite denials by city, county, and state authorities that she had been taken. Clyde had been quoted by some of his captured cronies as having said he would "kill any person that ever harms a hair of her head." Although the announcement was said to have no connection whatsoever with the disappearance of Mrs. Barrow, United States District Attorney Clyde Eastus said that federal agents were making a systematic investigation which was expected to result in the prosecution of many people for giving aid to the West Dallas gang.

"We have sent a number to the penitentiary for helping George (Machine Gun) Kelly and his wife, Kathryn Kelly, last summer, and there's no reason why we can't do the same with some of the friends of Barrow, Parker, and Hamilton," Eastus said.

"There is no doubt," he continued, "that the help they have been receiving from friends and their innumerable relatives is one of the main reasons they have been able to evade capture. It's a penitentiary offense for any person to aid a fugitive to escape arrest, and we mean to invoke the power of the law to decrease the number of hideouts the gang can find."

Eastus said anyone found giving help to Bonnie and Clyde or Raymond Hamilton would be charged with conspiracy to harbor a federal fugitive. Dallas officers stated they felt Mrs. Barrow probably would not be prosecuted, even if it was learned definitely that she had been helping her son. They did feel, however, that she could give information which could be used in the effort to capture him. Henry Barrow said he did not know the men who took his wife away.

"Four men drove up and said they wanted to talk to my wife," Barrow said. "I thought they were Texas Rangers. They had their pants stuck down in their boots. They said they'd bring her back in a few minutes, but I haven't seen her since. I'll just have to wait here until I hear some word from her. I haven't any money to spend on lawyers, even if I did know where she is. They can't do anything to her anyway. She hasn't done any crime."

Mrs. Barrow was returned to her husband on Saturday, May 12. She had been in the custody of officers at Tyler. Bonnie's sister Billie, sister-in-law Edith Parker, and aunt Mrs. Leila Plummer also had been held for questioning at Tyler before being released.

Mother's Day, May 13, 1934, brought a report that Bonnie and Clyde had been sighted. Lawmen shifted their primary search grounds from the Wichita Falls area to the Cleburne area south of Fort Worth when the desperadoes and three others were sighted. Police in the Dallas–Fort Worth area were told to be on the lookout for a black V-8 Ford sedan, but the search for Raymond Hamilton's friends turned up nothing.

Also on Mother's Day, Alice Hamilton Davis learned her youngest son was still on a collision course with the electric chair. News came he was to be tried later in the week at Denton for the Lewisville bank robbery and that once again the death penalty would be sought.

The twenty-year-old demanded that Denton County give personal service to the 100 veniremen called for his trial Friday. Albert Baskett, once again managing Ray's legal fight, notified County Attorney Judge Gambill of Denton County that his client would not waive personal service, and Sheriff G. C. Cockrell's deputies began immediately the job of notifying the 100 men in person. The usual practice was for defendants to waive personal service on their veniremen, who then were notified by mail to appear in court. It was announced that a special term of Judge Ben Boyd's district court would hear the case against Raymond. Gambill said he would urge the jury to assess the death penalty for the five-time convicted Hamilton. Gerald Stockard, assistant county attorney for Denton County, was named to assist in the prosecution.

John R. West, attorney for Floyd Hamilton, began attempts that same Monday to obtain the release of his client from county jail on a writ of habeas corpus. Judge Noland Williams granted the writ, but set no date for hearing to determine whether bond should be allowed. Floyd was under indictment for the Grand Prairie robbery and was being held in the Houston County jail, where authorities were planning to file charges against him in connection with the Eastham break.

On Tuesday, May 15, word arrived that disputed Clyde Barrow's disclaimer of the killing of the two state highway patrolmen. The information came from none other than Clyde himself in the form of a letter he sent to Assistant District Attorney Winter King:

> Mr, King
>
> So Raymond Hamilton never killed anybody. If he can make the jury believe that I'm willing to come in and be tried myself. Why dont you ask Ray about those two policemen that got killed near Grapevine, And while you are at it bwetter talk it over with his girl friend. Bonnie and me were in missouri when that happened but where was Ray? coming back from the West bankjob wasn't he? Redhot too wasn't he, I got it straight. And ask him about that escape at Eastham farm where that gard was killed Giess he claimes he doesn't know fire any shots there don't he? Well if he wasnt too dum to know how tp put a clip in a automatic he'd hace fired a lot more shots and some of the rest of the gards would got killed too. He wrote his lawyer he was too good for me and din't go my pace, well it makes a me sick to see a yellow punk like that playing baby ad making a jury cry over him. If he was half as smart as me the officers couldn't catch him either/ He stuck his fingerprint on a letter so heres mine too just to let you know thjis is on the leve;
>
> X   Clyde
>
> P s Ask Ray why he was so dam jumpy to get rid of those yellow wheels on his car and akshis girl friend how they spent easter

Barrow's disclaimer concerning the Grapevine murders was controverted by evidence in the hands of Sheriff Schmid. The print on the letter was identified as Clyde's left thumbprint by Douglas Walsh, head of the Dallas Police Department identification bureau. Schmid said that prints found on a whiskey bottle on the side road off Northwest Highway where the patrolmen were killed were those of Barrow. The sheriff added that as soon as Hamilton was captured, a new set of his prints was sent to Fort Worth, where the whiskey bottle was held as evidence, and Raymond's prints did not match those.

"One of the patrolmen was shot with a shotgun and with a machine rifle," Schmid said. "The machine rifle is one of Barrow's favorite weapons."

The sheriff also pointed out that on the day of the killings, Hamilton was in South Texas, having kidnapped Mrs. Gunter following the West holdup. Raymond had reminded interviewers of this, even though it involved admission of the West robbery.

"I had robbed the West bank and taken that woman with me," Hamilton said. "We drove to Houston in her car and Sunday morning I stole a car in Houston."

Hamilton went on to say he released the Gunter woman at 9:30 A.M. and drove northward over country roads, arriving at Cleburne at daylight Monday. Assistant D.A. King said Mary O'Dare's story of the happenings of that fateful Easter weekend matched Raymond's.

"Well, Clyde's just degenerated into a low down skunk," Hamilton said when shown a copy of the letter. "I didn't think he'd do a thing like that. If he's mad at me I didn't know anything about it."

"It seems that Clyde has turned rat," said Mary O'Dare in reference to the Barrow letter.

While the furor concerning the Barrow letter was on, Floyd Hamilton, in jail in Crockett, arranged to have a hearing before Judge Williams on his application for release on a writ of habeas corpus. Sheriff Schmid received warrants from H. Betts, justice of the peace at Crockett, Houston County, for Hamilton's arrest. The warrants showed Hamilton was charged April 24 for aiding in the escape of prisoners from Eastham prison farm, and as an accessory to Joe Palmer, who had been charged with murder in connection with the killing of Major Crowson. Raymond had also been charged in connection with Crowson's death. The application for Floyd's release claimed he was held without any charges pending against him.

Under heavy guard, Raymond Hamilton was transferred from Dallas on Wednesday, May 16, 1934, to the county jail at Denton. There, for the second time since his most recent capture, he would go on trial for his life. Ray had hardly been locked in his cell in Denton when Sheriff G. C. Cockrell and his deputies were called out on a report that Bonnie and Clyde had been seen nearby. No trace of them was found, but Sheriff Cockrell announced that sufficient guards would be maintained to ensure protection of Hamilton and prevent any escape attempt.

On Thursday Mary O'Dare was allowed to visit Raymond. A few cells down from Hamilton was T. R. Brooks, who was awaiting trial for his part in the Lewisville robbery. Brooks had admitted his involvement in the crime. Sheriff Cockrell kept close watch over Mary and Raymond during their thirty-minute visit. Mary had been jointly charged with Raymond in connection with the West robbery. She was free under bond pending the trial for that job.

Special guards were stationed around the Denton County jail that evening, and armed men were assigned to patrol the courthouse Friday when Hamilton went on trial for the Lewisville holdup. It was learned Ray intended to plead not guilty to the charge, despite the fact he had freely admitted committing the crime. His reason for a plea of innocence, according to his attorney, was to establish a basis for an appeal in the event of conviction. County Attorney Gambill reiterated that the state would demand the death penalty. Whether Brooks would be called as a witness was being kept secret, and Gambill refused to say if the youth was on his witness list.

With Raymond attempting to sidestep ol' Sparky one more time, the name of James Mullen resurfaced. Mullen, alias Jimmie Lamont, who several weeks earlier had given officers a lengthy statement concerning activities of Clyde Barrow and of the plot to free Hamilton from Eastham, was placed in the Dallas County jail Thursday by U.S. Marshal J. R. (Red) Wright. Mullen was held in various Texas jails for several weeks by state officers and was now held by the federal government in connection with the robbery of the Eastland National Guard Armory. He was held in Dallas for an appearance in federal court. Also, three friends of Raymond Hamilton were convicted Wednesday in federal district court on charges of concealing two guns that allegedly were government property and that were identified as having been stolen from armories.

Sixty-eight veniremen had been questioned but not one juror selected to hear Raymond Hamilton's trial in Denton as court recessed Friday night, May 18. Formed opinions and unwillingness to inflict the death penalty excused most of the veniremen. From the group of farmers nine were disqualified for having formed opinions and forty-seven said they could not inflict the death penalty on a robbery case where no shots were fired or no one was hurt by the person committing the crime. Hamilton, under heavy guard, sat next to his sweetheart, Mary O'Dare Pitts, who held her hand on his shoulder throughout the long day.

At the start of the trial, defense attorney Albert Baskett moved for a continuance on the contention that the defendant had not been served with a copy of the indictment. District Judge Ben Boyd overruled this motion, and immediately afterward, the judge overruled motions to quash the indictment and the special venire. Guards stood at doors of the courtroom as the trial proceeded, keeping close watch over the defendant and the crowd which jammed the room. Hamilton followed proceedings closely, at times turning to survey the crowd and glance at guarding officers. Every precaution had been taken to prevent the slippery criminal from making a break.

On the same Friday that Raymond Hamilton was tried in Denton, the still elusive Clyde Barrow and Bonnie Parker were indicted in Fort Worth by the Tarrant County grand jury for the slayings of E. B. Wheeler and H. D. Murphy.

On May 19 state prosecutors failed again in their attempt to send Raymond Hamilton to the electric chair, but they had the satisfaction of seeing another ninety-nine-year sentence added to the total of 263 years in sentences already handed him. Ray pleaded guilty in district court in Denton to the Lewisville robbery after state's attorneys spent most of Friday and Saturday trying to find a jury willing to assess the death penalty for robbery with firearms. After questioning 109 veniremen and finding only one juror willing to impose such a heavy punishment, County Attorney Gambill decided there was no chance of getting such a jury in Denton County. Judge Boyd called time out in court proceedings while lawyers discussed possible ways to work out the problem. A change of venue was considered, but finally the state agreed that if Hamilton would plead guilty to robbing the bank and would accept a life term in prison, efforts to have him sentenced to death for the crime would be discontinued.

The only juror found Saturday who had no scruples against imposing a death sentence on a robber who used firearms in a holdup was an elderly farmer, Floyd Byrom. After the death sentence qualification was removed, attorneys quickly obtained eleven other farmers to fill out the panel.

As soon as Raymond pleaded guilty and testimony from a few Lewisville witnesses had been heard, the jury promptly handed out the prison term. To Hamilton the sentence meant nothing — escaping the electric chair was another matter.

Hamilton said he was pleased with the outcome of the trial. He admitted he was apprehensive due to the possible consequences when he was brought to Denton, but seemed greatly relieved as Mary remained at his side throughout the trial.

Sheriff Cockrell announced that Raymond would be kept in Denton until officers of other counties wanted him. McLennan County authorities had asked that he be delivered to them for trial on the West charges, but Lee Simmons, prison director, told them that Hamilton would be taken to Huntsville on June 14 to face charges in connection with the fatal shooting of Major Crowson. District Attorney Willard McLaughlin said McLennan County would postpone plans to try Hamilton for the West robbery in order to allow Huntsville authorities to place him on trial.

What was said to be a positive identification of Mrs. Billie White, alias Mace, and Floyd Hamilton as the couple who shot to death the highway patrolmen resulted in the state filing charges of murder against the pair on May 21. William Schieffer, the farmer who witnessed the shootings, identified the two suspects. Billie was placed in the Tarrant County jail, while Floyd was already in the Crockett jail.

Tarrant County District Attorney Jesse Martin said Schieffer, whose home overlooked the place where the killers' automobile was parked for several hours, had never identified photos of Bonnie and Clyde. Martin said fingerprints on a whiskey bottle found near the scene of the killings had been partially but not positively identified as those of Barrow, and this had given false credence to the letter written by Barrow denying any part in the slaying of the patrolmen. Even though Floyd Hamilton and Billie White had been charged in Fort Worth, the Highway Patrol still planned to make an investigation before it ended its hunt for Barrow, Chief L. G. Phares announced. The search for Barrow and Parker was predicated on the belief they committed the crimes, Phares added, saying that the patrol had put much faith in the accuracy of fingerprints identified as Barrow's which were found on the whiskey bottle. A minimum reward of $1,500 had been posted for the arrest of persons convicted of the double homicide. Phares said he had actually received about $4,000, a large amount of which might be used for expenses incidental to the apprehension of the slayers.

Aided by Dallas county officials, Martin and members of his staff questioned many witnesses in their efforts to bring about conviction of Floyd Hamilton and Billie White for the murders. Special Investigators Denver Seale and M. L. Miller and Assistant District Attorney King worked up evidence which was submitted to Martin in Fort Worth and which resulted in the filing of charges against the elder Hamilton brother and Billie.

Appearing unworried and claiming to have an airtight alibi, Billie Mace talked readily on Tuesday about Bonnie and Clyde but had little to say about her own problem with the law. Billie said both she and her mother, Emma, had tried in vain to "reason with Bonnie" to come home and lead a law-abiding life instead of running with Barrow.

"But she won't listen," Billie said. "I guess she's too much in love with Clyde."

Why anyone would accuse her of complicity in the Grapevine slayings was a mystery to her, Billie told gathered newspaper reporters.

"I don't see why anyone would even think I chased around with Floyd Hamilton," she said. "No, I don't care anything about him or where he is. I was taking snapshots at my mother's house that day and I won't have any trouble proving it in court. Sure I was surprised when I was arrested. If I had been in any killing I wouldn't have been working in that Gladewater sandwich stand. I'd have been where they couldn't find me."

Her husband, Fred Mace, was still serving time at Huntsville. D.A. Martin said Billie would be given an examining trial if she desired it.

On Wednesday, May 23, 1934, the trail ended for Clyde Barrow and Bonnie Parker on a lonely country road between Arcadia and Gibsland, Louisiana. They were ambushed in a hail of bullets fired by six officers who had been trailing them for weeks. The officers were Frank Hamer, a retired Texas Ranger who had been placed on the case secretly by Lee Simmons and Texas Governor Ferguson; Manny Gault, retired Ranger and current member of the Texas Highway Patrol, who was chosen by Hamer to join the chase; Ted Hinton and Bob Alcorn, Dallas County deputies; and Sheriff Henderson Jordan of Bienville Parish, Louisiana, and his deputy, Prentiss Oakley. The lawmen had caught up with Barrow through relentless detective work, as well as tips received from the Dallas area, East Texas, and Louisiana. One of the chief tipsters from Dallas was Joe Bill Francis, Clyde's brother-in-law. Francis hated and feared Barrow and was only too glad to put him on the spot.

Lawmen figured they could find Bonnie and Clyde in northern Louisiana because Henry Methvin's father had a place there. Methvin had been with them off and on but was not present on the morning of the twenty-third. The officers had hidden by the roadside near the Methvin farm for a couple of days and in the process stopped Methvin's father, Ira, handcuffed him, and chained him to a tree. They then took a wheel off his truck to make it appear as though he had stopped to fix a flat. The old man roundly cursed the officers for their actions. At 9:15 A.M. on the fateful morning the officers had

R. T. PAINE FARM — This field along the banks of the Arkansas River, northeast of Muskogee, was a familiar sight to the Hamilton family in 1918. Lillie and Floyd, the two oldest children, worked the farm using mules and Belgian mares. Raymond was too small to help.

— Photo by Sid Underwood

GOLDMAN HOME — The home of Ben (Boots) Goldman and Roxie Goldman, southwest of Dallas, was a temporary home for Raymond Hamilton during the late 1920s. Steve Davis, Raymond's stepfather, and Roxie were siblings.

— Photo by Sid Underwood

HAMILTON CHILDREN — This photograph was taken in a Henryetta, Oklahoma, studio in 1914. One-year-old Raymond Hamilton is seated, surrounded by Lucy, left, Lillie and Floyd. Within four years, daughters Audrey and Maggie would be born to John and Alice Hamilton.

— Photo courtesy Floyd Hamilton

RAYMOND'S BIRTHPLACE — The Deep Fork River just east of Schulter, Oklahoma. Raymond Elzie Hamilton was born in a tent to John and Alice Hamilton May 21, 1913, not far from here.

— Photo by Sid Underwood

SENTENCED TO DEATH — Raymond Hamilton, in handcuffs, stands before the bench in court at Huntsville on April 9, 1935, while Judge S. W. Dean, standing at left, sentences him to death for the murder of a prison guard. Beside Hamilton, in far right-hand corner, is prosecutor Max Rogers.
— Photo courtesy United Press International

FINAL SENTENCING — Hamilton is shown with his mother, Alice Hamilton Davis, April 8, 1935, in a Huntsville courtroom. The court turned down pleas by his mother concerning his death sentence in connection with the killing of Major Crowson, a prison farm highrider. Raymond proclaimed innocence, but his plea fell on deaf ears and he was later electrocuted.
— Photo courtesy United Press International

NOT LONG — Raymond Hamilton and his mother, Alice Hamilton Davis. Hamilton was executed not long after this photo was taken.
— Photo courtesy Dallas Public Library

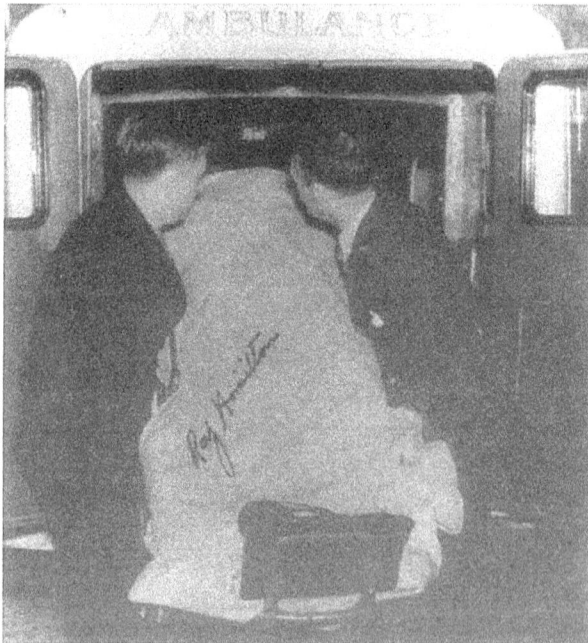

END OF THE LINE — Huntsville prison officials load the body of Raymond Hamilton into an ambulance for the trip to Dallas following his execution May 10, 1935.
— Photo courtesy Ken Woodall

THE HUNTERS — *The men who ambushed Clyde Barrow and Bonnie Parker between Arcadia and Gibsland, Louisiana, May 23, 1934: (standing from left) Prentiss Oakley, Bienville Parish deputy sheriff; Ted Hinton, Dallas County deputy sheriff; Bob Alcorn, Dallas County deputy sheriff; Manny Gault, Texas Ranger; (kneeling from left) Frank Hamer, former Texas Ranger, and Henderson Jordan, Bienville Parish sheriff.*

— Photo courtesy Ken Woodall

RAYMOND'S ADVERSARIES — *These men and Raymond Hamilton did not get along. Shown from left are R. A. (Smoot) Schmid, Dallas County sheriff; Lee Simmons, Texas prison director; W. W. Waid, Texas prison warden; and Bill Decker, Dallas County chief deputy.*

— Photo courtesy Ken Woodall

DAY IN COURT— *Raymond Hamilton had many days in court. Following several court appearances and convictions early in his career, he received more than 300 years in sentences. Later he received the death penalty.*

— Photo courtesy Marvin Jones

FINAL CAPTURE — *Raymond at the Fort Worth city jail shortly after his capture in the Fort Worth railyards April 5, 1935, by Dallas County Deputy Sheriff Bill Decker and other Dallas and Tarrant county officers. Raymond was executed May 10, 1935.*

— Photo courtesy Ken Woodall

THE CATCHER, THE KEEPER, THE BAD BOYS — *Raymond Hamilton, seated, far right, shows little interest in Dallas County Sheriff Smoot Schmid's (seated, far left) story in this shot from the Dallas County jail. Murray Fisher, Dallas County jailer, stands at far right. Hamilton's associates in crime, between him and Schmid, are (from left) Oscar Lafferty, Roy Thornton (Bonnie Parker's husband), Clarence Chance, Bud Mace, and Dewey Hunt.*

— Photo courtesy Dallas Public Library

ON THE ROAD — *Clyde Barrow and Bonnie Parker. Barrow and Raymond Hamilton knew the backroads of North Texas.*
— Photo courtesy Dallas Public Library

TWO-GUN BONNIE — *The diminutive companion of Clyde Barrow, Bonnie Parker was less than five feet tall and weighed eighty-five pounds.*
— Photo courtesy Ken Woodall

BONNIE AND CLYDE — *One of the best known criminal duos in modern times, Bonnie Parker and Clyde Barrow are shown at one of their "motels." Camping out was a way of life for the desperadoes. Clyde is rolling a Bull Durham cigarette while Bonnie strikes a pose.*
— Photo courtesy Ken Woodall

THE TEXAS RATTLESNAKE — The son of illiterate parents, Clyde Barrow was the most hunted criminal in America in April and May of 1934.
— Photo courtesy Ken Woodall

BONNIE PARKER — Portrayals of Bonnie as a cigar-smoking gun moll who ruthlessly shot down anyone are exaggerated. She seldom was directly involved in the gunplay, and the cigar-smoking story was the result of a photo in which she jokingly posed smoking a cigar.
— Photo courtesy Ken Woodall

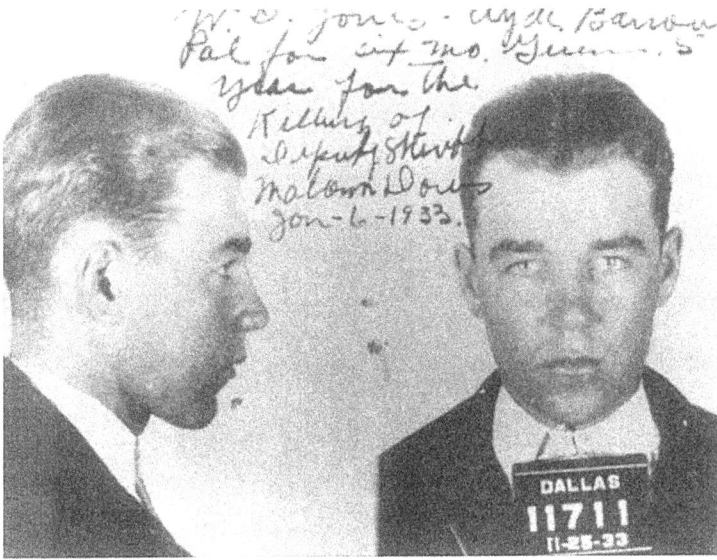

THE KID — W. D. (Deacon) Jones, a trigger-happy seventeen-year-old, traveled with Bonnie and Clyde during some of their crime sprees in the Midwest, and was also involved in murders credited to the gang in Dallas and Belton, Texas. Following his capture in Houston, he told authorities Barrow forced him to help commit crimes.

— Photo courtesy Ken Woodall

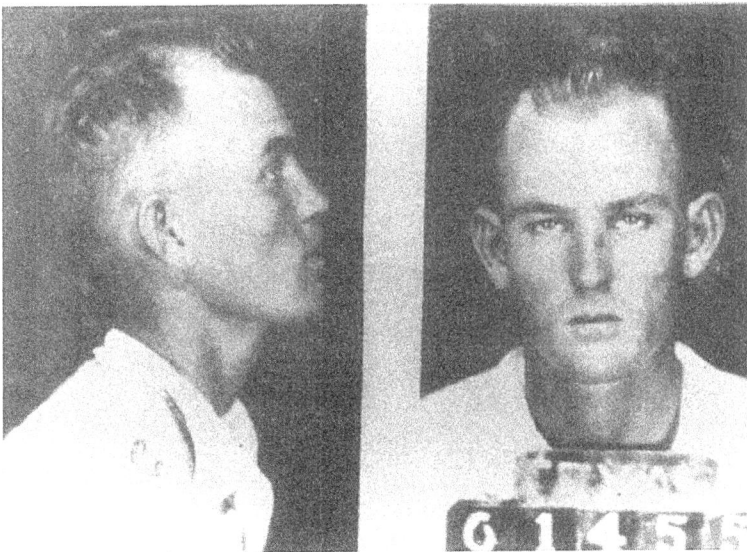

JOE PALMER — An accomplice to Raymond Hamilton during the infamous January 16, 1934, break at the Eastham Prison Farm near Weldon, Texas, Palmer admitted killing Major Crowson, a highrider, during the break. Crowson confirmed this before he died, but Hamilton was convicted in the shooting as an accessory. He and Palmer were executed May 10, 1935.

— Photo courtesy Ken Woodall

THE LEWISVILLE JOB — Raymond Hamilton, left, and T. R. Brooks robbed the Lewisville, Texas, bank April 25, 1934. Following a wild chase across North Texas, the men were captured at a roadblock near Howe, Texas.
— Photo courtesy Dallas Public Library

WHERE DID HE GO? — On March 19, 1934, Raymond Hamilton, Floyd Hamilton, and John Basden robbed the state bank in Grand Prairie, Texas. Basden held a gun on bank employees while Raymond gathered the money. Floyd stayed in the car.
— Photo courtesy Dallas Public Library

SHOOTOUT SCENE — At this site, near Stringtown, Oklahoma, a wild shootout occurred between Raymond Hamilton, Clyde Barrow, and Oklahoma authorities in August 1932. The building partially pictured was a saloon. As Atoka County Sheriff C. G. Maxwell and Deputy E. C. Moore approached, shots rang out. Moore was killed instantly and Maxwell was seriously wounded.
— Photo by Sid Underwood

HIDING PLACE — Hamilton hid his car in this old barn when he visited his relatives and friends in southern Dallas County. An older cousin of the author, who used to play with one of Raymond's stepcousins during the 1930s, said that one time he peeked in the car and saw more guns in one place than he had ever seen in his life.
— Photo by Sid Underwood

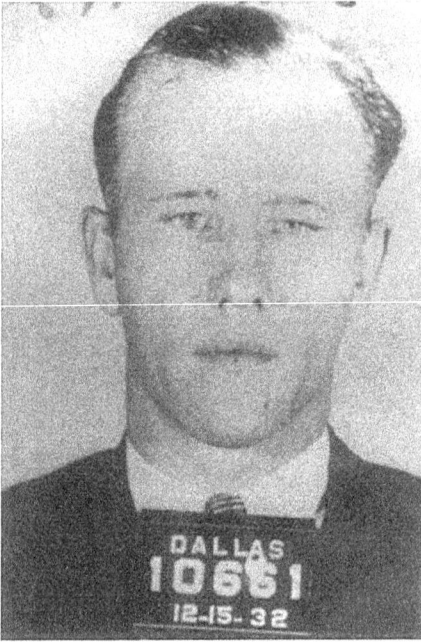

FIRST MUG SHOT — Nineteen-year-old Raymond Hamilton is shown in this December 1932 mug shot, taken following his arrest in Bay City, Michigan. Hamilton and Gene O'Dare were arrested in a skating rink and extradited to Texas to face charges of robbery and murder.
— Photo courtesy Ken Woodall

DEPRESSION DESPERADO — This mug shot of Raymond Hamilton was taken at the state prison at Huntsville, Texas.
— Photo courtesy Ken Woodall

BANDIT'S JAIL — Raymond Hamilton was locked up many times during his life. Occasiona. he turned the tables. Shown is th door to the vault of the First Sta. Bank of Cedar Hill, Texas. Hamilton robbed this bank twic and locked his victims in the va. both times.

— Photo by Sid Underw.

CEDAR HILL BANK — On October 8, 1932, Raymond Hamilton entered the First State Bank (still Citizens Bank in this photo) of Cedar Hill, Texas, and demanded money. He escaped with more than $1,000. On November 25, Hamilton and an accomplice, Les Stewart, returned to the bank and got away with nearly $2,000.

— Photo courtesy Ann Permenter

TRINITY LEVEE — In his teens Raymond Hamilton helped with construction of the levee on the Trinity River. The levee curbed floods that plagued Dallas and West Dallas.

— Photo by Sid Underwood

BARROW SERVICE STATION — This station on the West Dallas Road (now Singleton Boulevard) was owned and operated by Henry Barrow, Clyde's father. Besides gasoline and sundries, Henry also sold home brew beer to those willing to pay.

— Photo courtesy Dallas Public Library

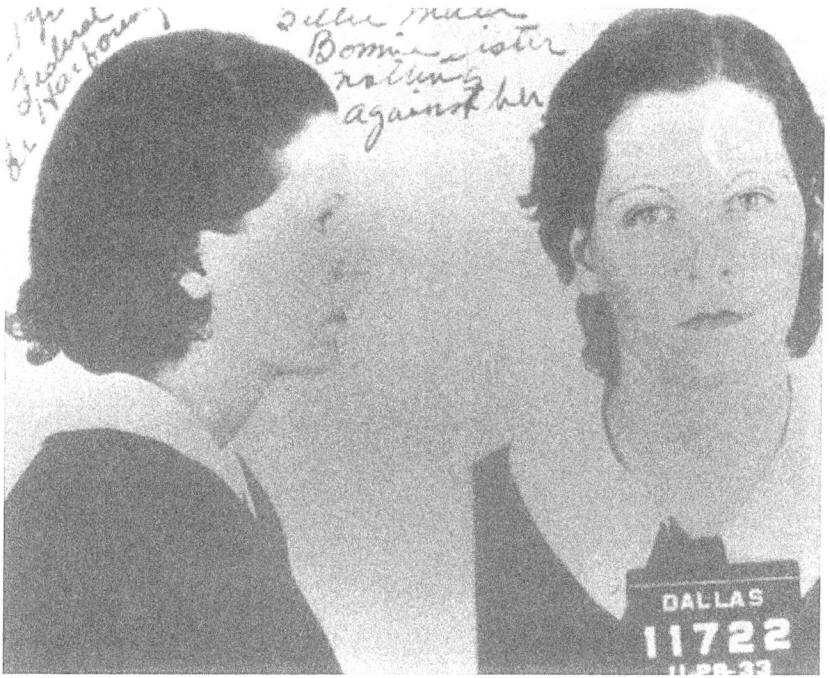

BILLIE MACE — *The younger sister of Bonnie Parker, Billie got into trouble as much for who she was as what she had done. Billie and Floyd Hamilton were falsely accused of killing two highway patrolmen Easter Sunday, April 1, 1934, near Grapevine, Texas. The patrolmen had been killed by Clyde Barrow and Henry Methvin.* — Photo courtesy Ken Woodall

RARE MOMENT — *Bonnie and Clyde enjoying a light moment. When Raymond Hamilton realized his friends were headed for a fatal shootout with the law, he went his own way and declared himself a "gentleman bank robber."* — Photo courtesy Ken Woodall

IN CHAINS — When law enforcement authorities got their hands on Raymond Hamilton, they took no chances because he was hard to catch and harder to hold.
— Photo courtesy Ken Woodall

HOME AWAY FROM HOME — The Dallas County jail was like a second home to Hamilton. Once, he nearly escaped from his sixth-floor cell. After sawing cell bars with hacksaw blades that had been smuggled in, he fashioned a rope from sheets and managed to lower himself to the second-floor level before running out of "rope." He climbed back up to get more sheets, but alerted officers were waiting for him.
— Photo by Sid Underwood

about decided to call it quits when they heard a car approaching. When the car, which was slowing to inspect Methvin's truck, got close enough for the occupants to be identified, Alcorn and Hinton alerted the others it was Barrow and Bonnie. As Clyde pulled along-side the truck, Alcorn yelled "Halt!" Clyde, who had been eyeing the truck, jerked his head toward the voice and floorboarded his vehicle. The six lawmen emptied their firearms into the outlaws' car, striking Barrow and Parker some forty to fifty times each, killing both instantly.

Two of the most interested people in the news of the end of Bonnie and Clyde were Deacon Jones and Raymond Hamilton. Jones, who had given officers some valuable information concerning Barrow's movements, was still telling the ludicrous tale that he was a virtual prisoner of Barrow. Hamilton, who had given authorities only the vaguest of information concerning his former partner in crime, appeared downcast at the news.

"I knew it was gonna happen; I just didn't know when," Raymond said from his Denton County jail cell. "Me and Clyde had our differences but we was still friends no matter what it looked like."

The day following the killing of her sister and Clyde Barrow, Billie Mace found herself in a Fort Worth courtroom. Mrs. Leila Plummer, Billie's aunt, testified at the examining trial that Billie was with her on Easter Sunday.

"It wasn't possible for her to have gone to Grapevine and taken part in that shooting," the aunt declared. She was the only witness placed on the stand during the hearing before Justice Faulkner. In the meantime, attorneys for Billie sued out a writ of habeas corpus to free her, and a hearing was set by Judge George E. Hosey for Friday or Saturday. Mrs. Plummer, Emma Parker's sister, said Billie went with her to the scene of the killing during the latter part of Easter Sunday when they heard about the shooting. Emma Parker, with her oldest daughter lying in state in a Dallas funeral home, looked on somberly at the proceedings in Billie's trial. District Attorney Jesse E. Martin announced he had sent for Clyde Barrow's guns and would have ballistics experts compare shotgun and rifle shells found on the Grapevine roadside with shells fired in those weapons.

"That should tend to prove or disprove whether Clyde Barrow and Bonnie Parker killed the two peace officers," Martin said. "If they don't check we will have a better case against Billie Mace and Floyd Hamilton."

Martin sent police identification superintendent Barney Finn to Dallas to take fingerprints from the bodies of Barrow and Parker.

Finn planned to compare those prints with marks on the whiskey bottle found at the scene.

On Friday, May 25, Raymond Hamilton was taken from Denton back to Huntsville. Warden W. W. Waid was there to greet him, giving him his old number along with a striped suit. Arriving about noon, Ray was pushed out into the southeast Texas heat and humidity. Hamilton was sweating and giving a scowl because he had been sent down chained to a common forger. Raymond hobbled inside to see Warden Waid.

"Well, Ray," said the warden, "they want you to hurry back to the Eastham farm and finish up that crop you planted before you escaped in January."

A smile replaced Ray's scowl.

"I'm ready, Warden," he said. "I was a good worker when I was there before, you know."

Raymond was known in the prison system as a 200-pound-a-day cotton picker, but it would be several weeks, if ever, before he got his fingers on a cotton boll again. First, the warden ruled, he must chop wood. The desperado was held behind the prison walls until the various trials for robbery and murder pending against him were held. He was scheduled to be tried in June for the murder of Major Crowson. Prison officials said Hamilton dreaded the Crowson trial more than any. The state was prepared to demand the death penalty, and Raymond feared he might get it.

Raymond Hamilton was a curiosity to the other inmates. Some of the hardened criminals remarked, "He's not so tough." Others chatted with the talkative one from West Dallas.

Private funeral services for Clyde Barrow were held on Friday, May 25, at the Sparkman-Holtz-Brand Funeral Home on Ross Avenue, with only members of his family and about 100 neighbors and friends from West Dallas admitted. Police lines held back a crowd at the funeral home both during the services and as the casket was brought out and placed in the hearse. The service was concluded at the grave in the Western Heights Cemetery in West Dallas. The Rev. Clifford Andrews, pastor of the Oak Cliff Gospel Church, conducted the services. Andrews revealed that during one of his visits to see Raymond Hamilton the desperado intimated that Bonnie and Clyde had prayed often in his presence.

The Barrow-Parker family woes did not end with the ambush in Louisiana. Although a Fort Worth police identification expert testified on May 26 that fingerprints on the whiskey bottle found at the scene of the Grapevine murders were those of Clyde Barrow and

Henry Methvin, it was insisted by William Schieffer, the Grapevine farmer who had witnessed the shootings, at the habeas corpus hearing for Billie Mace that it was she and Floyd Hamilton who had fired the fatal shots. The hearing concerning Billie and Floyd Hamilton was recessed until Tuesday, May 29, after District Attorney Jesse E. Martin asked for time in which to obtain the opinion of ballistics experts on whether the exploded shells found at the Grapevine shooting scene did or did not come from guns carried by Clyde Barrow at the time of his death. If both Schieffer and identification expert Barney Finn had been right, the authorities could have contended that Floyd and Billie carried with them to the scene of the killing a whiskey bottle out of which both Barrow and Methvin drank in order to pin the crime on them.

Rising from the witness stand, Schieffer pointed his finger at Billie and declared, "There is no doubt in my mind but that this is the woman."

The farmer went on to explain that he had picked Floyd Hamilton out of twenty-five prisoners in the Dallas jail as the other slayer.

"I recognized him instantly and he seemed to recognize me," said the farmer.

Bonnie Parker was buried Saturday, May 26, 1934, in the Fishtrap Cemetery in West Dallas. Many of the friends and relatives of the Barrows, Hamiltons, and Parkers were in attendance. Only about a hundred of her relatives and friends were present at the private funeral services at the McKamy-Campbell Funeral Home. Her sister Billie was allowed to attend under heavy guard. Several hundred others milled about the neighborhood, outside the police lines, or remained in parked cars to join the procession to the cemetery. The Reverend Andrews also conducted this service. After reading the ninetieth Psalm, he spoke briefly along the line of his talk at the Barrow funeral, stating that he loved Bonnie because God loved her, and reiterated Raymond Hamilton's statement that Clyde and Bonnie often prayed together. The pastor then related briefly the story of the prodigal son and spoke of the love of God for sinners. Vocal music was provided by Vivian and Douglas Hughes and by a quartet composed of J. T. Turner, L. L. Stroup, George M. High, and Joe Richardson. Clad in a new blue dress, Bonnie lay in a steel coffin with plush interior. She was viewed by those present at the funeral home before the procession to the cemetery. Pallbearers were Joe L. Snow, Louis Cook, Clarence Clay, Harvey Gamble, Philip Hodges, and Dink Biddle.

Shortly after the Walker County grand jury convened in Huntsville on May 28 it returned an indictment against Raymond Hamilton, charging him with the murder of Major Crowson. The highrider guard had died in a Huntsville hospital, giving Walker County jurisdiction in the case. The indictment set out the conviction of Hamilton in Fayette County for the Carmine robbery, and his conviction in Hill County for the Bucher slaying. The case was set for June 11, and the district attorney said he would ask for the death penalty. A venire of seventy-five men was ordered from which to select a jury. On the same day he was indicted in Huntsville, Raymond Hamilton's name surfaced in Dallas as Sheriff Schmid revealed a second letter addressed to Ray in the Dallas County jail and purportedly written by Bonnie and Clyde. The sheriff believed the letter strengthened his theory that Barrow and Parker killed the state highway patrolmen. Of course, he was wrong about Parker firing shots, and too, the letter, if authentic, contained some inaccuracies.

"You exposed your hole card when you stole the money from us on the Lancaster bank job," the letter said in reference to the Barrow-Hamilton squabble on the division of loot. "When I demanded a shake down, you offered such strange excuses for having the money on you I should have killed you then. After you writing that letter saying you didn't stoop so low as to rob filling stations I have done nothing but look for you."

Schmid took the incorrect position that Barrow was at the Grapevine hideout waiting to kill Hamilton when the patrolmen approached. In fact, Barrow, Methvin, and Parker were there so that Bonnie could give her mother a white rabbit for Easter. The sheriff claimed Raymond identified the letter as having been written by Bonnie Parker. At the same time the authenticity of the letter was discounted because of its good construction, whereas the letter identified by Barrow's fingerprint contained misspelled words and poor grammar. The most recent letter was handwritten and postmarked 4:00 P.M., April 27, DeSoto Station, Memphis, Tennessee. Schmid said he was attempting to obtain specimens of Bonnie's handwriting in order to compare it with the letter to Hamilton with a view to further authenticating it.

"Raymond," the letter said at its beginning, "I'm very sorry to hear of your getting captured, but due to the fact that you offered no resistance, sympathy is lacking. When I came to the Eastham farm after you I thought maybe the 'joint' had changed you from a boastful punk. However, I soon learned of the mistake I had made. The first thing that aroused my suspicions was your suggestion of shooting Joe Palmer in the back while he was asleep. You soon learned how I felt about such cat ideas." There is no way to be sure Raymond actually made the threat. Hamilton was classified as a "yellow punk" in other portions of the letter. One sentence said he had proven it when he hid in the bottom of the car instead of preparing to offer a fight when officers nearly hemmed the gang in at the Ozark Mountains. This portion was fiction because Raymond was not with Barrow during brushes with the law in Arkansas and Missouri. If this letter was authentic, then it indicated Ray and Clyde were jealous enough of one another's notoriety to snipe at each other through the newspapers.

On Monday, May 29, in Fort Worth it was learned that if necessary Police Chief Percy Boyd of Commerce, Oklahoma, would be brought to Texas to testify in the habeas corpus hearing of Billie Mace on May 31. Clyde Mays, attorney for Billie, made the announcement after he failed to have Henry Methvin subpoenaed through the Dallas sheriff's office. Mays accurately claimed that Methvin was with Bonnie and Clyde and that they were on the scene when the officers were slain near Grapevine. Bob Alcorn and Frank Hamer had also been subpoenaed to testify in the Mace case.

On statements from Houston ballistics experts that the slugs which killed the two highway patrolmen came from the guns of Bonnie and Clyde, the murder charges against Billie Mace and Floyd Hamilton were dismissed May 31 in criminal district court in Fort Worth at the habeas corpus hearing. Billie's mother, Emma, broke into sobs when the district attorney asked that charges be dismissed. Judge George E. Hosey apologized to Billie.

"You have been wronged, locked in jail, and held for nearly two weeks because possibly somebody swore to a lie," he said. "The law made a mistake and I apologize. I have been on this court seventeen years and this is the first time that anything like this has happened. If I can ever make amends, don't fail to call on me. I am sure that Mr. Martin feels the same way about it."

The packed courtroom cheered the judge's words and was not restrained. Billie, who had refused to eat after Bonnie had been killed, changed her mind following the dimissal.

"I'd like to get ahold of some fried chicken," she said.

When Billie was asked if she would go back to her job at the sandwich stand in Gladewater, her mother broke in and said, "No, sir, she's going back to Dallas with me."

On the Friday following Billie's dismissal, Cumie Barrow and Emma Parker asked an injunction against further exhibition of motion pictures of the events connected with the slaying of Bonnie and Clyde, claiming they were humiliated by pictures displaying the bodies of their slain outlaw children.

With Clyde Barrow dead and Raymond Hamilton behind bars, the nation's crimestoppers were concentrating on catching (Two Gun) John Dillinger, the bank robber from Crown Point, Indiana. The United States Department of Justice was even said to be negotiating with Frank Hamer and Manny Gault to join in the search for the elusive Dillinger. Henry Hutchins, adjutant general of Texas, said he understood the department had been considering using the services of the two Texas officers. Hamer maintained he had had no direct contact with the federal agency, but he did not hesitate when asked about his chances of nabbing Dillinger.

"Sure, I believe I could catch Dillinger if they gave me a chance."

Department of Justice officials in Dallas denied any attempt to recruit Hamer or Gault for the Dillinger chase.

Albert S. Baskett said on Sunday, June 10, that he would represent Raymond Hamilton in his trial opening the following Monday in Huntsville on a charge of murder for the killing of Major Crowson. Baskett said Hamilton would enter a plea of not guilty. He said other defense plans would be decided after he reached Huntsville and "looked the situation over." Prosecutors had declared they would make a determined stand to have the death penalty assessed against Raymond, who already had sentences totaling more than 300 years. A jury to try Ray on charges of being a habitual criminal was half completed when court adjourned late Monday in Huntsville. A special venire of seventy-five was exhausted by the time the sixth juror was selected. Fifty more veniremen were summoned for Tuesday as Hamilton was facing the third attempt by the state in little more than a month to obtain the death penalty for him.

An expense account of $250.95 for Denver Seale, special investigator for Dallas District Attorney Robert L. Hurt, was approved Monday by the commissioners' court as the second item in Dallas County's part in the trailing of the Barrow-Parker-Hamilton gang. The account involved Seale's operations from April 1 to May 23. The court approved an account a week earlier of $557.50 for Ted Hinton and Bob Alcorn.

On June 12 James Mullen in Huntsville said Raymond Hamilton planned the Eastham break but denied the latter fired any shots. Mullen, the state's chief witness, testified more than an hour, relating in detail the escape. He said Floyd Hamilton and Bonnie and Clyde helped Raymond make his getaway. Mullen testified that Joe Palmer held the only weapon and that Joe had said, "We shot two guards." The state countered at Hamilton's defense and at a portion of Mullen's testimony with the statement of Ed Frizzell, prison guard at the time of the break, that Hamilton and Palmer each fired eight or ten shots at both Ollin Bozeman and Major Crowson. In several details Frizzell corroborated Mullen's statements. Hamilton watched Mullen closely as he testified, and the courtroom was crowded when the testimony began.

"They told you that Raymond didn't fire any shots?" asked Baskett.

"Yes, sir," Mullen answered. He said Palmer's gun had been fired but that there was no clip in Raymond's pistol. Mullen asserted that he was promised immunity from prosecution in Houston County in connection with the prison break, for his testimony, but said he had not been promised safety in other counties. The witness testified he served prison terms for burglary in Michigan, Pennsylvania, and Texas, and for narcotics law violations in federal prison.

On June 13, 1934, twelve Walker County men, led by a Baptist preacher, convicted Raymond Hamilton and assessed the death penalty for the fatal shooting of Major Crowson. The jury deliberated three hours before returning a verdict. Four ballots were taken before the jury agreed on the electric chair for Hamilton. The jurors stood deadlocked at six to six for death and life imprisonment on the first ballot. The count changed to seven for death and five for life on the second poll. It was ten for death and two for life on the third ballot, and the fourth ballot brought a unanimous decision to exterminate the accused killer in the electric chair.

Hamilton, gritting his teeth, slumped in his chair and eyed the jurors as they filed into the box. George C. Montgomery, a Baptist minister, arose and announced the jury had found Hamilton guilty and assessed death as punishment. Mrs. F. W. Robinette, district clerk, walked to Hamilton's side and asked, "Do you want me to telegraph anyone?" At first Hamilton answered "Yes," but then scowled, "They'll all hear about it too soon." Testimony was completed late in the day. Arguments of counsel were comparatively short. Baskett announced he would seek a new trial Thursday. If that move failed the decision would be carried on appeal to the Supreme Court, Baskett said. As Hamilton was led down the corridor to the courtroom before the jury officially reported its verdict, he asked his guards, "Well, what's the verdict?" They answered they did not know.

"Well, it looks pretty bad for me," Hamilton remarked.

They led him through a packed courtroom and he took his customary place as the verdict was read. Immediately after the verdict

was announced and the jury polled, Hamilton was hurried back to
the state penitentiary — three blocks down the street from the
courthouse. Max Rogers, district attorney of Groveton and prosecutor in the district for the last four years, said the verdict gave him
his first capital punishment conviction. He had asked for the death
sentence only once before, he said.

The crowds that surged in the courtroom and corridors over-
flowed onto the lawn, where an electrician had installed a loudspeaker
so outsiders might hear courtroom proceedings. Baskett closed the
defense case without testimony of several convicts, witnesses to the
shooting, who had been subpoenaed. The state closed after Britt
Mathews, Eastham farm guard, testified he saw Palmer shooting
Bozeman and Hamilton firing at Crowson.

"Did you see anyone shooting at Crowson?" asked Rogers.

"Yes, sir, Raymond Hamilton," Mathews replied.

"How many shots did Hamilton fire at Crowson and Palmer at
Bozeman?"

"Must have been five or six shots before they finished their guns
at me."

Lee Simmons, general manager of the Texas prison system, testified Crowson said Joe Palmer shot him but added others were shooting and he didn't know who they were. Dr. W. D. Veazey, prison
medical supervisor, said Crowson died eleven days after he was shot
in the abdomen with a large caliber pistol. Crowson's mother, Mrs.
T. W. Crowson of Lovelady, related that her son was thirty-three and
was planning to be married.

CHAPTER XI

Free from "The most damnable place on earth"

Working toward a final cleanup of those who allegedly contacted Clyde Barrow during his career of crime, Texas Rangers Jim Shown and W. R. Todd arrested five people and placed them in jails in other counties. One of the five, a resident of West Dallas, was released Wednesday, June 13, after a hearing before Judge Grover Adams on a writ of habeas corpus. He and the others had been arrested Tuesday night and taken to jails, the location of which the Rangers declined to reveal. While the Rangers were working on the remnants of the Barrow gang, they were also investigating various cigarette thefts and it was indicated some of their prisoners might be wanted in connection with that investigation.

District Judge S. W. Dean Thursday, June 14, in Huntsville overruled a motion for a new trial for Raymond Hamilton, and Baskett gave notice of appeal. Baskett's motion carried objections to testimony of James Mullen and H. A. Weatherley, Hill County filling station attendant, terming their statements irrelevant. Baskett also objected to the court's overruling of a motion for an instructed verdict of not guilty. The Court of Criminal Appeals in Austin planned to adjourn June 30 for the summer vacation of three months, starting a new term October 1, 1934. This made it certain that Hamilton's death penalty appeal would not reach the court in time to be decided by the end of the month, and therefore it would be held over until fall.

Highest praise for the work of District Attorney Rogers in getting the death penalty for Raymond was voiced in a statement issued in El Paso June 14 by William McGraw of Dallas County, candidate for attorney general. McGraw also wired his congratulations to Rogers, who was manager of the McGraw campaign in the 12th Judicial District.

"This is a splendid victory for the state of Texas against her public enemy number two," McGraw's statement said. "The fact that Texas is ridding herself of this hoodlum in a lawful and orderly manner bespeaks an aroused public conscience, and a new day in which such terrorism as was Hamilton's and Clyde Barrow's will not be possible. It has long been my plea, as district attorney of my own county and as president of the County Attorney's Association of Texas, that there should be greater coordination among the prosecutors of the state, as well as among the law enforcement officers."

Peace officers of four states on Friday night, June 15, sought custody of Joe Palmer, who was captured in St. Joseph, Missouri, after releasing three men he had kidnapped in Davenport, Iowa. Texas officers were en route to return the former companion of Bonnie and Clyde and Raymond Hamilton to Texas to answer charges of murder in connection with the Crowson slaying. Palmer's capture ended a twelve-hour chase through Iowa and Missouri following the kidnapping of patrolman Elmer Schleuter of Davenport; Al Schultze, secretary of the Davenport baseball club; and Dr. W. H. Fitch, veterinarian. Palmer first commandeered Schultze's car. Later overtaking Dr. Fitch, he changed his human cargo to Fitch's smaller coupe. Schleuter was forced to ride in the turtle back of the car with the rear deck closed. Palmer was captured by St. Joseph officers fifteen minutes after he left the car at the Missouri River bridge.

On June 18 Joe Palmer was brought to the state penitentiary from the Dallas County jail and his dressing in started at once under supervision of Lee Simmons. Simmons said he would be kept at Huntsville until some disposition of the case against him charging murder for the Crowson slaying was made by the courts. He also said Palmer would not be quartered with Raymond Hamilton.

"We don't want those two parties together," Simmons said.

Sheriff Henderson Jordan of Bienville Parish, Louisiana, was ordered by Judge Ben C. Dawkins in Federal District Court in Shreveport on Wednesday, June 27, to produce the Clyde Barrow automobile and turn it over to United States Marshal George W. Montgomery not later than Thursday morning on penalty of being held in contempt of court. Sheriff Jordan was cited for contempt for failure to deliver the car to Montgomery at Arcadia, Louisiana, in a suit for possession of the car instituted by Jesse Warren of Topeka, Kansas, who claimed ownership. Warren asserted the car, valued at $5,000, was stolen by Bonnie and Clyde during the month of March. The sheriff previously had declined to deliver the car to Warren, his wife, or his agents.

Joe Palmer fought to escape the electric chair at Anderson on June 28 as he sought to refute the dying statement of Major Crowson. Palmer's court-appointed attorneys, H. L. Lewis, Jr., of Anderson and Robert Smither of Huntsville, said they expected to call only three or four witnesses and that Palmer would not take the stand. The convict was being tried as a habitual criminal. Joe was assessed the death penalty on Friday, June 29, 1934, by a jury in Anderson which convicted him of the murder of Major Crowson. The jury deliberated only twenty minutes. Palmer, who had frequently predicted that the extreme penalty would be imposed, forced a wan smile as the verdict was read. When sentence was pronounced, Palmer said, "I can go to the chair at Huntsville. It won't bother me at all. I had far rather die in the electric chair than spend four and a half years more in that prison, the most damnable place on earth."

Ted R. Brooks, the Wichita Falls youth who participated with Raymond Hamilton in the Lewisville robbery, pleaded guilty July 9 in Denton to complicity in the robbery and was given a seven-year prison sentence. Brooks told the jury he aided Hamilton in fear of his life and against his will. He related how he met a young man in the railroad yards at Fort Worth one Sunday while hoboing about the country. He said the young man suggested they travel together. They boarded a freight train for Wichita Falls and, as they rode along, Brooks said he learned his companion was Raymond. Brooks testified that from the time he learned the identity of his companion he acted under duress, afraid to try to leave Hamilton and afraid to refuse to obey his suggestions. He said they took another freight train to Henrietta and there stole an automobile, which they drove back to Fort Worth and then to Denton County. The sentence was only two years more than minimum for such a crime. The jury was out thirty minutes. Brooks appeared vastly relieved when he heard the verdict.

Claiming Bonnie Parker met an accidental death when she and Clyde Barrow were killed, Mrs. Emma Parker, her mother, filed suit Saturday, July 21, in County Court at Law No. 1 in Dallas to collect $339 on the basis of a double indemnity clause in an insurance policy. Mrs. Parker claimed in her suit against the National Life and Accident Insurance Company that it had refused to pay her the double indemnity. She asked the payment and $40.68 penalty for refusal, plus $150 attorney's fees, making a total of $529.68.

Sunday, July 22, 1934. In less than twenty-four hours John

Dillinger would be killed by FBI agents in Chicago and Raymond Hamilton would escape death row at Huntsville. While Dillinger was betrayed by "The Lady in Red," Raymond was befriended by fellow inmates. A break from Huntsville was being planned by Whitey Walker and Charlie Frazier, two men with extensive criminal records and many years behind bars. Frazier had a long history of escapes and attempted escapes. Walker wanted to save his partner in crime, Blackie Thompson, who was on death row. Together they had paid off prison guard Jim Patterson to supply them with three .45 automatic pistols. Word was sent through the prison grapevine to death row. Would Raymond Hamilton be interested in participating in a break — one with only a limited chance of success? Walker and Frazier received the response they had hoped for: count Hamilton and Joe Palmer in.

In a break unparalleled in Texas prison history, Raymond Hamilton, Blackie Thompson, and Joe Palmer, the three most desperate killers in the Southwest, escaped from the death house of the penitentiary in Huntsville on July 22, 1934. Three other desperate convicts, all bank bandits and life-termers, were mowed down by gunfire of guards as Hamilton, Thompson, and Palmer scampered over the wall, where two fast automobiles waited.

"We know that they raced through the streets here headed north," Lee Simmons said that evening, "but we have not received any word of them being sighted since they got out of Huntsville."

Charlie Frazier was the man who made the escape of Hamilton and his pals possible. At 4:30 P.M. inside guard Lee Braswell had approached the death house to feed the five inmates. Inside guards were not permitted to carry weapons since they came in close contact with the convicts. As Braswell approached the door, Frazier, crouched against the wall, stepped forward, and thrust the muzzle of a .45-caliber pistol against his ribs. In his other hand the convict held another .45. Frazier marched Braswell into the death house and compelled him to unlock the cells in which Hamilton, Palmer, and Thompson were held. They came out and Frazier handed Hamilton his extra gun, and Braswell was locked in Hamilton's cell. The quartet of desperadoes dashed from the death house and were joined at the door by Walker and Roy Johnson. A few feet from the death house they encountered W. T. McConnell, also an unarmed inside guard, and forced him to go with them to the back wall of the prison, traveling unseen the distance from the death house to the wall.

"Do as we say and keep quiet or we'll drill you," Frazier told McConnell as Hamilton tickled the guard's ribs with a gun.

Picket guard C. E. Burdeaux, on duty on the back wall, sighted the convicts and their prisoner as they crept along, but, with the hapless McConnell as a shield, Frazier and Hamilton covered him with their weapons and forced him to drop down to them his guns — a sawed-off shotgun, a .30-.30 rifle, and a six-shooter. Forcing Burdeaux to stand to one side with upraised hands, the convicts hastily raised a ladder they had brought with them. Hamilton, Palmer, and Thompson shinnied up, with Frazier following next and then Walker and Johnson. Ed Roberts, a picket guard on duty on the wall about 150 yards from the Burdeaux station, saw the convicts as they started up the ladder and opened fire. He was unable to reach them successfully with his pistol and seized his .30-.30 rifle. His first shot and accompanying shout caught the attention of H. E. George, picket guard 150 yards on the other side of Burdeaux's position, and he also joined in the fire. The convicts, all but one armed now, returned the fire as they swarmed up the ladder. Hamilton, Palmer, and Thompson lost no time in dropping off on the other side. Frazier was shot off the ladder as he reached the top and dropped with several slugs in his body. Whitey Walker was toppled off a second later and fell to the ground, killed instantly. The gunfire caught Roy Johnson just as he was starting up the ladder. One of the convicts, it was not known who, had seized the rifle dropped by Burdeaux and with this weapon shot George, inflicting a minor scalp wound. The impact, however, temporarily stunned the guard and took him out of the battle.

All of the armed convicts joined in the shooting. Guard Roberts, coolly advancing upon the convicts along the wall, firing his rifle as he ran, then loading and firing again, kept up an incessant fire until the wall was clear. By the time he reached the spot where Hamilton and his pals climbed over the wall, the cars in which they escaped had rounded the corner and sped away. Roberts fired about thirty shots at the convicts, but the distance and his running movement rendered them difficult targets. It was not known whose shots dropped the three lifers.

Warden W. W. Waid and Lee Simmons, summoned from a prison ballgame, took immediate charge of the pursuit. Heavily armed squads of officers raced out the Dallas highway in search of the killers and their confederates, and police departments throughout Texas were hastily notified. On every road leaving Huntsville, squads of heavily armed officers were racing to intercept the trio within twenty minutes after their elusive heels had disappeared over the wall. Dallas and Fort Worth police departments sent squads racing south in hopes of intercepting them. Houston police and deputy sheriffs raced north, fingering machine guns, rifles, and shotguns. L. G. Phares, Highway Patrol chief, said from Austin following a long-distance telephone talk with prison officials at Huntsville that Sunday afternoon's prison break apparently had been engineered from the outside. Phares said he was informed that an automobile was waiting outside the prison to whisk Raymond Hamilton, Blackie Thompson, and Joe Palmer away. Prison authorities, Phares said, were unable to say in what direction the prisoners fled.

News of the escape was broadcast by Phares, and all patrolmen were ordered on duty to aid in the search. D. E. Hamer, captain of the Headquarters Company, Texas Rangers, said he was informed the escape was made in two black Ford sedans and in a small gray Ford coupe. Hamer was trying to contact a Ranger company at Rio Grande City to cut off any attempt of the prisoners to get into Mexico. The Dallas County sheriff's department, city police, and detective departments hastily organized Sunday afternoon to throw a barricade around Dallas County against the possibility that the escaped convicts might try to pass through Dallas toward Oklahoma. Dallas police were notified after the three had escaped and had started toward Dallas in two automobiles with three other men who had been waiting for them, Lee Simmons said. The Dallas officers were armed with repeating rifles, shotguns, and machine guns and were told to take no chances with the three desperate men.

A general alarm was broadcast by Station KVP, the Dallas police radio station, for police squad cars and other North Texas officers. Detective Lt. Will Fritz directed the stationing of city officers on highways leading into Dallas, while Sheriff Smoot Schmid called all deputies to station themselves at strategic points on main and county roads. Both Fritz and Schmid warned their men to take no chances, but to bring in the three convicts and their companions if they located them. Officers who knew Hamilton, Palmer, and Thompson on sight were stationed on the most likely highways.

An aged black woman sitting on the front porch of her home directly across the street from the state prison was an eyewitness to the sensational escape. The woman said the two cars in which the three desperadoes whirled away had been waiting outside the prison wall about fifteen minutes before Hamilton, Thompson, and Palmer scaled the wall. The woman related the story:

> I had been sitting on my front porch. I noticed the two cars, one a sedan and the other a coupe, with a single driver in each, but there was a baseball game going on nearby and I thought nothing of it.

Just as the ball game was breaking up I saw the two men jump out of their cars and start shooting at a picket guard who was standing on top of the prison wall. He fell and three men appeared at the top of the wall and dashed down the steps toward the waiting cars.

All three men jumped in the sedan and the two cars drove away. They were going fast and I watched them go west about four blocks and then turn north.

Before the men in the cars started firing at the picket I could hear shots inside the prison walls.

Officers learned that one of the cars bore a Dallas County license plate, while the other license had been registered in Houston.

At the time of the escape, the Prison Tigers and the Humble Oilers from Brenham were going into the ninth inning, with the score at 5–1, Tigers. The Oiler batter had three balls and two strikes on him as the Tiger pitcher wound up. Before he could let go the ball, three rapid shots came from within the Walls. The crowd foamed to its feet like soda pop out of a bottle. Lee Simmons was going down the grandstand steps two at a time. By the time he reached the street all hell had broken loose. Thirty to forty shots crackled on the west side of the prison. He raced for his car, with his driver, Luther Berwick, and Tom Tennison, the cashier, hard on his heels. As they came to the scene of the break, someone called out: "A bunch of men went over the wall and some men and women hauled them off in two automobiles." Just then Warden Waid and Night Warden T. T. Easley ran up. The men hurried up the long flight of steps outside the wall to the picket stand of guard C. E. Burdeaux to find out what had happened. They looked below and saw Whitey Walker lying dead. Burdeaux told them that several other prisoners had escaped, taking his .45 pistol, his shotgun, and his Winchester. They didn't tarry with him; Simmons gave him his gun and ran back down the steps to rejoin Waid. The two rushed inside the Walls to investigate. They found the door of the death house standing wide open. But inside the death house, one of the guards, Lee Brazil, and two black convict waiters were locked in cells. Two prisoners, Pete McKenzie and Ira Rector, were still in their cells. But Raymond Hamilton, Joe Palmer, and Blackie Thompson were gone.

More investigation cleared up the story. Brazil had gone through three prison gates, each of them locked, and got the death-cell keys. He returned, unlocking doors to let cooks bring in the prisoners' food. Just as he opened the death cell door, Charlie Frazier stuck a gun in his back, warned him not to touch the alarm button, and told him to give up the keys without making any trouble. Brazil obeyed. Frazier then unlocked Thompson's cell, forced Brazil and the two waiters inside, locked the three of them in, and gave a .45 automatic to Thompson. Next he freed Hamilton and Palmer. He asked Pete McKenzie (the killer of Detective Chief Sam Street, of San Antonio) and Ira Rector if they wanted to go along, but both declined. Frazier, Hamilton, Thompson, and Palmer marched quietly through the prison yard until they met Whitey Walker, who was also armed with a .45 automatic, and Roy Johnson and Hub Stanley, both of the latter unarmed. In the lower yard they surprised guard McConnell, and marched him around to the machine shop to get a pair of steel snippers. With these they proceeded to the fire department quarters, where they cut the chain securing one of the fire ladders. Carrying the ladder with them, they advanced on the west-wall picket manned by Burdeaux.

Raymond Hamilton, Joe Palmer, and Blackie Thompson had vanished on the Monday following their Sunday escape. Their mad dash to freedom made front-page news nationwide, including one of the lead stories in *The New York Times*. Prison authorities started a thorough investigation, seeking specifically to learn how three pistols used by the fugitives were brought into the institution. W. A. Paddock, chairman of the prison board, and Lee Simmons headed the inquiry. Frazier, who in some unexplained manner obtained two pistols with which he started the escape scheme in motion, refused to say where he obtained the weapons, and Johnson likewise was silent. The only information as to where Hamilton and the other two escapees went was provided by a Houston man who said he believed they were in a car which collided with his vehicle there late Sunday. From what the man, H. M. Dry, said, it was indicated one of the men in the car might have been wounded. But Houston officers were unable to pick up any clues to the whereabouts of the fleeing desperadoes. They were able to keep under cover from 4:30 P.M. Sunday, when they escaped, until darkness.

Officers were speculating Monday on just how long it would be before Hamilton resumed his raids on small-town banks. Thompson, Walker, and Johnson were fugitives from an Oklahoma penitentiary and had committed several robberies in Texas before being arrested in Florida. Thompson had been given the death sentence at Marlin the previous March for robbing the First State Bank there of $41,000. Walker and Johnson were under sentences to ninety-nine years' imprisonment for the $10,000 robbery of a Bryan jeweler, and all three had long criminal records. The leader of the escape scheme apparently was Frazier, who gained a reputation for such things by his former breaks from the Arkansas and Louisiana prisons. He recently had tried to flee from Huntsville but guards frustrated the attempt by wounding him. Officers were also looking for Mary O'Dare. She was reported to have left Wichita Falls earlier, hitchhiking toward Dallas or Fort Worth, and officers believed she might try to rejoin Raymond Hamilton. Officers wanted to question her and learn, if possible, whether she knew anything about the plot to liberate Hamilton and the other convicts.

M. O. Barrett, filling station operator and eyewitness, said he was positive the first man to reach the sedan was wounded.

"He was a short, black-haired man and was bending over holding his stomach," Barrett said. "He shouted to the other two men, 'Come on, Ray and Joe, let's go.'"

While prison officials and state authorities were noncommittal, a strong rumor persisted that Frank Hamer would be put on the trail of Hamilton and his companions. On Monday, Paddock issued a call for a meeting of the board in Huntsville Tuesday to conduct an investigation of the escape. Paddock and W. R. Dulaney, another Houston member of the board, spent most of the day getting information concerning the daring foray. Paddock and Dulaney conferred with Simmons and Waid. They also questioned the guards who killed one and wounded two during the escape. Convicts suspected of knowing something of the escape plot were subjected to severe questioning.

Billie Mace was detained by officers in Tyler on Monday afternoon for questioning in connection with the escape. Billie had been running around with Mary O'Dare.

Raymond Hamilton would most probably still be in the hands of the law and safely locked behind the bars in the Dallas County jail if a Dallas jury had given the captured convict the death penalty when he was tried in Dallas the previous May, District Attorney Hurt said Monday, July 23. "Except for those two jurors weakening and refusing to give him the death penalty," continued the prosecutor, "Raymond Hamilton would today be in custody and not at large to prey on society and threaten the lives of thousands.

"I say this because with the death penalty inflicted in Dallas, Hamilton would have been forced to remain in the Dallas County jail pending his appeal to the Court of Criminal Appeals."

The district attorney said that Hamilton's sensational break for freedom from the state penitentiary underscored his belief all along that Hamilton was one of the most desperate criminals alive:

I never did take any stock in the sob stories about Hamilton being a soft-hearted kid, which were current at the time of his capture and trial in Dallas. Such mawkish sentimentality as went the rounds then, including the common remarks that "Hamilton never killed anybody," largely defeated the handing out of exact justice to him both in the trial here and at Denton where a jury could not be found willing to give him the death penalty.

I believed then as now that he is a killer and I had affidavits at the time of the Dallas trial convincing me that he was a killer of two peace officers at Atoka, Oklahoma. With Clyde Barrow and John Dillinger dead, Hamilton is easily number-one public enemy in the United States today.

He is easily the most dangerous criminal we have ever had in the Southwest. He's got more nerve in handling a gun than Clyde Barrow ever had; as cool as a cucumber and as a bank robber he made Barrow look like a novice. Banks in Texas and over the country had better watch out, now that he's free again, for he'll knock 'em over at the first chance.

Hurt pointed out that the appeals of both Hamilton and Joe Palmer were automatically dismissed by their prison break.

Working on the theory that the three escaped desperadoes might yet head for Dallas, police and deputy sheriffs continued on Monday, July 23, to guard strategic points in and near Dallas. Virtually no dependable clues had been received, detectives said, by which they could trace the fugitives. A report that they took part in a gunfight with officers at Oklahoma City appeared in error, as later developments indicated it was another group the officers encountered there. Another report said a group resembling them had been seen near Palestine. The last report concerning them that appeared authentic, detectives said, was of them being sighted at 8:40 P.M. Sunday at Hearne. Officers were under instructions to take no chances if they encountered the escapees. Detective Lt. Will Fritz, head of the homicide squad, was in charge of police details assigned to the search and spent most of the day with them. They were armed with submachine guns, automatic rifles, and pistols.

The Texas Prison Board on Tuesday night, July 24, absolved Lee Simmons and W. W. Waid of any blame in connection with the break. The board said it found no evidence of negligence on the part of the management or of collusion between the convicts and guards or prison officials. A preliminary report of the board's findings after an investigation which lasted most of the day was given by W. A. Paddock. He said a formal report would be issued later.

While the Texas Prison Board hurriedly convened in Huntsville to investigate the escape, the discovery of a coupe abandoned near Vernon led officers to believe the fugitives might have fled across the northern boundary into Oklahoma. Abandonment of the gray Ford V-8 coupe was coincident with the theft of a new Ford V-8 coach from Vernon, and officers were of the opinion that whoever had abandoned the coupe had driven away with the coach. The coupe was stuck in a ditch on a side road a few hundred yards from Highway 5. Its license plates were missing, and officers found some shotgun shells and an automatic pistol shell in it. A charge of buckshot had riddled one side of the car. Discovery of the coupe was the first clue officers had found to work on in their hunt for the desperadoes.

In Tyler, police were holding Mary O'Dare incommunicado. They were trying to elicit information from her as to the plot which led to Hamilton's liberation. Officers were particularly interested to know if she could identify the two men who drove the getaway cars which parked just outside the prison walls before the break.

Still of the opinion that Raymond Hamilton might yet guide Palmer and Thompson to Dallas or its vicinity, city and county officers remained grimly on watch for them Tuesday night, July 24. A description of the car they stole at Vernon was broadcast over station KVP, and all officers warned again to take no chances if and when they encountered the three escaped convicts. Most Dallas officers were of the opinion that the fugitives were without funds and believed they would try to rob a bank at the earliest opportunity. In this connection they recalled the tendency of Hamilton to prey on banks in the vicinity of Dallas, and were of the opinion that he might try to include his companions to strike near Dallas. The fact that the fugitives apparently stole an automobile at Vernon caused some officers to comment that they appeared to be following about the same path that Clyde Barrow did after Hamilton and five others from Eastham escaped.

A group of workmen engaged in the innocent occupation of beautifying a highway caused a false report that Raymond Hamilton and his fellow fugitives from the Huntsville death house were in the Lampasas vicinity — on the same day that John Dillinger was buried at Maywood, Indiana. The workmen had an automobile similar to the one used by Hamilton, Joe Palmer, and Blackie Thompson in their escape. They parked their car in the shade of some bushes while they went down the road to work. Passersby saw the half-hidden automobile and immediately reported that "Hamilton's car is out there in the bushes." Officers rushed to the scene and found the beautification workers preparing to get in the automobile and go home.

A report that Frank Hamer and M. T. Gault, former Rangers who were in the group of officers who killed Bonnie and Clyde, had gone after the fugitives spread almost as fast as the report that Hamilton's automobile had been found. Hamer and Gault, who were in Austin, were notified about the finding of the car, but before they had a chance to leave Austin the owners of the automobile had been found.

Interest in the investigation of the daring break shifted to Dallas when it was learned that one of the cars in which the inmates drove away was stolen in Dallas. The coupe which was abandoned at Vernon had been identified as one of the two autos they used and was stolen on the night of July 9 from a driveway at St. Paul's Hospital. It was the property of Dr. P. L. Goodnight of Caldwell, Burleson County, who was at the hospital when his car was stolen. Apparently, police said, the coupe was stolen by members of the Dallas underworld, friends of Raymond Hamilton.

Three women and two men, three of whom were suspected of having aided the escape at Huntsville, were arrested in Monroe, Louisiana, on July 26 by Sheriff Milton Coverdale. J. R. Corbett, twenty-one, Dorothy Davis, twenty-three, and Estelle Davis, twenty-one, who gave their address as Houston, were arrested in a tourist camp, and were held at the request of Warden Waid pending completion of the prison break investigation. The Davis women and Corbett were charged with violation of the Mann Act. E. M. Warner, a paroled convict from the Louisiana penitentiary, and Berly Ione Kerns, twenty-six, of Houston, were arrested at a hotel. They were held by Monroe authorities on charges of violating a local anti-vice ordinance. Sheriff Coverdale said he received a tip that Dorothy Davis had put in four long-distance calls at the tourist camp shortly after midnight to towns in Texas. One of the calls was to Huntsville, where she attempted to learn the condition of Charlie Frazier. The woman paid for three of the calls, but failed to pay for another, which amounted to more than $17. This excited the suspicion of one of the attendants at the camp, and he called the sheriff. When Sheriff Coverdale communicated by long-distance telephone with Warden Waid, the warden said that he believed the three occupied one of the two automobiles which waited near the prison when the break was staged.

One of the automobiles used by Hamilton, Palmer, and Thompson was located Friday, July 27, in a pine thicket thirteen miles west of Huntsville. John Ward, a cattleman, first discovered the car Monday following the break, but he failed to notify officers because he believed it belonged to some person working nearby. The car, a Ford V-8 sedan, bore license number 524-388 and was identified as one stolen from W. C. Allison of Houston the previous Sunday. The rear window of the car had been smashed, apparently to allow the fugitives a place for firing at pursuers. A five-pound sack of tacks, ready for use to disable pursuing cars, was found in the rear seat. Three prison uniforms marked "D.C." (death cell) were in the car. The price tag off a new shirt indicated the trio had changed to new clothing. Two .30-.30 shells, ten .45-automatic shells, and a shotgun shell were found. The shotgun shell and two of the .45s had been discharged. Officers, in tracing the convicts' flight, said they went five miles north toward Dallas and then took the Bedins Road west before abandoning the car.

Prison officials said that Charlie Frazier, the man who engineered the daring break, probably would recover from wounds received in the gun battle.

Belief that Raymond Hamilton might have fled to Houston after his automobile crashed Friday night on the Hempstead Road led police to keep a watch in that city. So far, however, no trace of the desperado had been found in Harris, Grimes, Waller, or Montgomery counties, where peace officers were conducting a vigorous hunt. A man known to Dallas police, captured after a car in which he and another man were riding crashed on the Hempstead Road, told conflicting stories about his companion. He first named the other occupant, described by a truck driver as resembling Hamilton and as having escaped in a Houston-bound car, as Hamilton. Later the man denied his companion was the notorious outlaw. He next said he had obtained a ride with Hamilton in hopes of getting him drunk and effecting a capture. Later he declared he had been picked up in Dallas, but did not know the motorist was Hamilton until they were seventy-five miles out of the city. The car was wrecked when it struck a mule. Two machine guns and ammunition were found inside. A couple called Sheriff Fred Blumberg of Waller County and reported that they had driven by the scene of the wreck, but as they halted to investigate they were fired on five times by a man with a pair of pistols. They were not hit.

A man resembling Hamilton caught a ride in a car which sped away toward Houston. Frank Brown, Gatesville truck driver, informed Sheriff Blumberg.

"I was driving toward Houston when I approached the scene of the automobile-mule collision," Brown said. "My headlights played on a passenger car just ahead of me. Then I saw a man standing by the roadway, hailing the car with two six-shooters. The car stopped. The man leaped into it and the machine drove off at rapid speed."

The wrecked automobile that was found in Waller County on the Hempstead-Houston highway was identified as the car which was stolen in East Dallas from Louis Cert, 4344 Westway, Highland Park. Investigators believed Raymond Hamilton and Blackie Thompson were in the car when it crashed. The man who had been arrested near the auto and who admitted he was one of the occupants riding with Hamilton had not been positively identified by Saturday night. If Hamilton and Thompson were in the car they probably escaped on a freight train that passed near there shortly after the accident, officers surmised.

According to Frank J. Blake, head of the Department of Justice in Dallas, two machine guns found in the wrecked car were identified as having been stolen Friday morning from the armory of the 112th Cavalry, Texas National Guard, on the Lemmon Avenue road. Five automatic pistols and 1,000 pounds of ammunition also were taken. The machine guns were described as the kind that must be mounted on tripods and provided with substantial bases for operation. Investigators believed the armory was raided by Thompson and Hamilton, and that the two had separated from Joe Palmer, who was said to be in ill health.

CHAPTER XII

Captures and Confessions

All available deputy sheriffs, heavily armed, were hastily scattered over the western and northern sections of Dallas County early Tuesday night, July 31, following apparently authentic reports that the elusive and slippery Raymond Hamilton was returning to his old haunts in Dallas County.

Evidence in the case was twofold. At 10:00 P.M. the sheriff's office and Dallas police were notified by Fort Worth officers to be on the lookout for Hamilton, who had been identified by two Cleburne youths as their kidnapper earlier that afternoon. O. B. Throneberry, one of the Cleburne boys, said he was a spectator at Hamilton's trial at Hillsboro for the Bucher killing, and was positive of his identification. Throneberry, with John Cain, was hitchhiking when picked up by the man identified as Hamilton. The youths told police they were kidnapped near Alvarado and were released on the outskirts of Fort Worth at 8:00 P.M. Tuesday. They identified Hamilton's picture after giving officers a description of their kidnapper which fitted the desperado. Hamilton was driving a Ford V-8 coupe and told the boys as he released them that he was going to Dallas. While no squads were being sent into the West Dallas haunts of Hamilton, Dallas police were warned by radio to be on the lookout. This alerted other officers in the North Texas area.

Another bit of information which seemed to dovetail with the account given by the two youths was a communication received by Dallas and Fort Worth police from Houston that the car driven by the abductor of the youths had been stolen early Tuesday morning in

Houston by a man later identified as Hamilton. The car was taken from a Houston physician who told police he was kidnapped at 1:30 Tuesday and later released twenty miles north of Houston. The physician's description matched Hamilton's.

A car identified as the one stolen from Dr. J. L. Short in Houston and fitting the description of the one in which the two Cleburne youths were kidnapped was found in Fort Worth on Wednesday night, August 1, by police. Officers were checking the car to see if fingerprints of Raymond Hamilton were on the steering wheel or mirror. The coupe fitted exactly the description of the one said by the two boys to have been driven by their captor. Motor numbers telephoned to Houston police tallied with those belonging to the car taken from Dr. Short, who was robbed of his car, instrument case, and $21 in cash and left bound and gagged in a wooded area. Police found the abandoned car with doors locked.

The two boys let out near Katy Lake in Fort Worth repeated their belief that their kidnapper was Hamilton. The man had taken a filling station cap from one of the boys and given him an old felt hat. The two boys said the man drove them over several counties, buying gas at several stations and driving off without paying for it. They said he told them he had 265 years and a death sentence hanging over his head and that he often got on his knees and prayed to God for help when he thought of it. He told them prayer got him out of the penitentiary.

Lee Simmons made the following statements regarding escapes of criminals from the penitentiary:

1. The death house escape was the greatest personal tragedy of his life and the greatest public tragedy in the history of the Texas prison system.
2. His administration, believing in rehabilitation, had emphasized education and wholesome amusement.
3. He left guard selection to the warden and prison farm managers.
4. During his tenure as system manager, prison escapes had dropped off dramatically.
5. It was known Frazier was plotting escape but his method was thought to be by tunnel.
6. Keeping guns from being smuggled in by someone determined to do so was virtually impossible.
7. He accepted his part of the responsibility for the break.
8. The guard who surrendered his weapons had no regard for the safety of the public.
9. Prison guards were overworked and underpaid.

10. He would gladly have given his life to prevent it because he feared law enforcement personnel could be killed.

11. His organization would remain dedicated to the rehabilitation of prisoners and protection of the public.

Jim Patterson, a guard at the Texas prison, was under arrest Thursday, August 2, 1934, charged with smuggling the guns used by Raymond Hamilton and the others during the death cell break. Patterson was taken to the Harris County jail in Houston by fellow guards at the prison, under orders to let him talk to no one. Patterson was charged with smuggling three pistols into the prison. These guns, it was alleged, were used by Raymond Hamilton, Joe Palmer, and Blackie Thompson in their sensational escape from the death house July 22. Before orders were given that Patterson could not talk to anyone, he denied that he was guilty.

"Someone had to do something, so they passed the buck to me," he said.

Three unmasked bandits, heavily armed, and who officers believed may have been Hamilton, Palmer, and Thompson, held up and robbed the bank at Robeline, Louisiana, at noon on Thursday, August 2, and escaped with a small amount of money. The robbery occurred at a time when George C. English, bank president, and Pauline Johnson, acting cashier, were alone in the bank. Two of the robbers, clad in khaki work clothes, entered the bank and at pistol point forced Johnson to hand over the money, while the third waited in an automobile parked in front, with motor running.

Mary O'Dare remained in federal custody Friday night, August 3, in Wichita Falls despite a state court writ of habeas corpus designed to effect her release. Frank J. Blake, Department of Justice agent in Dallas, said she would be charged soon with harboring a fugitive from justice in connection with the widespread travels of Clyde Barrow and Bonnie Parker. The traveling companion of Raymond Hamilton was arrested by Perry Browning, sheriff, Thursday night at the request of federal agents. Her attorney filed the writ of habeas corpus in district court Friday. When she was not produced for a hearing, Judge Irvin Vogel ordered a Department of Justice agent under Blake and a captain of the Texas Highway Patrol to appear in court Monday to show reason why they should not be held in contempt.

Two men believed to be Raymond Hamilton and Joe Palmer kidnapped W. E. Low of Fort Worth on Friday, August 3. They drove him nine miles out on the Grapevine road, robbed him, and sped away in his car. Low, who was picked up by a passing motorist and returned to Fort Worth, gave police descriptions of the men which led them to believe the kidnappers were Hamilton and Palmer. The men told Low they were accused of a job over in Louisiana that they "didn't do" (referring to the Robeline robbery). After letting Low out of the car, the kidnappers said they were going to Oklahoma but might leave his car in Dallas, where they intended to get some guns.

Guard Patterson admitted to Warden W. W. Waid in a signed statement on August 5, 1934, that he smuggled three automatic pistols into the prison for an unannounced amount of money. Lee Simmons said the statement was obtained from the guard after hours of questioning. Patterson admitted in an earlier signed statement he was paid $500 to point out to a convict implicated in the break a spot on the prison baseball diamond where some letters were cached.

A special term of court and a special grand jury to investigate the break was expected to be requested by Max Rogers, district attorney of Walker County. Rogers was en route to Huntsville from Kerrville, where he had been vacationing.

A statement issued by Lee Simmons said:

> Warden W. W. Waid and I are indeed sorry for the recent prison break July 22 when three prisoners, Raymond Hamilton, Joe Palmer, and Irvin (Blackie) Thompson, escaped from the death cell.
>
> We have found after going into every detail that those responsible for the escape are Guard Patterson, for smuggling in the three automatic pistols, and Guard Carey Burdeaux, for failure to discharge his sworn duty when occasion demanded same.
>
> We have found no dishonest acts whatever in regard to the conduct of Burdeaux but we have obtained a sworn statement from Guard Patterson that he did deliver the guns inside the walls and that he received pay for the same.
>
> The penitentiary proper is Warden Waid's unit and he is honest and efficient and we both have worked hard and long hours to give to the State of Texas the best service possible.
>
> At the proper time all the facts of the case will be given.
>
> District Attorney Max Rogers of Groveton will arrive here Monday from Kerrville and will take charge of the case and we will assist him in every way possible in this, the most serious break of the Texas prison system.

Simmons declined to discuss Patterson's statement further. "There are many details of this we do not care to divulge at this time and this is all I will say about it to anyone. Max Rogers will be in charge of the case Monday," the prison manager declared.

Patterson, formerly a Highway Department official in East Texas, had been working at the prison since December. He came under suspicion when he left the prison on a leave of absence a few hours before the break. From his home in Paris, rumors surfaced that the guard had paid overdue bills and was flashing a roll of money, Warden Waid said. The warden made a hurried trip to the Paris area and recovered $100 of the money Patterson paid his creditors. Serial numbers of the bills were checked by authorities to determine if any of it was a part of the loot stolen from one of several banks robbed by bands headed by Charlie Frazier. The payoff man, a former inmate of the prison, had delivered the money to Patterson in a flour sack at a Huntsville beer parlor. He and several women, also suspected in the break, were being sought. Authorities believed the plot was hatched by Walker, who contacted a man released from the prison and told him to contact friends on the outside. Guards McConnell and Burdeaux had resigned.

Successful in a skirmish with a state court, the federal government on August 6, 1934, went ahead with plans to prosecute Mary O'Dare for conspiracy to harbor Clyde Barrow. District Judge Irvin J. Vogel in Wichita Falls dismissed the contempt of court citation against E. J. Dowd, Department of Justice agent who failed to produce O'Dare at a habeas corpus hearing on application of her attorney, John Davenport, when the following Supreme Court ruling was cited: "No state judge or court, after they are judicially informed that the party is imprisoned under the authority of the United States, has any right to interfere with him or to require him to be brought before them."

Davenport had filed the application on the previous Friday, and Judge Vogel set the hearing for the same afternoon. Dowd, however, did not appear at the stipulated time, keeping custody of the woman until M. E. Peters, United States commissioner, could be located and charges filed. Clyde O. Eastus, United States attorney for the northern district of Texas, and his assistant, J. H. Jones, came to Dallas to defend Dowd because officials at Washington had taken a great interest in the case. After Eastus obtained Dowd's release, he said he had agreed to a reduction from $10,000 to $5,000 in the bond by which Mary O'Dare had been held. A formal hearing on the reduction was scheduled before federal judge James C. Wilson at Fort Worth. Commissioner Peters set her bond at $10,000. O'Dare was to be held in jail in Wichita Falls until the bond was perfected or until her examining trial before Judge Wilson on August 28, 1934. Others besides Mary O'Dare faced arrest on charges of harboring Clyde Barrow and Bonnie Parker, it was indicated on August 7 by U.S. District Attorney Eastus on his return from Wichita Falls.

A man arrested near Paducah, Kentucky, on Saturday, August 11, while sleeping under a tree, was positively identified the following Sunday night as Joe Palmer. It previously had been thought the man was Alvin Karpis, notorious outlaw wanted on charges of kidnapping Edward G. Bremer of St. Paul, Minnesota. Identification of Palmer was established through an anonymous telephone caller who told police in Paducah to look on a certain page of a detective story magazine. They did and found Palmer's likeness. Fingerprints of the Texan were then sent to Paducah from the Kentucky state penitentiary and confirmed his identity. Officers said that even though Palmer's fingertips had been bruised by rubbing them on concrete, it still was possible to identify him after federal officers questioned him.

The desperado was captured after Chris Burger, a truck gardener, reported to police, "There's a dead man out in my field." Palmer, exhausted after days of fleeing from the prison, had fallen asleep and was using a bundle of newspapers for a pillow. He awoke and in a dazed manner reached first for the gun, then for his hip pocket in which the officers found a crude blackjack. Palmer had only twenty cents in his pockets when arrested. At the jail he refused to answer questions and told officers, "You've got my picture, now find it." Chief of Detectives Kelly Franklin said the resemblance between Palmer and the description broadcast of Alvin Karpis was so marked that it had misled everyone.

"There is no doubt about it now, however," he said. "Everything — fingerprints, pictures and all — show that this man is Palmer, although he still refuses to give his name."

Because of threats which Palmer made to "be out tonight," two guards were kept near him constantly. Officers telephoned prison authorities at Huntsville and said they were told that guards would leave at once to come after Palmer. They, too, considered the identification positive.

Notified that Palmer had been caught, prison authorities expressed confidence that Hamilton and Thompson would be apprehended eventually or would be killed resisting arrest.

Guard Patterson was to go on trial in Huntsville on August 13, 1934. In the characteristic swiftness that attended the trials of Hamilton and Palmer, District Attorney Max Rogers planned to handle the case of Patterson. A special grand jury, called by District Judge S. W. Dean of Navasota Saturday night, August 11, 1934, met to consider charges against Patterson. The prosecutor said he planned to ask the inquisitional body to return three charges against Patterson

—a separate charge in the escape of each of the trio—and that the trial of Patterson would be concluded by nightfall.

Patterson, forty-three, was sentenced to fifteen years in Huntsville after he pleaded guilty to providing pistols used in the daring break.

Expressing belief he had only thirty days to live, the man whose identity had baffled local authorities since his arrest finally admitted to officers that he was Joe Palmer. Confronted with prison classification records which officers said proved his identity, Palmer broke his silence and talked freely. He went into detail concerning the activities which led to his being sentenced to death for a killing during the Eastham break. Palmer said he did not know whether or not he killed the guard during the January break but admitted he was shooting at him.

"They sentenced me to death," he said. "Railroaded me because they threatened witnesses that might have saved me."

While in Joplin, Missouri, recovering from a head infection, Palmer narrated, he heard of the death of Clyde Barrow and Bonnie Parker. He termed Barrow the best friend he ever had.

"I wanted to go to his funeral and I did," he continued. "I got a pair of smoked glasses and went to Dallas. Out at the old French Cemetery I stood in the mob while scores of police, all looking for me, roamed around. Then I hit north, was caught in Saint Jo, and sent back to Texas to be found guilty of murder and sent to the death house."

Barrow, he said, helped him escape from prison in January.

"Guy had just gotten out," he said, "and Ray and I knew he was to plant some guns for us. Clyde and Bonnie knew it too. It was a dull, foggy morning when Ray and I edged to a ravine, got a gun apiece, and went back towards two guards, Ollin Bozeman and Major Crowson. We got to them, then covered them. Bozeman shot at me twice but I escaped. Ray and I stepped back and then started shooting. Everybody was shooting and we started to run. Two others were with us. As we got to the highway, Clyde stood up and opened fire with a machine gun. Pursuing guards fell back, we got into the car, and got away."

After his escape in January, Palmer said, he kidnapped three people in Davenport, Iowa, before being captured. As soon as Palmer was returned to Huntsville, he was taken before a judge and resentenced to death. His execution was possible within thirty days.

CHAPTER XIII

Home Strikes and Harborers

Police and deputy sheriffs of North Texas renewed with vigor their hunt for Raymond Hamilton after a man answering his description held up a gas station in Bonham at 8:00 P.M. Thursday, August 16, 1934. Armed with pistols, three men drove up to the station in the center of town just as the attendant was closing for the night. They took three or four dollars in change and forced him to unlock the station pumps and put ten gallons of gasoline and several quarts of lubricating oil into the car, a new V-8 black Ford. Then the robbers sped out of town, headed west toward Sherman. The attendant said he recognized one of the bandits as Hamilton from numerous newspaper pictures.

C. M. Watson, who ran a filling station several blocks from the one that was hijacked, said he noticed the men circling his station continuously earlier in the evening. He thought their actions peculiar, but did not report the incident until after the robbery. Sheriff Podd Chaffin of Bonham said he notified officers in surrounding counties to be on the lookout for the trio, but police at Dallas had not heard of the robbery three hours later until informed by newspaper reporters.

Floyd Hamilton was indicted Friday, August 17, 1934, on charges of aiding his brother and four other convicts in the Eastham break. It was charged he planted the guns which made it possible for the outlaws to break for liberty. Date for the trial of Floyd had not been set, but District Judge Ben Dent of Crockett said it probably would come up during the August term of court. Floyd was free under $5,000 bond.

A petty filling station holdup, in which the money taken amounted to only $27.85, was the latest crime credited to Raymond Hamilton. Photographs of the slippery outlaw and Ed (Perchmouth) Stanton were positively identified as those of two of the three robbers who raided W. E. Hoffman's service station in Vernon on Tuesday night, August 21, 1934. The other robber was tentatively identified as Irvin (Blackie) Thompson. Driving a black sedan with Oklahoma license plates, the three men ordered gasoline at the station and then covered the attendant, Martin Lowke, with pistols. They took all the money he had and forced him to ride with them several blocks down a street before releasing him. Stanton was a fugitive from the Lubbock jail.

A young man suspected by operators of a local lunchstand as being Raymond Hamilton dined in Waxahachie Wednesday afternoon, August 22, it was revealed the following Thursday. He and another young fellow dropped in at the lunchroom and consumed six hamburgers each, with a liberal amount of soda water. The suspect peeled money from a hefty roll of greenbacks, talked freely, and soon the discussion of who he was came up.

"You've seen my picture in the papers lots of times," he said. "Just think back when you've seen write-ups about big robberies."

One person in the restaurant asked point blank, "Are you Raymond Hamilton?"

"I could be," he replied.

Those at the cafe at the time said they considered his appearance to tally with identifications printed about Hamilton. Peace authorities were notified of the incident, but by then the suspect and his companion had departed.

Raymond's troubles were added to on August 23, when his former sweetheart, Mary O'Dare, expressed a desire to remarry the Wichita Falls tailor B. A. Pitts, whom she divorced with the intention of marrying Hamilton. That morning Mary telephoned J. R. Wright, United States marshal, asking for permission to remarry Pitts. She was in jail in Wichita Falls.

Stuart W. DuBois, companion of Raymond at the time of their automobile wreck near Hempstead, remained in jail in Houston Friday, August 24, awaiting federal grand jury action after a preliminary hearing before United States Commissioner W. F. Carothers. His bail was fixed at $2,500. DuBois was charged with receiving and concealing two machine guns stolen July 26 from the federal armory at Dallas. He said he had the opportunity and the idea to shoot

Hamilton in the back shortly after the wreck four weeks earlier, but did not have the nerve. DuBois was captured a short time later.

Austin L. Avers, thirty-three, who was captured August 26 at Love Field in Dallas, and who was accused of having aided in the escape of Raymond Hamilton and the others from the Walls, was identified the next day in connection with the $2,500 Metropolitan holdup at Fort Worth several weeks before and was being held in the Dallas city jail for questioning concerning other holdups, detectives said. Charges were to be filed against him as soon as the investigations were complete. Shortly after his arrest he was identified as the one who held up three employees of the Progress Laundry and robbed them of $814. Victims of at least one other hotel holdup in Fort Worth and several robberies in Dallas were to be asked to view Avers, Detective Lt. J. W. (Will) Fritz said. Avers was wanted by the penitentiaries of both Oklahoma and Texas as an escaped convict and was under indictment in Walker County on charges of aiding Hamilton and others to escape, Dallas detectives said.

A bandit gang which chose as its hunting grounds the strange, rounded knobs of the Arbuckle Mountains, and whose leader declared he was Raymond Hamilton, was sought August 31 near Ardmore, Oklahoma. Their first victim was R. D. Williams of Allen. He was held prisoner in his automobile while the outlaws cruised the evergreen-studded hills in search of an out-of-state car. Successful at length in their search, they made prisoners of Mr. and Mrs. Harry E. Newman, and Mrs. J. W. Price and her son Calvin, all of Parsons, Kansas. The five victims were taken on a lonely mountaintop ranch, where $14 and personal belongings were taken from them. The outlaws left directions for finding the two cars and fled northward. Williams said one of the men told him he was Hamilton and that the group planned to rob a Texas bank. All the hoodlums expressed hatred for Frank Hamer and swore they would shoot him on sight.

Itinerants, bumming rides on freight trains in South Dallas switching yards, were given the scare of their lives Friday afternoon, August 31, when heavily armed detectives went scurrying through a number of their side door Pullmans on a search for Raymond Hamilton. Trainmen sent word to police that a man they believed to be Hamilton had swung a Texas & Pacific freight train in the Union Terminal yards. The man was described as of medium build, wearing a gray suit and gray cap, and armed with two pistols, one on either hip. The guns were seen as his coat tail flew straight outward in the breeze when he swung the car. Armed with automatic pistols, Detectives L. G. Delk, J. T. Luther, and G. A. Bates met the train on Spring

Avenue and began a systematic search. They failed to find the armed man, he having apparently changed to another train, but they did find numerous other people taking free rides on freights. Many of the riders turned pale with fright as the officers suddenly swung into their midst with their grim-looking weapons. One man, accompanied by his wife, became so frightened he jumped from the top of a car to the ground. A number climbed hastily out of cars and fled from the yards.

The long fight of Joe Palmer to escape death in the electric chair at Huntsville entered its legal phase Wednesday, October 3, 1934, in Austin. State's attorneys presented the Court of Criminal Appeals with a motion to dismiss Palmer's appeal from a death sentence assessed for the murder of Major Crowson. Dismissal was asked because Palmer escaped from the death house at the prison and failed to return voluntarily within ten days. The court was expected to act on the motion for dismissal of the appeal the following week. If the motion was granted, the trial court probably would issue its mandate within the following fifteen days and would fix the date for the execution not less than thirty days from the day of the sentence. Dismissal of the appeal of Raymond Hamilton also was sought.

Texas Rangers believed Hamilton and Blackie Thompson were in the Carolinas, pointing to a marked similarity in a series of bank robberies in those states to the methods pursued by Hamilton in his raids on Texas banks. Ranger Capt. D. E. Hamer said the Carolina bank robberies were executed by three men and that he believed Thompson and Hamilton had associated themselves with a desperado familiar with Carolina localities.

Henry Methvin, held in the slaying of Constable Cal Campbell of Commerce, Oklahoma, in the summer of 1933, was taken to state prison at McAlester, Oklahoma, from Miami, Oklahoma, on Tuesday, October 2, 1934, for safekeeping. Methvin's transfer came after Sheriff Dee Waters received a tip that Methvin's friends planned to liberate him from the Ottawa County jail. Sheriff Waters and Deputy Gerald Hodge, armed with a machine gun, took Methvin to McAlester handcuffed to Estell Mashburn, Picher, Oklahoma, sentenced to five years in prison for burglary.

Mary O'Dare, sweetheart of Raymond Hamilton, was expected to be brought to trial in Dallas in the near future on the charge of aiding a federal fugitive, Clyde Barrow, announced U.S. Marshal Red Wright on October 9. O'Dare was transferred by Marshal Wright from the Wichita Falls jail to the Dallas County jail Tuesday. She had been in the Wichita Falls jail since her arrest immediately after the escape of Raymond Hamilton from the death cell at Huntsville. The charge against the woman resulted from assistance given Barrow, who was a fugitive from justice. She was charged with interstate transportation of stolen cars, a Dyer Act violation. Members of the U.S. district attorney's force who were queried in Dallas as to when the trial would take place said no definite date had been set.

The Court of Criminal Appeals in Austin denied the state's motion for dismissal of the appeal of Joe Palmer on October 10. The law provided that if recapture of an escaped convict was made within thirty days, an appeal would be considered by the court. The appeal of Hamilton was dismissed because he was still at large, having escaped July 22.

Six others might have been charged along with Mary O'Dare for their parts in harboring Clyde Barrow and Bonnie Parker, according to U.S. District Attorney Clyde O. Eastus. Eastus refused to name the other persons being investigated in connection with the case, but said: "We won't be satisfied until we have all those who helped Barrow behind the bars." Eastus said he was going to make a thorough prosecution as it was his belief that "the best way to break up such criminal activities is to offer a stern warning to those who would harbor such criminals in the future." Eastus intimated that federal officials were in possession of much incriminating evidence against numerous people who had aided the recently killed Dallas bandits. Much of it had been gained from two former members of the Barrow gang, who themselves had earned immunity from the state by selling out their former pal in disclosing information which played a major part in his capture and execution. The federal prosecutor said intense investigations would follow before filing of further charges. O'Dare and any others who might be indicted on the harboring charge would stand trial in Dallas at the January 1935 term.

Two Overton newspapermen said that Raymond Hamilton was their host on an early Sunday morning ride on the Tyler–Dallas highway. W. H. Grayson and Harry Miers were afoot near Tyler when the person they identified as Hamilton drove up and offered them a ride. In the car was another man who was addressed as "Cotton" by his companion. Grayson said he recognized Hamilton the minute he entered the car. The latter at once demanded some money.

"We need some liquor," Grayson quoted him as saying. Grayson gave him $1.35. After that, Hamilton appeared friendly and carried on a casual conversation while speeding along, Grayson said.

The car was stopped at a hamburger stand near Forney, Kaufman County, where the two hitchhikers were informed Hamilton had changed his mind about going to Dallas and was going to Mesquite instead. "Cotton" then spoke up, Grayson said, and demanded some "coffee money." Grayson and Miers gave up thirty-five cents more, got out, and the car sped away. Hugo Ghormley, proprietor of the stand, agreed with the two newspapermen that one of the travelers strongly resembled Hamilton. William Edwards, a motorist who took the pair on into Dallas, said their description of the man fitted that of Hamilton, whom Edwards said he had known for several years.

City detectives and members of the sheriff's office said they had no knowledge of the affair. Some of the detectives, however, commented "that it sounded like Hamilton," who had a known liking for traveling with hitchhikers.

Belief that he had encountered Raymond Hamilton near Lisbon late Wednesday night, October 24, was reported by radio patrolman J. B. Burns and was responsible for a hasty search of Dallas by city and county officers. The man, who was in a V-8 Ford, had driven into a stand near Lisbon and ordered coffee to be taken to a sick person. When Burns drove up to the cafe, the man gunned the car. Burns, declaring the man appeared to be Hamilton, gave chase but was distanced.

Another attempt to trap Hamilton failed on Thursday, October 25, near Texarkana. The Texas Rangers, Louisiana State Highway Patrol, and Arkansas sheriffs and deputies participated in the unsuccessful attempt. Shortly before dawn the officers approached a farmhouse in Miller County, Arkansas, where they had been informed Hamilton might be found. As they neared the dwelling an automobile drove hurriedly away. Whether Hamilton was in the machine was plain conjecture. No trace of the desperado was found. Quickly, the officers descended on three other farmhouses in the vicinity, some fifteen miles south of Texarkana in the timbered country, but their search was fruitless.

The raids were made after a farmer notified Texarkana authorities a man who might be Hamilton had been seen frequently in that section. When shown photographs of the bandit, the farmer said, "That's the man." Hamilton was reported to have lived most of the time in an auto. The farmer said he had noticed the outlaw slept in it nightly. Another farmer told authorities a man resembling Hamilton had sought to buy a machine gun from him. The man was accompanied by a one-armed companion, the farmer said.

Missouri officers on Friday night, October 26, were seeking two men, one of whom they believed to be Raymond. The two had kidnapped William Lane, rural mail carrier, near Halfway, Missouri, and later released him unharmed beyond Yahola, Oklahoma, late Thursday, October 25. Identification of one of the kidnappers as Hamilton was made by two Missouri highway patrolmen. They reported their identification to Capt. William J. Baxter of the Highway Patrol in Kansas City, Missouri.

Highway patrolmen were in a gunfight Wednesday, October 24, with the two kidnappers near Buffalo, Missouri. The men escaped after abandoning their car and seizing Lane's car, taking him with them. Lane's car was found containing several unopened mail sacks near Columbus, Kansas, on Thursday, October 25. At Parsons, Kansas, police said they were convinced Hamilton and his companion, whom police had not identified, were in Parsons on Wednesday. They reported the two men stole the car of Mrs. Willard Kanitz and that both cars, with Lane lying captive in the rear seat of his car, were driven to Columbus, where Lane's car was abandoned. The Kanitz car later was found by officers at Muskogee, Oklahoma.

The First State Bank of Temple, Oklahoma, was robbed of $1,200 Thursday, November 1, 1934, by three young bandits who escaped after kidnapping three bank officers and two customers. The kidnapped men were released unharmed at the edge of town, and the bandits fled eastward in a small sedan. Six or seven customers were in the bank at the time of the robbery. Eyewitnesses of the robbery said they believed the leader of the gang was Raymond Hamilton

Returning from a vacation to New York, Dallas Assistant District Attorney D. A. Templeton was awakened early Thursday, November 1, in his Pullman berth by a man who was gently but firmly shaking his shoulder.

"I beg your pardon," the shoulder-shaker said, "but would you mind turning over?"

"I don't mind turning over, but what in the world do you want?" answered Templeton.

The man explained he was a United States Department of Justice agent and that he was investigating a tip that Raymond Hamilton had gotten on the train at St. Louis.

"Well!" replied Templeton, "I might be able to help you some, if you'll let me. I helped send him to the penitentiary twice and know him personally. I could help you identify him if you let me go with you and find him."

The agent accepted and Templeton continued with him on the rest of the search, but no trace of Hamilton was found.

Two men, one of whom officers believed was Raymond

Hamilton, and a woman companion were encountered near Columbus, Kansas, early Tuesday, November 6, by a posse in search of chicken thieves. Several rifle shots were fired at members of the posse, who said they were too far away to return the fire with the small arms they carried. The trio escaped, but later abandoned their car. It was through this car that officers made tentative identification of one of the desperadoes as Hamilton. Members of the posse reported the three opened fire on them as they were driving along the highway. Some of the shots struck the car in which the posse was riding, but no one was injured. Sheriff Dave Hasenplaugh and several deputies took up the chase, and the abandoned bandit car was found south of Columbus. Officers in this district had been on the lookout for Hamilton since he was identified several days before as the alleged kidnapper of a Missouri mail carrier.

Austin L. Avers, thirty-two, alleged to have been the payoff man in the escape of Hamilton from the death house, pleaded guilty on November 7, 1934, in Fort Worth to the $2,500 Metropolitan holdup on June 29, a month after Avers had made his getaway from the Huntsville lockup, and was given a life sentence. It was generally concluded by peace officers that part of the money taken from the hotel safe was used to pay prison guard Patterson to assist Hamilton and the others escaping.

Three men, one identified by the bank president as Raymond Hamilton, robbed the First National Bank of Okeene, Oklahoma, of $1,000 on Thursday, November 8, and escaped amid a flurry of shot in the direction of Clinton, Oklahoma. The trio took C. C. Wisdom, president of the bank, Bill Westfall, a customer, and Wisdom's sister, a bank employee, to the edge of town as hostages. They first turned southeast toward Kingfisher, but were met by a force of deputies who engaged them in a running battle, causing them to swing southwest toward Clinton. An airplane and deputies and police from Oklahoma City joined in the chase along with officers from the Okeene area.

Raymond Hamilton was a visitor in Ennis Friday night, November 9, according to E. O. Brown, manager of a gas station on Highway 75. Brown said a V-8 containing two men, one of whom he identified as Hamilton, ordered gasoline and oil at his station. The driver asked Brown to see if his tail light was burning and then drove rapidly away without paying his bill.

Raymond bobbed up again, this time in a revelation on November 21, by Waxahachie authorities that he had kidnapped and robbed George M. Taylor of Wichita Falls, between Dallas and Waco, on

November 17. Taylor told local authorities he picked up Hamilton on the outskirts of Dallas while en route to Austin and that after their arrival in Waco, the youth robbed him of $10 at pistol point. Taylor told officers that Hamilton forced him to drive back to Dallas and, after warning him not to call officers, directed him to leave Dallas on the Waco highway. When Taylor arrived in Waxahachie, he told officers of the incident. He identified Hamilton from pictures. Taylor said Hamilton attempted to steal an automobile he was towing but when told special wrenches were required to loosen the trailing machine, he gave up the idea.

On November 22, 1934, the federal government definitely entered the hunt for Raymond Hamilton. C. H. Baker, postal inspector in Springfield, Missouri, conferred with William Lane, post office carrier at Long Lane, Missouri, who recently had been kidnapped by bandits and taken into Oklahoma. Lane identified a picture of Hamilton as that of one of the bandits. Thousands of circulars were sent that night to police departments throughout the country, and Department of Justice agents were advised, "The government wants Hamilton."

Another bank robbery was charged to Raymond on Friday, November 23, when Clarence Clay, twenty-three, was held without bond on a federal charge of robbing the First National Bank of Okeene, Oklahoma, of $1,165 on November 8. Hamilton was identified from photographs as one of the three men who robbed the bank, and Clay was pointed out by bank employees as one of the trio who kidnapped two men and a woman and escaped after a spectacular airplane chase and gunfight. Two Missouri highway patrolmen, J. M. Wherritt and J. A. Hensen, testified at Clay's preliminary hearing in Oklahoma City that he and Hamilton escaped after a gunfight with them near Buffalo, Missouri, on October 24.

Clay, who was a connection by marriage of the late Bonnie Parker, was arrested at Gladewater on November 12, 1934, as the result of information obtained by Denver Seale, special investigator for District Attorney Robert L. Hurt. Seale, having information that Clay was connected with Hamilton in the kidnapping of a U.S. mail carrier at Halfway, near Springfield, Missouri, telephoned Texas Ranger Jim Shown at Gladewater and asked him to arrest Clay. Clay was a brother of the wife of Buster Parker, brother of Bonnie.

The search for Raymond and an outlaw companion centered in Bexar County on Friday, November 23, after a bloodstained car taken from G. E. Shilket of Joplin, Missouri, was found in Alamo Heights, Texas. Shilket identified a picture of Hamilton as one of a pair of hitchhikers he picked up near San Marcos on Thursday, November 22. The bandits took a $500 diamond ring, $12 in cash, his clothes, and his car and left him gagged and tied to a tree nine miles south of Belton. He had been struck on the head by one of the robbers. Shilket was en route from San Antonio to Dallas, where he had relatives, when he was robbed.

A $1,000 bond stood between Mary O'Dare and freedom on November 30, 1934, following a hearing before United States Commissioner Lee R. Smith. Raymond Hamilton's light o'love previously had pleaded not guilty to charges of conspiring to harbor and conceal the late Clyde Barrow. On recommendation of U.S. Attorney Clyde Eastus, the bond was granted and set at $1,000 by Commissioner Smith. She said she hoped to "raise the bond within two or three days. I'm going back to Wichita Falls," but added, "if I ever get out of here." Mary had been transferred to Dallas about one month before from Wichita Falls, and new charges were filed in Dallas when similar complaints were dropped in Wichita Falls, putting the jurisdiction of her case in the Dallas Federal District Court. Commissioner Smith said she would be tried before Judge W. H. Atwell during the January 1935 session.

Three bandits, one of them identified as Raymond Hamilton, shot nightwatchman Gene Mills, fifty, when he sought to question them on Sunday, December 2, in Maud, Texas. Mills, shot in the side but not critically injured, identified Hamilton's companions as Julius Bohannon, Oklahoma bandit charged with killing two officers near Sallisaw, Oklahoma, and Chester Elliott, Texarkana youth sought under charges of assault to kill and robbery. The shooting occurred early in the day, when Mills saw the three men sitting in an automobile parked in front of the post office. He flashed his gun in the car and the trio opened fire. The automobile then sped out of town. It was traced to Marshall, but officers lost the trail there.

Reports had been made for some time that Hamilton was operating in East Texas. Police believed he might have intended to rob the Maud post office when Mills interfered. Police in Shreveport, Louisiana, Sunday, December 2, 1934, found the automobile used in the Maud shooting, The car was found abandoned, with the motor still warm, a mile west of the city, and police records showed that it had been stolen several weeks before in Houston.

In Fort Worth, fingerprints on a half-gallon fruit jar left a telltale calling card of Raymond Hamilton. Apparently he had abandoned a late-model coach on a side street Friday, November 30. Residents of the neighborhood said the car had been there since then. The car was recovered by city detectives the following Monday. The fruit jar and six containers for automatic rifle clips were found inside the car. License plates on the vehicle were issued in Smith County, near where Hamilton and two companions were believed to have shot the watchman.

Hamilton came out of his hole Thursday afternoon, December 6, 1934, long enough to stage a robbery in his old stomping grounds, West Dallas. The blond bandit was identified by a man who knew him as one of two men who entered the Continental Oil Company warehouse on the Eagle Ford Road, herded all employees out of the building, and escaped with $182 in a V-8 two-door sedan driven by a third man. The robbery took place less than five hours before Hamilton's partner, Blackie Thompson, was shot to death by police near Amarillo, leaving Raymond as the only death house escapee unaccounted for.

Hamilton's foray was carried out quickly. When he and an unidentified companion entered, H. P. Forrest, cashier, who knew Hamilton, was at a desk just inside the door and facing it. H. R. Bates, warehouseman, was walking from one table to another to look at a record book. Forrest reported what followed:

> I looked up and saw them. I recognized Hamilton immediately. He had a sawed-off shotgun strapped to his shoulder and the other fellow was carrying a .38 hammerless pistol. Bates and I both put up our hands, but Hamilton said, "Put 'em down and you won't get hurt."
>
> Then Hamilton asked, "Where's the money?" and I told him it was in the desk drawer. There was thirteen dollars in silver there and he took it.
>
> "Where's the rest of the money?" Hamilton asked again. "You tell us where it is and you won't get hurt. If you don't there'll be some trouble."
>
> I had the keys to the floor safe in my pocket and told him and he said to get the money. I started to put my hand in my pocket for the keys and this other fellow jerked his gun up and told me to be careful. Hamilton put his hand out and knocked the gun down and told him to be quiet.
>
> "Go ahead and get the money," Hamilton said. "We won't hurt you."
>
> I got the money and gave it to them and Hamilton asked again if that was all.

M. A. Cummings, driver, had been working in another area when he came on the scene. Hamilton and his companion forced Forrest, Bates, and Cummings to walk toward Eagle Ford Road, while the hijackers walked to the car that was waiting across the railroad tracks to the south of the warehouse.

While Forrest was telling a *Dallas News* reporter of the hijacking the news telephone rang and Forrest answered it. "I don't appreciate your telling the newspapers that was Raymond Hamilton," Forrest quoted the telephone caller as having said. "I'm going to get you, too. I'll be watching you."

Forrest said he could not account for the call and declared his belief it was Hamilton or a friend of the hijacker threatening him.

As quickly as possible after the hijackers fled, Forrest had telephoned the sheriff's office and police. Sheriff Smoot Schmid and Deputies Bill Decker and Bob Alcorn had gone to the company office, and all other available deputies attempted to find the trail of the desperadoes. Detective Capt. Will Fritz and other members of the police and detective departments joined in the hunt.

The car used by the bandits was found about 8:30 P.M. on Thursday, December 6, by members of the sheriff's department on the old Colony Road near Cement City. The old Colony Road was between the Commerce cutoff and the old West Davis pike. The car contained a few shotgun shells loaded with buckshot and was identified as the one used in the robbery both by its appearance and by the license plate. It was a new vehicle and had been driven only 2,000 miles. The car was found in a clump of underbrush some distance off the road, and deputies declared that the bandit probably changed to another car at that point. A check of the records showed the owner of the car was C. R. Kendrick of North Lancaster. Kendrick said it was stolen from his garage sometime Wednesday night, December 5.

Schmid said the description given by Forrest indicated the leader of the hijackers was Hamilton, but he could not identify the other man who entered the oil company office. Forrest said the man was very dark. The cashier said neither hijacker addressed the other by name while they were in his presence. Captain Fritz said the description he obtained of the bandit automobile indicated the license plates were stolen: the back of the machine, the only part seen by the holdup victims, was dirty, whereas the license plate was clean. The car was black and had yellow wire wheels. The tract on which the oil company warehouse was situated was at the intersection of Eagle Ford Road and a narrow crossroad giving access to the Commerce Street cutoff of the Fort Worth pike. The bandit car was waiting across the railroad tracks to the south of the warehouse, and pointed in the direction of the cutoff. Forrest and the other employees were unable to give officers much information as to the direction taken by the fleeing men other than that they drove toward the highway.

It must have been mortifying to Raymond to learn that he was the "cheapest" public enemy in the country. Though wanted for numerous bank robberies and other holdups, not to mention a date he had broken with the electric chair at Huntsville, to the officer of the law who brought him down, dead or alive, only the measly sum of $25 would be paid. This reward was the standing offer for the capture of any escaped state convict; otherwise Hamilton's death or capture would not return a thin dime. Local law enforcement agencies in Dallas expressed the opinion that Hamilton was not looked on as a murderous desperado, despite his sentence to the chair for the killing of Major Crowson, and that was the reason for the small price on his head. The lone hope officers had of making the missing bandit pay dividends was to kill him in the act of robbing a bank. They could collect the standing $5,000 reward offered under such circumstances by the Texas Bankers' Association.

An attempt by a Wichita Falls attorney to secure release of Mary O'Dare failed December 8, 1934, when U.S. Commissioner Lee R. Smith refused to accept sureties who signed the $1,000 bond unless they were approved by the Department of Justice agents. Frank Blake, chief of the department in Dallas, notified Smith that he would not make a recommendation until he had investigated the sureties. In the meantime, Mary O'Dare spent another peaceful weekend at Dallas County jail.

The price on Raymond went up. It developed December 10, with the posting of reward notices in the Federal Building in Dallas of $2,000 for the arrest and conviction of offenders for assaulting persons in charge of United States mail. Hamilton had been identified as one of two men who kidnapped the post office employee in Missouri. The other identified man, Clarence Clay, was awaiting trial in Okeene, Oklahoma, for bank robbery. Clay was arrested on information obtained by Denver Seale, special investigator for District Attorney Hurt.

In January 1935 word came that Mary O'Dare would remain in the Dallas County jail until brought to trial following unsuccessful efforts to gain her release on bond. A $1,000 bond signed by several Wichita Falls persons was turned down on January 2 by Commissioner Smith after Department of Justice agents refused to approve the signers.

Wheels of federal justice started grinding in Dallas on January 14, 1935, when Judge W. H. Atwell opened a lengthy civil court term and the grand jury assembled to either indict or clear persons charged with offenses which ranged from dope peddling to income tax evasion. The grand jury's indictments were to come to the attention of the court starting February 19, 1935, though it was unlikely that Judge Atwell would hear a number of guilty pleas from those not wishing to contest their cases prior to that time. Though the ensuing criminal term loomed as one of the lightest in several years, sensations were expected. U.S. District Attorney Clyde O. Eastus had been investigating the means and methods whereby Barrow evaded justice for so long. The previous September Eastus said he would press charges against at least eight persons for harboring and concealing Barrow. Only one person had been charged on that count so far — Mary O'Dare. It was known that federal investigators had secured evidence that several persons not publicly connected with the slain bandit helped conceal him during his reign of terror. This information could have been turned over to the grand jury for action without public charges being filed.

Raymond Hamilton was hunted near Buffalo, Texas, on Wednesday, January 16, after four bandits took $7,011.50 from the Citizens State Bank early in the day. Officers were skeptical of reports that Hamilton was in the gang, but several witnesses believed he was. The weak point in the description was that two different men were said to have resembled the fugitive killer. Hamilton also was identified as one of two men who stopped at a filling station in Mexia late Tuesday, January 15, 1935. The automobile in which the bandit escaped after the robbery was found late in the day in some woods eight miles south of Buffalo. Officers believed the group transferred there to another car, believed to have been driven by a woman. While investigators could not be certain from descriptions of the bandit whether Hamilton was in the party, the victims said they could identify three of the robbers if they were caught. Some of the holdup victims were in the same room with the bandits for an hour and a half.

The bandits were waiting at the bank when President Robert E. Burroughs arrived. While two of the gang remained on guard outside, the other two forced Burroughs to open the vault and then go into a small room. As the other two people entered the bank, they were forced to join Burroughs. By the time the holdup was over, the captives included cashier G. E. Bowers, his wife, two bank examiners, and almost a dozen customers. Meanwhile, the bandits leisurely searched the entire place.

Investigators believed the bandit gang probably included two men who kidnapped J. C. McCracken and Forrest Palmer at Tyler early Wednesday and stole Palmer's automobile. Two telephone calls to the United Press office in Dallas indicated the robbers came from there. The calls were made by a woman, who apparently knew the robbery was taking place. On the first call she inquired, "What happened at Buffalo?"

"Who's calling?" she was asked. Without answering she hung up.

A few minutes later she called again, with the same question. Told that there was a bank robbery at Buffalo, she said, "Thanks," and hung up again. At that time Dallas police had not yet heard of the robbery and newspapers with the story had not appeared on the street, causing officers to believe the woman had knowledge of the holdup.

State highway patrolmen stole quietly into a remote wooded section of East Texas Friday night, January 18, 1935, with the expectation of capturing Raymond Hamilton, or some members of his outlaw band who had looted the Buffalo bank. An outlaw hideout described by Patrolman Neal Arthur of Huntsville as being somewhere in the East Texas woods was to be raided by officers, who had been informed Hamilton was in hiding in that section of the state. Hamilton was identified positively by two black men, who were shown photographs of the desperado. The men were held at bay by Hamilton as he directed the bank raid. Fingerprints found on an automatic abandoned by the gunmen, two of whom entered the bank while two more remained on the outside, had been identified as those of Raymond and a former prison pal. The prints also were found on a bottle in the car. The pal, Arthur said, had been released from the Eastham prison farm, where he and Hamilton had been held.

Detective Capt. M. Burton revealed that two Waco men, both with penitentiary records, had been held for several hours Friday in the city jail as suspects in the Buffalo robbery, but were released during the afternoon. President Burroughs and cashier Bowers of the bank had failed to identify either. Attention was directed toward one of the men when he went into a local bank Friday morning and exchanged $300 in bills of small denomination for three $100 bills.

A self-confident young bandit, armed with a submachine gun and a pistol, held up the First National Bank of Handley at 9:30 A.M. Saturday, January 19, 1935. His helper, who drove him away in a coupe, was believed to have been Raymond Hamilton. The getaway car bearing a Dallas license number was found at 11:00 A.M. five miles east of Handley and brought to Fort Worth.

Stalking in out of the rain soon after the bank was opened, the dark-haired young gunman pulled the machine gun from under his overcoat and ordered Ben Merrett, cashier, and two customers, W. T. Johnson and Ray Jones, Texas Motorcoaches bus drivers, to hold up their hands. Assistant cashier Ray McCleskey was told to scoop up the money in the cashier's cage. McCleskey bundled up $500, but left $700 behind. The bandit then ordered him to open the safe. This he could not do, McCleskey answered, because of the time lock. The gunman didn't insist. At this point William D. Weiler, vice-president of the bank, walked in and was told to raise his hands and join the others. Ruth McLeod, bookkeeper, was in the woman's restroom and remained there when she heard what was taking place outside the door. Forcing McCleskey to walk ahead of him, the bandit went out to the coupe where his companion waited. Getting in, the bandit said goodbye and they drove north on the Ederville Springs Road. Merrett snatched up a single-action Colt and a Winchester as soon as the car started. He fired the pistol out the window of the bank and then tried to get in a shot with the rifle, but the gun jammed, he said.

Joe Winters, employee of Tate's Dairy north of Handley, reported he had pulled the robbers' car out of a ditch earlier in the morning and that one of the men offered him thirty-five cents, saying that was all the money they had. Winters refused the tip. Handley citizens told officers they had seen the bandit around town Friday. The car, bearing license number 228-837, was missing a rear tire when it was recovered, and the bandits had wired around the ignition switch. United States Marshal J. R. (Red) Wright and Department of Justice agents joined in the chase of the bandits. Robbery of a national bank was a federal offense, and the hijackers, if apprehended, would be brought to trial in federal court.

Ranger Capt. Tom R. Hickman and four other Texas officers left Gainesville Monday night, January 28, 1935, for an unannounced destination with two men, Corey (Curley) Hudson, two-time ex-convict, and Arthur Whitten, ex-convict, captured Monday near Pauls Valley, Oklahoma, and held in connection with the Buffalo robbery. Hudson and Whitten had been arrested that day at a farmhouse thirty-five miles from Pauls Valley after officers surrounded the house. The ex-cons surrendered without a fight, although armed with pistols. Officers said they found nearly $1,300 in cash, believed to be part of the Buffalo loot, at the house. Several women and babies and three men were in the two-room structure. Two of the women were identified as Rose Marker, twenty-eight, and Minnie Rogers, twenty, both of Overton. They also were taken into custody. Officers had hoped they also would find Raymond Hamilton but were disappointed.

Both prisoners had flesh wounds, which Hickman said he believed were caused by bullets. Officers said Hudson had served time in Texas and Ohio prisons and Whitten in Arkansas. Both were about twenty-eight. Assisting in the capture of the men was Frank

Smith, Department of Justice agent and only surviving officer of the Kansas City Union Station Massacre. Officers with Hickman and Smith were Sheriff Ike Allred of Van Zandt County, Jum Harris, city marshal of Wills Point, Sheriff Lee Thompson of Lean County, Sheriff Claude of Pauls Valley, and two of his deputies, James Kemp and H. A. Beddo.

Hudson and Whitten admitted participation in the holdup as they were placed in the Tarrant County jail Monday night. Both men told reporters they took part in the robbery and said that money found where they were arrested was part of the loot.

Eighteen people, recently named in a secret federal indictment alleging conspiracy to conceal, harbor, and aid Clyde Barrow and Bonnie Parker, were placed under arrest January 28, 1935, it was announced by U.S. District Attorney Clyde O. Eastus. Those indicted included Mrs. Cumie Barrow and Mrs. Emma Parker, mothers of the slain bandits; Billie Mace, sister of Bonnie; L. C. Barrow, young brother of Clyde, already under a five-year robbery sentence; and several other members of the Barrow and Parker families. Those indicted and the amount of bond set in each case were: John Basden, $5,000; Lillian McBride, $5,000; Joe Francis, $1,500; Marie Francis, $1,000; Beulah Praytor, $5,000; Mrs. Cumie Barrow, $1,500; Mrs. Emma Parker, $1,500; Steve Davis, $5,000; Mrs. Steve Davis, $5,000; Billie Mace, $5,000; Henry Methvin, $5,000; S. J. Whatley, $5,000; L. C. Barrow, $5,000; Audrey Fay Barrow, $5,000; William D. Jones, $5,000; W. H. Bybee, $5,000; Blanche Barrow, $5,000; and Mary O'Dare, $5,000. The case was to be called for trial Friday, February 22, 1935, Eastus said. Maximum penalty which might be assessed in each instance was two years in the penitentiary and a $10,000 fine. Filing of the charges followed the line of the government's policy to stamp out crime by not only wiping out the criminals but also by penalizing those who aided such fugitives to evade justice, Eastus said.

The return of the indictment followed a thorough investigation of the dead bandits' careers by the grand jury. Many of those charged, as well as officers who hunted the elusive Barrow during his bloody flight from the law, paraded before the federal investigating body. All named in the complaint were well known to law enforcement officers. Federal officials, including District Attorney Eastus and Department of Justice agents, had been working on the case for six months. During that time they had delved into minute activities of the slain pair, attempting to learn how and by what means the bandits eluded capture for so long. The search had revealed the fact that the pair had much outside help, according to Eastus:

The attorney general regards this character of prosecution as highly important in the drive to stamp out crime and banditry. The government is deadly serious in its campaign against harborers and concealers of such criminals. The indictment alleges eight overt acts and set forth the fact that many banks would not have been robbed and eight or nine police officers would have been living had persons named in this complaint not helped Barrow and Parker to evade the law.

We have definite evidence that practically every person named in this indictment was to have met Barrow and Parker on the highway near Grapevine where two highway patrolmen were killed in cold blood last Easter. We also have definite evidence that Barrow was furnished with funds secured in the robbery of the West, Lancaster and Grand Prairie banks.

Rounding up the Barrow gang to face trial for harboring the slain outlaws was thought to mean a quicker meeting with his ultimate fate for Raymond Hamilton — death or capture at the hands of law enforcement officers. The government's action would make it harder for Hamilton to maintain contacts with criminal associates. Several people from whom he might expect aid were being held among the eighteen arrested on the Barrow conspiracy charges. Also, other underworld characters, realizing Ray was "red hot" and that dealings with him might mean subsequent federal prosecution for them, would not be so willing to lend him assistance. Without such aid officers figured the bank-robbing desperado would find it more difficult to keep from the law's clutches. District Attorney Eastus on January 30, 1935, issued a warning addressed to possible offenders in this class: "The government means business. We will not only press the Barrow case vigorously but we will also seek new indictments if we can get evidence that any person or persons are aiding Hamilton to evade justice. The Barrow case proves conclusively that criminals must have assistance in keeping their liberty. We are going to continue to crack down on all who shelter or aid such desperadoes."

Aid of any kind furnished Hamilton would mean eventual trouble for those providing it if the matter came to the attention of government authorities, for Ray, like Barrow and Parker, was a fugitive from justice. He was, among other things, under federal indictment for robbery of a national bank at Amarillo.

Hunted by both federal and state officers and now faced with a complete withdrawal of the underworld support which previously had stood him in good stead, the obvious ending of a criminal career was believed nearing for Hamilton. The lone mystery about it was whether he would die at the hands of capturing law enforcers or in the electric chair at Huntsville.

Raymond was cleared of one of the numerous charges blackening his name on January 31, 1935, with the capture of the last of the quartet believed to have robbed the Buffalo bank. Ranger Capt. Tom Hickman announced the arrest of two men believed to have been implicated in the stickup.

CHAPTER XIV

Lightning, Love and Loss

Raymond Hamilton and Floyd Hamilton, one or both possibly wounded, escaped from a carefully laid ambush of city and federal officers at 10:30 p.m. Monday, February 4, 1935, on Harrison Avenue near Grand, South Dallas.

Six law enforcement officers had secreted themselves in a duplex apartment at 2614 Harrison after arresting Mrs. Mildred Hamilton, Floyd's wife, and another woman there during the afternoon. They awaited the return of the Hamiltons. A car drove up at 10:30 P.M. and a roughly dressed man, wearing a ten-gallon hat, stepped out and knocked on a side window.

"Hello! Hello! Hello!" he called.

He did not appear to resemble Floyd Hamilton, officers said, because he apparently was forty years old and not clad in the immaculate garb the Hamiltons were known to favor. The officers were afraid to shoot immediately, fearing he might be an innocent friend of the present or former tenants.

"Stick 'em up," Detective Jack Archer ordered.

Dazed, the man did not seem to comprehend. Archer was forced to repeat his order twice before anything happened. At the third command, Floyd jumped back and reached for his pistol. The officers let loose their blast at the car in which Raymond Hamilton was seated, and also fired at Floyd. Raymond tumbled out of the car and started to run. Floyd ran down the alley also, but the two apparently separated. The officers, firing through the windows of the house, were at a disadvantage, and the elusive brothers quickly got away. One of the brothers leaped into a gas company truck at Atlanta and Logan, and sped away while the other fled on foot. Detective J. F. Daniels was struck in his trigger finger when one of the Hamilton brothers returned the fire. The bullet hit the stock of his shotgun and glanced off, jamming the gun. He was treated at the Emergency Hospital and immediately rejoined the search for the elusive pair. The other detectives were L. G. Delk, J. T. Luther, Jack Archer, T. N. Bedell, and C. O. Buchanan.

No bloodstains were found on the car or in the alley, but officers said it would have been a practical impossibility for Raymond to escape unscathed, having been seated behind the shattered windshield. One thing that disarmed the ambushers was that the brothers were in a four-cylinder, 1931 model Ford. They were expected in a V-8.

The escape of the two was practically a miracle inasmuch as a dozen or more city and federal officers were scattered over the vicinity as well as at the ambuscade. Officers were stationed on Harrison Street at the end of each block in which the house was located and at other places. The party was in charge of Frank J. Blake, chief investigator of the local branch of the Department of Justice; city inspector E. V. Bunch; and Detective Capt. Will Fritz. Just previous to drawing up in front of the house where the battle occurred, the two bandits had circled the block several times in their car to look the locality over. After the battle, state patrolmen were thrown into a search by order of L. G. Phares, chief of the State Highway Patrol at Austin, in addition to city, county, and federal officers.

The car abandoned by the brothers in their hasty flight housed a veritable arsenal. Included were two automatic shotguns, fully loaded, with the stocks and barrels sawed off to make them easier to handle; two .351 caliber automatic rifles; and hundreds of rounds of ammunition for pistols, shotguns, and rifles. The car also contained tear gas bombs, three fully equipped physicians' kits, a toy machine gun, and a huge box of household utensils, including blankets, sheets, tablecloths, and clothing. A gas bill made out to Floyd Hamilton, Route 6, and a letter from the Anderson County district attorney to a Dallas lawyer discussing Floyd Hamilton's record were found in the apartment.

Officers had known for some time that Raymond and his brother had teamed together. It was the second successful brush with the law within a week for Floyd. He was trapped a week earlier by federal agents, but he eluded his pursuers with the aid of an accident, which wrecked the pursuing officers' car when a man in an old model Ford turned directly into their path. Department of Justice agents refused to say where the skirmish took place or whether Raymond was with

Floyd at the time. Floyd was under federal indictment for harboring the Barrow-Parker clan.

The motor number of the car abandoned by the West Dallas desperadoes had been changed. Among its contents was a bottle of black hair dye, indicating that both brothers had tried to alter their appearance.

Floyd and Raymond had been seen at the apartment frequently during the last week by Mrs. Brown, the landlady, and her husband, who occupied the other half of the duplex.

"They seemed such nice tenants," Mrs. Brown commented.

She said she paid little attention to the men other than to notice that both were clad in greasy overalls. The women said the men were working at local factories, and one of them called herself Mrs. King. An abandoned Chevrolet coupe was found in the rear of the apartment. It was the third car they had taken to the house since their arrival, Mrs. Brown said. In it were more tear gas bombs, a submachine gun, and several pump shotguns. All her dealings in renting the apartment were made with the women. They had paid their rent for a second week. Scattered through the rooms were detective magazines, a popular woman's magazine, soft drink bottles, and a brown fur jacket. The two scantily furnished bedrooms were in great disorder.

In an earlier Carthage bank raid, laid to the Hamiltons, three roughly dressed men participated. Two entered the bank with automatic pistols in their hands while the other waited outside in an automobile. These pistols were believed to be the only weapons the Hamilton brothers escaped with after the Dallas battle. Cashier A. L. Ross of the Carthage institution complied with an order to unlock the vault, and the robbers were preparing to rifle it when two customers walked in. The robbers collected all the cash they could find in the cages, about $1,000, and fled to their car. They sped out of Carthage on the Henderson highway, abandoning their car sixteen miles west of Carthage and changing to another vehicle. Officers learned that three men fitting the description of the bandits had been camped since Saturday at a hideout sixteen miles from Carthage on the Henderson highway. The men, accompanied by a woman, had posed as oil scouts.

Arrest of Floyd Hamilton, twenty-six, at Shreveport, Louisiana, Tuesday, February 5, 1935, and the discovery of the Dallas Gas Company's red truck bearing evidence that Raymond Hamilton, twenty-one, probably was badly wounded when he escaped in it from the South Dallas police trap caused officers to redouble their search for the elusive desperado. The alertness of two Shreveport deputies making a routine inspection at the Shreveport bus station resulted in Floyd's capture. Chance discovery of the getaway car by two Dallas County farmers revealed that Ray might be so severely wounded that his capture would be facilitated.

An attractive Dallas brunette, who was arrested Monday with Floyd Hamilton's wife, still was held incommunicado in the city jail. No charge had been filed against her, the police insisted, and they even denied that she was there. Nevertheless, it was known that she was held in the woman's quarter of the jail, that she had been allowed to see no one, and that strict orders had been given that no information about her be made public.

The truck was found at 8:15 P.M. Tuesday in a clump of trees and underbrush on a side lane off the Second Avenue road near Rylie, a small community fourteen miles southeast of Dallas. Smears of blood shoulder high on the back of the seat to the rear of the driving wheel of the truck indicated the desperado might be badly wounded, Capt. Will Fritz said. Other stains, identified as human blood by Dr. J. L. Howley of the Emergency Hospital, were found on the seat cushions and on the floor board. It also was evident that Hamilton had been wounded slightly above the knee, according to the smears, Captain Fritz said. Each of the cars was equipped with soap, water, and a wash brush, and Hamilton did his best to clean up traces of his wounds before he abandoned the car. It was evident, detectives said, that he had scoured the floorboard with the scrub brush. The water bucket was empty when found. An examination of the car revealed that Hamilton drove it straight to the place where it was abandoned at a speed no greater than thirty miles an hour. The speedometer showed the truck had traveled only thirty miles from the time it left the garage until it was returned to the city hall. A governor, limiting the speed, was not molested.

Floyd was suffering from a slight wound in the left forearm, believed inflicted during the Monday night skirmish. Deputy Sheriffs Stone and Prudhomme of Shreveport, veteran Caddo Parish officers, were making a routine check of the bus station at 4:55 P.M. when they noticed Floyd Hamilton seated in a bus bound for Texarkana. He had bought a ticket to Vivian, Louisiana, thirty miles from Shreveport, where his father was employed at a refinery. Both officers entered the bus, pressed guns close to the fugitive's midsection, and said, "Come on, Floyd." The youthful desperado, indicted with twenty-three others in federal court in Dallas for conspiracy to conceal and harbor Bonnie and Clyde, instantly raised his hands.

"Don't shoot, I haven't a gun," he said.

Officers found $300 in bills and almost $100 in silver on his person. Most of the money was hidden in his shoes, socks, and trouser legs. He was wearing a yellow leather jacket. Until three weeks before, Floyd worked at the refinery where his father was employed. Since that time he had been suspected of being in several bank stickups with Raymond, particularly in the holdup of the Carthage bank. Floyd told Shreveport officers he was not with his brother at the time of the battle with Dallas police and denied he or Ray had anything to do with the robbery of the Carthage bank. He admitted contacting Raymond a few days before and claimed that the missing desperado gave him the $400 which was found on him at the time. He could offer no explanation of how he received the wound near his elbow. He told of boarding a bus at Dallas for Shreveport sometime Tuesday and said he had spent most of the day in Shreveport.

"Raymond will resist to the last any attempt to capture him," Floyd said. "It's all he can do. What would you do if you were facing the electric chair? Shoot it out, of course."

Sheriff R. A. Schmid and Deputies Ed Caster and Bill Decker, who left for Shreveport immediately on learning of Floyd's arrest, started back for Dallas with the prisoner at 11:30 P.M. Tuesday after remaining in the Louisiana city less than an hour. He was wanted by the state on charges of assault to murder, but Schmid said he thought he would be tried on the federal harboring charge first. Floyd's arrest left at large only one of the four persons who had occupied the South Dallas hideout.

Mildred Hamilton was in Dallas County jail under $5,000 bond. She was under indictment in the Barrow harboring case. A young woman identified as Katie Jenkins was in the city jail. Mrs. Hamilton was taken to the Federal Building in Dallas Tuesday morning and questioned briefly by federal agents. Unlike many other people in the blanket Barrow indictment, it was understood she gave officers little information about either of the Hamiltons. Floyd's quick capture cheered Dallas police and federal agents, disconsolate earlier in the day at their failure to land the number-one bad man.

While Ray made good his escape from Monday night's trap, officers were confident he would soon be captured. They pointed out that his hurried escape left him without arms, with the possible exception of an automatic pistol; that any automobiles he picked up would be "hot"; and that with most of his pals already in jail he could bank on little outside assistance in his efforts to evade capture.

Investigation Tuesday revealed that the 1931 Ford sedan in which Raymond and Floyd drove to their hideout had been stolen January 24, 1935, from Elva Davis of Fort Worth. The Chevrolet coupe found stored in the garage was stolen from Dr. C. P. Smith of Nacogdoches on January 30, 1935. The Ford was equipped with a shortwave radio tuned to receive police broadcasts. License plates had been changed on both cars. The federal indictment under which Floyd was charged alleged that he and James Mullen, arrested a week prior, placed the two pistols under a culvert near the Eastham prison farm.

Raymond's actions Monday night convinced law enforcement officers that the man who faced the electric chair if caught would shoot it out rather than be arrested. Previously, Hamilton had not been rated a dangerous killer, as was Barrow, but with death staring him in the face, hunted and harried, police now stamped him fully as great a menace as was his late West Dallas hoodlum pal. They rated the missing outlaw a far smarter criminal than Barrow. As to his whereabouts, opinions and theories differed. Many officers believed he was in hiding in or near Dallas. Some thought he was wounded and holed up. Others thought he had stolen another car and was hundreds of miles away.

A report that Raymond had been seen at Bryan and Harwood about 2:00 A.M. Wednesday, February 6, sent policemen scurrying to the scene, as well as all officers being posted on the lookout. The report was based on the meeting of two automobiles with a woman getting out of one car, handing a rifle to a young man, and saying, "Now, for God's sake be careful, Ray." The man addressed as Ray entered one of the cars, a 1931 or 1932 Chevrolet coach, and drove north on Harwood. According to the police informant, the stopping of the two cars and handing of the rifle by the woman to the man was preceded by a taller man standing on the corner for some time apparently awaiting something. When the two cars appeared, he turned and ran into an adjoining lot and immediately the man later called Ray ran out from the darkness of the lot, took the rifle, entered the car, and drove off.

Raymond and Floyd Hamilton were identified Wednesday night, February 6, 1935, by two of their victims at Carthage as the robbers who held up the Citizens' State Bank in the Panola County city Monday, according to the Associated Press. Pictures of the brothers were picked out of a group of more than 100 police photographs by a bank teller and a customer. Department of Justice agents and Panola County officers watched H. T. Hooker, customer, and J. P. Cook, teller, identify the pictures of Raymond and Floyd as the two men who entered the bank, held several persons at bay against the wall, and escaped with a third confederate and loot totaling $1,094. Hooker and Cook said Raymond Hamilton was the man who ran back of the teller's cage, bundled up the cash, and fled out the front door. Floyd, the two men said, was the man who trained the pistol on the bank employees and customers while he stood in the middle of the lobby. Sheriff J. T. Hughes of Shreveport told Sheriff T. M. Hurt of Panola County in a long-distance telephone conversation that several $20 bills taken from Floyd Hamilton when he was captured had been identified as part of the Carthage bank loot.

While federal and police officers grilled three of his companions in Dallas Wednesday, Raymond apparently had made good another escape from the law. Floyd was returned to Dallas Wednesday following his arrest at Shreveport.

Mildred remained in Dallas County jail. Katie Jenkins was still under guard at the city jail.

Department of Justice agents questioned Floyd through the morning and afternoon in an effort to secure information which would help them in their quest for Raymond. Floyd apparently gave them little satisfaction. He roundly denied being at the Harrison Street apartment at the time of the shooting, although he admitted he had been living there, and he also denied either he or Raymond had taken any part in the Carthage holdup. At one point of the questioning he admitted the elusive Raymond would be willing to trade out with the government and surrender if some means could be found of lifting the death sentence he was under.

"Take the 'heat' off and he'll come in," Floyd said.

He explained that by "heat" he meant Raymond would have to be promised a commutation of his death sentence to a life term. Led on by this line of questioning, he readily admitted that if permitted he could contact Ray to put the proposal to him. Floyd's proposal was quickly declined by District Attorney Clyde O. Eastus.

"Raymond Hamilton's death sentence is a state matter and we have no jurisdiction in the first place," he commented. "Then again, it is not governmental policy to make trades with gangsters. Raymond is at the end of his rope. It's just a question of time."

In the meantime a thorough check of local hospitals and other Dallas hideouts of the West Dallas desperado failed to give officers any lead as to his whereabouts. They offered conflicting theories. Many believed he was still holed up in Dallas. Others figured he wasn't far from Floyd when the latter was captured. While the search continued, details of how officers learned of the Hamiltons' hideout leaked out Wednesday. It was learned that the information came from a Dallas bootlegger, a well-known police character, who squealed for vengeance after Raymond had stolen his girl.

Arrest of Floyd Hamilton and his wife practically cleaned up the case of the federal government, which would bring them to trial along with twenty other defendants on charges of conspiracy to harbor Bonnie and Clyde. The trial was set for Friday, February 22, 1935. Of twenty-three indicted in the case, only Raymond Hamilton was free. Floyd Hamilton, according to federal officers, was going to see his father, who worked near Vivian, Louisiana, in an effort to get him to make bond for Mrs. Steve Davis, mother of the Hamilton boys, and Lillian McBride, their sister, held under $5,000 each in the Barrow case. The $400 found on Floyd's person at the time of the arrest was to have been used for this purpose, the agents said.

Katie Jenkins started the legal battle to regain her freedom. A habeas corpus writ application filed with Judge Noland G. Williams resulted in an order for Police Chief C. W. Trammello to produce the woman in Judge Williams' court at 10:00 A.M. Saturday, February 9, 1935. The application alleged that Jenkins had been held incommunicado for three days without charges being filed against her. Meanwhile, Mary Pitts, alias Mary O'Dare, one of the twenty-three indicted harborers, sent word to District Attorney Eastus that she was ready to plead guilty to the charges against her. Mary was told that she must wait until February 22.

Regardless of how many other charges were filed against the Hamiltons, Floyd was to be first brought to trial on the harboring charge, Eastus said. This was his answer to Wardlaw W. Lane, state district attorney from Center, who sought permission to have Floyd removed there where Lane hoped to indict him on the Carthage bank robbery charge.

While many rumors floated around concerning the will o'wisp Raymond, one that he was being secretly held in a Shreveport jail, actions in Dallas of close-lipped Department of Justice men did not indicate the search was over. They were busy all day questioning Hamilton's associates, among them Mildred Hamilton, who was closeted for some time with Chief Agent Frank Blake and his lieutenants. The sphinx-like investigators declined to reveal what information they had gained, but it was learned that all of them felt that if Raymond's capture was to follow as the result of Monday's poorly laid trap, the deadline hour was near. One reason for this theory was that if Raymond was as badly wounded as many officers believed, he would be forced to seek medical attention and hence reveal his whereabouts. City detectives, after a severe grilling of a former associate of Raymond Hamilton, placed little credence in reports that he was the third man in the robbery of the Carthage bank. Federal charges would not be filed against Jenkins, District Attorney Eastus said.

At the beginning of Governor James V. Allred's administration, the governor said on February 7, 1935, an offer for the surrender of Raymond Hamilton was made on condition that his death sentence be commuted to life imprisonment.

"The offer was made through underworld sources to a Texas Ranger," Governor Allred said. "I told the Ranger that we were not bargaining with Hamilton."

Three $20 bills definitely linked Floyd Hamilton with the Carthage holdup, Sheriff T. R. Hughes of Shreveport said Carthage officials told him February 8. The bills were identified through serial numbers as part of a shipment received at Carthage but never paid out. They constituted part of $300.12 taken from Floyd when he was arrested in Shreveport. Sheriff Hughes said his office would file a claim for the $100 reward offered by the bank's insurance company. All rewards, he said, would be divided among a man whose identity the sheriff refused to reveal, and Deputies Will Prudhomme and Bert Stone, the arresting officers.

Habeas corpus hearing scheduled February 9 for Katie Jenkins was passed by Judge Noland G. Williams on request of defense counsel and Detective Capt. Will Fritz. Fritz told the court police wanted a few more days in which to complete the investigation. In applying for the writ, counsel for Jenkins said she had been held incommunicado at the city jail since her arrest.

Charged with theft of government property, Stuart Whitaker DuBois, alias H. D. Daveham, twenty-four, Dallas youth who federal District Attorney Clyde O. Eastus said was a former associate of Raymond Hamilton, was placed under $5,000 bond by U.S. Commissioner Lee R. Smith on February 11. DuBois was charged with stealing pistols and machine guns from the 112th Cavalry armory on Lemmon Avenue road in Dallas July 26, 1934. DuBois waived hearing.

Joe Chambless, father of Mary O'Dare, and Beulah Praytor, both charged with harboring, were brought to Dallas on Wednesday, February 13, from Wichita Falls. They were placed in Dallas County jail to await the February 22 trial. Both were questioned at length by Department of Justice agents. Deputy L. N. McKelvy, Wichita Falls, delivered the two to Dallas.

Accused of having been with the much wanted Raymond and his imprisoned brother Floyd in the holdup of the Carthage bank, an ex-convict, formerly of Houston, was arrested near Tyler on February 14 by Dallas city detectives and delivered to the Dallas city jail. The man's wife also was taken into custody and was placed in the woman's ward of the county jail for questioning.

The two were in an automobile and said they had started on a pleasure trip when they were stopped by the party of Dallas officers, which included six members of the homicide squad and a detective inspector.

Sheriff J. B. Sample and a group of Shelby County officers seeking Raymond Hamilton returned unsuccessful Saturday night, February 16, from a hideout where they had hoped to catch the Dallas bad man. Sample said he was confident Hamilton was there as late as Friday. The officers surrounded Hamilton's hiding place after they received a report that a car similar to one he stole Saturday at Silsbee was seen passing through Magnolia Springs, Jasper County. Earlier in the day a man identified by fingerprints as Hamilton and a companion robbed a National Guard Armory in Beaumont of eight automatic rifles and 3,600 rounds of ammunition.

"That farmhouse down there in the tall pine timber, twelve miles from here, is a perfect place for Ray to hide," Sheriff Sample said. "It is off the main road, on a sandy country lane. He didn't show up Saturday night, however. We may know more about where he is Sunday morning."

The sheriff said he had information that Hamilton left the place earlier in the week, but returned to the cabin in the piney woods before his sudden raid Saturday on the armory at Beaumont. Reports from Beaumont indicated the Southwest's number-one bad man, the slight, shifty-eyed blond, had dyed his hair black and stained his face to give him a swarthy complexion. Officers had posted guards along the highways and admitted they were ready to shoot it out with Hamilton if he appeared. Officers said they did not believe Hamilton knew the hideout had been discovered or that his companion at the hideout several days before had been arrested and was in jail in Dallas.

Two farmers who lived near Hamilton's hiding place came to Center Friday and bought groceries enough to provision him for two weeks. They aroused the suspicion of the grocer who said "those two fellows never bought that many groceries before in their lives." Officers trailed them to be certain they took the groceries to the Hamilton cabin. Federal Department of Justice agents discovered the lair Wednesday, February 13. They learned that Hamilton left it Monday for another hiding place in Hardin County. His companion bought an automobile in Center and was trailed to Tyler, where he was arrested on suspicion that he participated in the $970 holdup of the Carthage bank. The man arrested, an ex-convict, told Dallas officers he was given sentences totaling eighteen years in nine burglary cases at Houston, but was freed from the penitentiary on a conditional pardon. He denied he participated in the Carthage robbery or that he knew Hamilton's whereabouts. Employees of the Carthage bank identified photographs of the man as one of Hamilton's companions during the robbery.

A party of officers returned to Center on Sunday, February 17, after a fruitless search south of there for Raymond Hamilton. Sheriff Sample said the suspected hideout of the bank robber and gunman was found deserted. Officers in the posse said a farmer living near the place had sold an automobile to a stranger Sunday and believed the buyer might have been Hamilton, obtaining the car for a getaway before the raid. They declined to discuss reports that federal agents participated in the raid.

Search for the elusive Hamilton was centered in East Texas by discovery near Center of a truck believed to have been used in the National Guard Armory robbery at Beaumont. Officers found a number of empty rifle cartridge shells near the truck, indicating the persons who stole a supply of automatic rifles and ammunition from the armory had been trying the weapons. The hunt was renewed in East Texas on February 29, after an automobile believed to have been used by Raymond in a robbery Saturday was found abandoned. The car was found on the Barker-Clodine highway west of Houston. License plates concealed in the car, and also the motor number, checked with those of an automobile stolen at Silsbee shortly after the National Guard robbery. Sheriff T. A. Binford said fingerprints on the car were so poorly defined it would be impossible to classify them. Hamilton fled in a truck after the Beaumont robbery, but apparently transferred to the Silsbee car a short time later, as the truck was found abandoned in a wooded section near Fletcher.

Reports that Hamilton had been seen at Arp also were circulated on February 29. A gasoline refinery attendant told authorities two men and a woman Tuesday forced him to refuel their automobile, and then drove away without paying. The woman was described as a blonde, and last reports of Hamilton indicated a blonde was acting as his chauffeur. The refinery attendant said he saw a machine gun and a shotgun in the car.

The inside story of Raymond Hamilton's Eastham escape marked opening testimony in the Barrow harboring trial in federal court in Dallas, February 22, 1935. During this testimony, James Mullen, forty-eight, ex-convict, indicated the nonchalance that Raymond displayed. During a meeting with the gang, after his Eastham escape, testimony showed that Ray was discussing the robbery of either the West or the Arlington bank.

"I'll rob the one I'm closest to in the morning," he was quoted as saying.

CHAPTER XV

Houdini Hamilton

The V-8 sedan used by Raymond Hamilton and a companion in their escape from a police ambuscade near McKinney Sunday night, February 24, 1935, was found abandoned near Weston, ten miles north of McKinney, the next morning. The car was covered with blood, indicating one or both of the fugitives was wounded. It also contained numerous bullet holes. Raymond sped through a gauntlet of machine-gun bullets on an abandoned highway near McKinney at nightfall and again escaped a police trap. Believed wounded by the seventy shots fired into his machine, Hamilton, accompanied by another man, slowed down, unloosed a clip of cartridges from a machine gun, and raced away. Officers, hampered in their chase by a driving rain, lost the outlaw at Weston.

Tipped that Hamilton would drive down the deserted road late Sunday, the officers, including two state highway patrolmen and four local officers, hid their automobile in brush and lay in ambush ten minutes before their quarry arrived. Constable John Record sprang in front of the machine, shouted a command to halt, and waved an automatic rifle. The slowly moving car speeded up and the six officers showered the machine with gunfire. Two hundred yards down the road the car slowed and machine-gun bullets whizzed back at the officers. The group sprang to the road and the machine started moving slowly away, running in first gear for about 400 yards. This led officers to believe the driver had been wounded. Before officers could get to their automobile, the outlaw had melted in gathering darkness. They gave chase for ten minutes down the slippery highway but said they did not spot the gray V-8 sedan, punctured by machine-gun bullets and pistol fire.

Constable Record said Hamilton had been reported in the McKinney vicinity for the last week and that Sunday he had been informed the desperado would drive along the road, unfrequented since the construction of the new Highway 75. The automobile had passed through Melissa, eight miles from McKinney, only a few minutes before the shooting. Those participating in the shooting were Constable Record, State Highway Patrolmen J. B. Truelock and K. D. Carr of Sherman, Sheriff C. J. S. Walker, and Deputies Arvie Sparlin and S. Allen.

Conviction that Raymond Hamilton's much-vaunted boldness and nerve were nothing but a bluff put up by a punk gunman, and that all his success in eluding capture laid in his phenomenal luck, was expressed Monday night, February 25, by three thrill-weary youths after eighteen hours as his prisoners. The boys, taken as hostages Sunday night after the battle with Collin County officers, were released at 2:00 P.M. Monday near Mansfield, Tarrant County, after Ray had stolen a getaway car. On their return to Celina they told their wide-eyed neighbors how the Southwest's number-one bad man had fallen asleep while menacing a peaceful rural family; how he had complimented with a smirk of ill-bred superiority the cuisine served by his unwilling hostess; and how he had cruised for six hours through the main residential sections of Fort Worth in an attempt to steal a car.

In making their escape from the Collin County posse, Hamilton and his pal, who subsequently left a cold trail after taking the car in Fort Worth, sought a hostage behind whom they might hide if cornered. They crowded L. B. Harlow, twenty, of Weston to the road's side and forced him to enter their bullet-torn automobile. Thus protected, they sought a different car and stopped J. C. Loftice, sixteen, also of Weston, just as their gasoline tank ran dry. Harlow was forced to enter the rumble seat of Loftice's roadster and the desperadoes climbed into the front. A driving rain was pelting the automobile, and Harlow objected to his position.

"Shut up and be quiet or I'll drill you," Hamilton said.

Loftice was given directions while the fugitives discussed their position. Both were nervous, the youth said, and jumped at every shadow at the roadside. The ace bandit was unable to offer a solution for difficulties, and his companion did little better. Suddenly, the lights of the home of William Mayes loomed nearby.

"Stop here," Hamilton ordered, and as the car pulled into the yard he told Loftice to call Mayes to the door. The farmer came out-side, expecting a friend. Instead, he faced a .45-caliber automatic, and was ordered back inside. There the bandits cornered Mrs. Mayes, wife of the farmer; his son, Jesse Roy Mayes, twenty-two; Mrs. Jesse Mayes, twenty-two; and their daughter, Mildred Ann, three. With typical cunning, the gunman said no one would be hurt. The road-ster was taken to the rear of the house and covered with a wagon sheet. Hamilton and his companion herded part of the family into a rear room, where the younger Mrs. Mayes lay ill. The boys were sent, one by one, into the front of the house and were instructed to call if they saw automobiles approaching. Now and then someone would snatch a bit of sleep, only to awaken at the grating of a shoe over the floor or a rustle of movement in a chair. It was a long and tedious vigil.

"Raymond talked about his mother," Mrs. Mayes said. "He told me she was on trial in Dallas. But he didn't seem to be bitter about it. He just told me as if it were some person he didn't know very well.

"He worked for a long time on his rifle, which he said had jammed while he was firing at the officers, and it brought Clyde Barrow to his mind. He said Clyde had been jumped three times, and the third time he was killed. 'This makes the second time for me,' he said."

While he was nervous when he first came in, Ray calmed a great deal, and even went to sleep with his rifle over his chest for a time. He awoke with a start and yelled, "I heard you," as if they had been plotting.

"I called him Raymond," she said, "because there was nothing else to call him. Mr. Hamilton would have been sort of funny under the circumstances."

At dawn the bandit pair forced Harlow, Loftice, and young Mayes to accompany them in the Mayes automobile, a 1929 Chevrolet. Mayes drove with Loftice beside him. Harlow and the other two sat in the rear seat.

"Nobody had much sleep, and we were pretty scared, but we joked and had a pretty good time," Harlow said.

First they went to Denton, where they stopped to buy gasoline. Hamilton paid for the fuel out of what seemed to the captives to be a sadly depleted purse, and sent Loftice to a sandwich stand several hundred feet away to get cigarettes and a morning paper.

"I went and got the things," Loftice said, "but I didn't tell any-one what was happening because I didn't think of it."

From Denton the quintet proceeded leisurely to Fort Worth.

The bandits considered going to Dallas, the youths said, but decided against the move because they feared the local police.

"We're too hot in that city," Hamilton mused.

At Fort Worth they sought a new car. Seven or eight tries were made before they were successful. Loftice described what happened:

> Hamilton is the boldest thief I ever saw. Several times he walked right up in garages and looked to see if cars had keys in them.
>
> They made no effort to conceal the weapons they had, nor the 150 pounds of ammunition they carried, but kept everything ready for instant use.
>
> When our fourth or fifth try failed, they sent Mayes to a stand to buy food. He brought it back and the two bandits ate heartily, but we didn't touch much.
>
> We cruised and cruised until finally we saw a man jump out of a car in front of a house and leave the motor running. Hamilton got out immediately, and drove off in the car, leaving the four of us in our automobile. We followed him out of Fort Worth and for about twelve miles. On a side road he stopped and told us to go home after giving us each a cartridge as a memento.
>
> As we left, they cautioned us not to say anything to anybody until we got home, and we didn't.

The three hostages agreed that Hamilton was fatalistic regarding his future, and had grown used to the shadow of death hanging over him. He seemed to be only slightly afraid, they said, and to trust fully in his abnormal luck which had brought him virtually unscathed through many battles. A scratch over the temple, where he was grazed by a bullet, and a few cuts from flying glass were the only injuries Hamilton received in the fusillade laid down by McKinney officers. His companion escaped unscathed, though his hat was pierced with bullet holes; he missed being slain literally by a hair's breadth.

Before leaving the trio, Hamilton presented to Mayes a collar pin which, he said, had been given him by Katie Jenkins. Hamilton and his friend sped toward Cleburne after freeing the three youths. From that moment, as far as authorities could learn, they vanished.

"Hamilton told us to say he was plenty mad about that McKinney thing," Mayes said after the boys returned home.

Meanwhile, officers took quick steps to cut off Hamilton's supply of harborers by arresting a youth believed to be a contact man for the death house fugitive. The man, twenty-five, was taken into custody at McKinney early Monday at or near the house where authorities uncovered Hamilton's cache of four Browning machine rifles he took in the Beaumont raid. The arrested man was being held in the city jail in Dallas, but police were careful to conceal all knowledge of facts surrounding the case. They said he was being held for federal agents, but no charges had been filed against him, either in government or state courts. It was learned he was a police character and a former bootlegger.

The three kidnapped youths reported they were treated well by the bandits. As the trio was given its freedom, Mayes complained of being without funds. Hamilton replied he, too, was short of ready cash, but gave the boy $2 of the $10 he said was his fortune.

Federal agents, city police and sheriff's deputies spent all day Monday in a fruitless search for the fugitives. The government men, it was reported, searched hideouts of Hamilton at Lake Dallas without success. The part they were playing in the drama of crime in the Southwest was not known, but J. Edgar Hoover, head of the Federal Bureau of Investigation, announced at Washington on Monday that his agents definitely wanted the blond West Dallasite. Local Department of Justice agents who joined in the search were under the command of Frank J. Blake, ace investigator who largely was responsible for the capture of Harvey Bailey and his gang for the Charles F. Urschel kidnapping. Included in his force was Charles Winstead, Chicago agent, who was in the party that snuffed out the life of John Dillinger in front of a Windy City theater.

Raymond Hamilton's companion during his battle with Collin County officers was identified as Ralph Fults, twenty-four, former convict who had intimate knowledge of the vicinity Hamilton had been frequenting recently, it was learned Monday. Fults was sentenced to ten years in the state penitentiary on May 29, 1932, on a robbery charge at Wichita Falls. He was said to have received a parole in December, but penitentiary officials at Huntsville could not substantiate that information when a newsman called them. They explained that the record bureau was closed at night.

Fults once lived at McKinney and his family still lived there. Harlow and Loftice, two of the boys kidnapped by Raymond and Fults, said they believed they recognized Fults. During their drive through North Texas, Fults inquired about a girl neighbor of his family. Harlow and Loftice explained they could not identify Fults positively because they had not seen him in several years. In an effort to substantiate its information, the newspapers phoned County Attorney H. H. Neilson at McKinney.

"I'd rather not answer," he said when asked if he knew the identity of Hamilton's companion.

"Do you know Ralph Fults?" he was asked.

His "No" came only after a long pause. Asked if Fults lived at McKinney, he replied, "His family does." As far as he knew, Fults had not been in McKinney recently, Neilson said.

Adding to the drama of the Barrow conspiracy trial in federal court Monday were shrill cries of newsboys from the streets below that officers were hot on the trail of the elusive Raymond Hamilton. Mrs. Steve Davis, mother of the desperado and one of the twenty defendants in the case, was visibly startled and for a few minutes lost complete interest in the prosecution attorneys' arguments to the jury when the newsboys' yells were heard above their demands. She straightened up in her seat and strained to hear what the newsies were yelling about her son's activities. Others who suddenly betrayed great interest in the newest chapter of the book of crime were Floyd Hamilton and Mary O'Dare.

Uncle Sam wrote a finis to Clyde Barrow's bloody career on February 26, 1935, when convictions and sentences were handed down in Dallas. Sentences ranged from the maximum, two years, assessed Floyd Hamilton, to an hour in jail, given his wife, Mildred. Each of the three mothers, Mrs. Cumie Barrow, Mrs. Emma Parker, and Mrs. Steve Davis, drew thirty-day jail sentences. Others were sentenced as follows:

Henry Methvin, fifteen months at Leavenworth to run concurrently with any future sentence he might receive.

Hilton Bybee, ninety days, concurrent with the life term he was serving at Huntsville.

Hilton Bybee, two years, concurrent with a fifteen-year Huntsville sentence.

John Basden, a year at Leavenworth.

S. J. Whatley, a year at Leavenworth.

Joe Chambless, sixty days in jail.

Mary O'Dare, a year at Alderson, West Virginia.

Blanche Barrow, a year to run concurrently with a current five-year sentence in Missouri.

L. C. Barrow, thirteen months at Leavenworth.

Audrey Fay Barrow, fifteen days in jail.

Marie Francis, an hour in jail.

James Mullen, four months in jail at Waxahachie.

Joe Francis, sixty days in jail.

Billie Mace, a year at Alderson, West Virginia.

Steve Davis, ninety days in jail.

In general comment before he started sentencing, Judge Atwell said:

> I read in the morning paper where a kinsman of some of you took three young Texans and made slaves of them. Now Texans are not that kind of people. Texans are not afraid of a man with a gun. I am astonished that one of the boys in this matter was afraid to tell people who was sitting out in the car when he was sent into a store.
>
> I have received a good many letters about you. You'd be surprised how many people are interested in seeing you go straight.

Clyde Eastus made this statement:

> The United States Attorney's office and the Department of Justice Bureau of Investigation are very pleased with the conviction of these persons.
>
> We feel that the result will have a wholesome effect on others who are harboring or concealing persons wanted by the government.
>
> We are serving notice on everybody that Raymond Hamilton is wanted by the United States for the robbery of the Ranger armory, robbery of a national bank at Darrouzett (Lipscomb County) and for harboring Clyde Barrow. A warrant for his arrest is in possession of the United States marshal and has been for some time. This verdict is notice to the world that no person, regardless of relationship, has any right to harbor any person who is a federal fugitive.

Federal officers grilled a McKinney man February 26, 1935, as they and three other law enforcement agencies groped blindly for clues by which they might end the careers of Raymond Hamilton and his companion, who was believed to be Ralph Fults, of McKinney. The federal prisoner was taken into custody by Collin County officers and was believed to be the one who was found with four machine rifles. Investigators refused to confirm or deny this report. The man was left in the city jail Monday night, but was taken from there Tuesday by federal officers.

Dallas city and county officers said they were without clues as to the whereabouts of Hamilton. Capt. Tom Hickman and Stuart Stanley of the Texas Rangers conferred with detectives and left for an undisclosed destination. Investigators declined to say whether they were in search of Hamilton's hideout or engaged in other business. They did reveal that they had been unable to establish ownership of the car in which Hamilton was riding when he drove earlier than expected into the Collin County trap. Detective Capt. J. W. Fritz said he had been told the car appeared to have been stolen in Tulsa, Oklahoma, adding that the report had not been verified.

Hamilton's weakness for pretty girls both led him into the Sunday night trap and saved his skin, according to a story being bruited about in Dallas on Tuesday. The date had been arranged by one of Hamilton's friends, so the story went, and Hamilton, in his eagerness for feminine company, hurried to the trysting place, arriving a few minutes early. The girl, instead of keeping the date, had notified an officer. If Hamilton had arrived at the time set, a larger group of officers would have met him and his avenue of escape would have been cut off, it was said.

A score of different groups of arresting officers were working at cross-purposes in the search for Raymond while the runt killer and bandit ran free, Judge Noland G. Williams declared Tuesday in a scathing indictment of the law enforcement agencies. "Every different agency is trying to capture Hamilton even if it's necessary to retard the efforts of the others," Judge Williams said. "They all want the glory of getting him. I say, to hell with the glory of catching him! Get the job done!"

It was Judge Williams who the year before, when Bonnie and Clyde were at large, secretly arranged for the financing of peace officers on their trail that led to their fatal capture. He continued his criticism:

> We had an example of the failure to cooperate, or the short-sightedness of the law enforcement agencies, in the reports that Hamilton and his pal, with three captives, cruised around Fort Worth for hours looking for a car to steal.
>
> Dallas has its own police radio and Fort Worth has its own, and they are on different channels. Neither has a set tuned on to the other. While Hamilton was cruising in Fort Worth the Dallas station was broadcasting the license number of the car he was in and the fact that he and his pal had their heads bandaged.
>
> Incidents like these call our attention to the need for a unified state police force and for cooperation between the different law enforcement agencies. They should be clear of politics and jealousy.
>
> The jealousy has become so bad that they have been arresting each other's informers. I have been releasing these informers on writs when I know they are informers because I know they have been giving officers tips on Hamilton's movements.
>
> When the officers jumped Hamilton in Collin County Sun-

day night, they should have caught him, but one of the officers wanted to get the glory so he did not stick to the plans for the trap. There were three officers waiting in a house they knew Hamilton was going to pass. The officer who caused the trouble knew they were there, so he went out on the road to meet Hamilton and messed up the detail. Hamilton got away.

These criminals are costing the people hundreds of thousands of dollars. I don't know how much longer the long-suffering public is going to stand for it, but until we have cooperation among the arresting officers, the outlaws will continue to run unmolested.

Judge Williams listed the following groups of officers as different entities that should be working together for the purpose of stopping crime: Dallas Police Department, Texas State Highway Patrol, Texas Rangers, Highland Park Police, University Park Police, four constables, Department of Justice agents, police forces of various towns in the county, and the sheriff's office.

"With that many agencies and the hundreds of officers at their command in Dallas County, it is a disgrace to a civilized community to have a man like Hamilton running at large," Judge Williams said.

Department of Justice agents also freely criticized the McKinney officers for their failure to notify them that they had spotted Raymond. The federal men pointed out that their agents had a fleet of fast automobiles and were equipped with the latest in criminal fighting equipment. Capt. Will Fritz of the Dallas Police Department likewise was critical that local detectives were not informed of the trap. Sheriff R. A. (Smoot) Schmid, who was notified about 6:00 P.M. Sunday, arrived at McKinney ten minutes too late with his deputies to help in the brief gun battle. Sheriff Schmid, on the other hand, was not notified when local police and federal agents planned the South Dallas trap.

In offering a $500 reward Wednesday, February 27, 1935, for information leading to the capture, dead or alive, of Raymond Hamilton, Governor James V. Allred asked all state, county, and city officers to cooperate in the search. The governor severely criticized the attempted capture of Hamilton by county officers near McKinney.

"State rangers were stationed a block and a half from the trap and never were called on to assist in the attempted arrest," the governor said. "The rangers were ready to help if they had been notified.

"Had the county officers not flushed Hamilton and his companion, the rangers would have killed both of them. I want no more of this lack of cooperation, but all state, county, and city officers should join in the hunt for Hamilton."

Previous to posting the $500 reward, only a $25 reward, made by the prison system for any escaped convict, had been offered for Hamilton's capture.

A staunch defense of Collin County law enforcement bodies was made Wednesday by Constable John A. Record as he reviewed facts surrounding the ambuscade. Constable Record came to his own defense after criticism was hurled at Collin County peace officers. Showing that all local agencies were combined, the constable pointed out that members of his department, the sheriff's department, state highway patrolmen, and city policemen united in the ambush. Police officers, Record said, were not looking for any personal glory in capturing or killing such rats as Hamilton but were uniting in a solid front to wipe out all would-be desperadoes. Record said the kind of cooperation shown in McKinney ultimately would result in the extermination of every bandit in the country. The only mishap, the McKinney officer explained, was the late arrival of Sheriff Schmid and his deputies, whose part it was to bottle up the outlaws after local officers had engaged them in a gun battle. McKinney officers, although regretting they did not get the frightened killer, recalled that Hamilton previously escaped the death cell at Huntsville and ran the gauntlet of two-score Dallas police in making a successful getaway.

While one of Raymond Hamilton's former girlfriends was starting to the penitentiary on February 27, 1935, another one was starting her first day of freedom in more than three weeks. Mary O'Dare was on her way to prison after being convicted of harboring Clyde Barrow. Katie Jenkins, allegedly a later associate of Hamilton, was released Tuesday afternoon from the city jail, where she had been held since February 4. No charges were filed against her during that time. She was said to have dropped from 101 pounds to 83 pounds during her confinement. Katie was quoted as saying that she barely knew Raymond Hamilton and that she had merely gone to the apartment for a visit with Floyd Hamilton's wife when she was arrested by officers.

Two more Browning machine rifles stolen by Raymond were found by Collin County officers in a brush heap on a lonely road two miles southeast of McKinney on February 28. Constable John Record, who received a tip about the location of the rifles, was careful to avoid any further charges of lack of cooperation when he staged the raid. He enlisted the aid of the sheriff's department, city police, and two Department of Justice agents, taking every peace officer in town with him. Texas Rangers who had been in McKinney since

Hamilton escaped left town several hours before the raid. Finding of the rifles accounted for all eight that Hamilton took from the Beaumont armory.

It was learned that a man arrested on February 25 and placed in the Dallas city jail might be charged with harboring Hamilton. The man, twenty-five, former bootlegger and police character who lived in McKinney, may have given the fugitive shelter, officers intimated.

Officers from half a dozen East Texas towns rushed to Peeltown Thursday afternoon in what proved to be a futile effort to capture Raymond Hamilton. A report from Mabank had tipped officers that a man fitting Hamilton's description had been seen near Peeltown, a tiny village twelve miles south of Kaufman. Officers from Terrell, Kaufman, Athens, and various other points encountered the suspect driving along a road, but it was not Hamilton. With the surprised youth was a young woman.

Two efforts to capture Raymond failed Thursday but furnished a lot of exercise for Sheriff Smoot Schmid and several squads of his detectives. At noon Sheriff Schmid was called from a luncheon of the High Noon Club on a report that Hamilton and a young woman had been seen parked in the woods near Athens. This turned out to be the alleged sighting near Peeltown. While the sheriff was gone, Deputies Guy Nowlin and John Chiess were called out on a report that Hamilton and a companion, armed with machine guns, had been seen near the Trinity River south of Dallas. They raced in an automobile to the neighborhood. Carrying heavy rifles and crawling laboriously through about 300 yards of Johnson grass, they approached a spot from different angles only to find two black women fishing with several cane poles.

A gunman, who told his victims he was Raymond Hamilton, and a companion on Friday night, March 1, kidnapped Edward Wells, twenty-two, and his companion, Bernice Gochnour, twenty, and drove them about Houston for several hours before taking them to a lonely spot near south Houston. The gunmen left the two bound after taking their auto, a speedy machine of the type fancied by the outlaw. Wells said he and Miss Gochnour were driving on a suburban street when an automobile occupied by two men forced them to stop. The men, one armed with a revolver, alighted.

"I'm Raymond Hamilton," the man with the pistol said. "Both of you get in the rear seat and remain quiet."

Wells said the second man drove the car while the man armed with the gun kept them covered during the long ride. The couple managed to free themselves of their bonds and reported to police shortly after midnight. A description of Hamilton tallied, police said, with that of the gunman.

Complete solution of bank robberies at Carthage and Handley, engineered by Raymond Hamilton, was claimed Friday by Dallas city detectives after federal charges had been lodged against four alleged accomplices of the hunted outlaw. Named in complaints filed with U.S. Commissioner Lee R. Smith was Wilford Boyce Lynn, alias Boyce Lynn, twenty-five, of McKinney, who was charged with "Ralph Fults and diverse other persons with conspiring to harbor and conceal Raymond Hamilton, a federal fugitive from justice." Also, John Bratcher, twenty-eight, of Dallas, was charged with entering and robbing the First National Bank at Carthage February 4, 1935. Raymond and Floyd Hamilton had previously been identified as his two confederates. Joe Carson, twenty, Dallas, Raymond's brother-in-law, was charged with "aiding and abetting a person or persons unknown by force and violence to take from the person of Ben T. Merritt, cashier of the First National Bank of Handley, the sum of $449."

Fults, named in the conspiracy charge with Lynn, had been identified as the man who was with Hamilton during the McKinney ambush, Capt. Will Fritz of the Dallas Police Department said. Each of the three men in custody were held on federal bonds as follows: Lynn, $5,000; Bratcher, $10,000; and Carson, $1,000. Lynn, who was arrested on February 25 by Constable Record of Collin County, denied any knowledge of why charges had been filed against him when interviewed at the federal building.

"It's a bum rap. I don't know anything about it. Why, I wouldn't know Ray Hamilton if I saw him," he commented.

"You know where we got those two rifles," a Department of Justice agent shot back at him. He was referring to the two Browning automatic rifles recovered in a house at McKinney, which had been identified as stolen at Beaumont.

Lynn claimed he was a truck driver, and said he had lived in McKinney all his life. He had been given a two-year suspended sentence for forgery in Dallas on June 10, 1933.

"Incidentally," Lynn remarked, "my name's Wilford Boyce Lynn, not Royce Lynn like the cops have been spelling it. Those guys can't get anything right."

Carson, a nice-looking blond youth, said he was a filling station operator. He had been married to a younger sister of the hunted outlaw for six months, he said. He was orphaned the summer before, when his mother and father were killed in an accident on Maple Avenue in Dallas. Like Lynn, Carson was given a two-year suspended sentence for robbery in Dallas on June 17, 1934. Carson said he lived at 4718 Maple.

Bratcher, also married, said he was a welder, resided in Lisbon addition, and had lived in or near Dallas all of his life. He said he had been kept in solitary confinement at the city jail since February 14, 1935. Bratcher received an eighteen-year penitentiary sentence at Huntsville on August 30, 1930. Filing of the charges followed investigations made by detectives working with Captain Fritz. Both Bratcher and Carson were arrested by local officers and had been held in city jail. Hearings for Lynn on March 12, 1935, and for Bratcher on March 13, 1935, were ordered by Commissioner Smith.

The charges against Lynn and Fults followed several warnings issued recently by federal officials that all persons aiding the missing Hamilton would be prosecuted.

CHAPTER XVI

An Interview
and an Invasion

Joe Carson, brother-in-law of Raymond Hamilton, was transferred to the Fort Worth jail by federal officials to await action following the filing of charges against him concerning the Handley robbery.

Police were searching Saturday, March 2, 1935, for the bandits, one of whom claimed to be Raymond Hamilton, who held up Edward Wells and Bernice Gochnour. Wells said he did not believe either of the bandits was Hamilton.

A report that Raymond had been seen near Richmond, Fort Bend County, late Sunday, March 3, causing posses of officers to start a new search, was exploded several hours later when a youth resembling Hamilton was arrested by officers and released two hours later. Paul Allison Abbott of Bogalusa, Louisiana, on his way to an engineering job in California, was stopped first at Victoria, where officers questioned him, and then was taken into custody at Lavernia, Texas. The license numbers on his automobile tallied with those seen at Rosenberg, where the search for Hamilton started after a former Texas prison official said he had recognized the fugitive. Abbott had stopped for a cup of coffee in Lavernia and was immediately taken into custody by Deputy Sheriff W. H. Robbins, who had taken the number of the car. Capt. Lee Miller of the state highway patrol came to Lavernia from San Antonio, thirty miles west, and after viewing the man assured officers they had been mistaken in their identity. Sheriff A. Hennigan of Richmond, who led the search for Hamilton, announced at midnight the posse had abandoned the hunt. After being released from custody, Abbott asked Captain Miller to escort him to San Antonio.

"I've been stopped enough for one day," he said. "The next guys that stop me might start shooting and ask questions later.

"When those policemen stopped me at Victoria I was sure they'd brought out the artillery. One of them yelled at me to stop and when I dropped my hand to the gear shift lever of the car he threw a machine gun up to his shoulder. I forgot about the gear shift lever right then. I'm not sure how the car stopped.

"Then when I pulled in here to get a cup of coffee, who should I meet but someone behind another of the biggest guns I ever saw. But I'm not arguing with anybody behind a gun."

Raymond Hamilton was reported on Monday, March 4, to have taken ten gallons of gas from a gas station at Lancaster without paying for it. The operator, who telephoned the sheriff's office, gave his name as Fitzhugh and said he knew Hamilton. He said Hamilton came to his station at 8:00 P.M. and ordered ten gallons of gasoline and then drove away without paying. Fitzhugh said Hamilton was in a green two-door 1935 Ford V-8. He said he did not think to get the number of the license plates. The sheriff's office transmitted the information to the Dallas Police Department, which broadcast it over the police radio, and sheriff's deputies and police were ordered out to search for the desperado.

Dallas police seemed to draw another blank with a feminine prisoner when word filtered in Monday night that Beaumont witnesses had failed to identify pictures of Maggie Lee Fairris, nineteen, sister of Raymond Hamilton, as a participant in the South Texas armory robbery. Inspector E. V. Bunch said he understood that the pictures which were taken Sunday, March 3, when the young woman was arrested, had been reported upon adversely. Investigation continued, however.

Federal officers made public Monday a week-old warrant for Ralph Fults, still wanted on a harboring charge.

Henry Johnson, of Houston, reported to Sheriff George Coy of Bellville on March 6 that he had been kidnapped by two bandits, one of whom resembled Raymond Hamilton. Johnson said the bandits jumped on his car at an underpass on the Hempstead-Bellville highway. They drove around four hours, he said, going to Navasota and then to the place where they released their hostage. They appeared to be trying to get into Houston without traveling on main highways, according to Johnson. The bandits released Johnson five miles north of Sealy and drove off in his automobile, he said. From his description of the bandits, officers believed Hamilton's companion was Ralph Fults. The bandits were armed with three automatic rifles and two machine guns. Reports of this encounter were broadcast throughout South Texas, and officers took up the trail.

Release of Wilford Boyce Lynn was effected Wednesday when his previous $5,000 bail was reduced to a $1,000 personal recognizance bond. Assistant U.S. District Attorney Joe H. Jones said the amount was reduced because Lynn already was under $4,000 bond in state courts. Lynn had been jointly charged with Fults in the conspiracy allegation.

A new V-8 found abandoned near Stepps Ford, Oklahoma, six miles northwest of Miami, Oklahoma, was identified on Monday, March 11, by Sheriff Eli Dry as one reported stolen at Fort Worth February 25 by Raymond Hamilton. Sheriff Dry said the license plates were missing, but the motor number corresponded. He was checking the machine for fingerprints. A farmer said the automobile was abandoned on Sunday, March 10. Its occupants were not seen. Another car abandoned by Hamilton was found in the same vicinity a few months before.

Three men, one of them described as resembling Raymond Hamilton, broke into a show window of a hardware store Tuesday night, March 12, and fled with a small quantity of ammunition in Grandview. Constable Homer Hunt said the men apparently were seeking .30-caliber ammunition. They escaped in a new V-8. Reports reached Grandview that the car was seen near Hillsboro and that it was going toward Waco.

The ex-Ranger captain who was Bonnie and Clyde's nemesis was to pursue Raymond Hamilton despite the refusal of Judge Grover Adams to allow Frank Hamer's salary and expenses to be charged to the present grand jury's cost. Judge Noland G. Williams, who engaged Captain Hamer on January 4, 1935, as a special grand jury bailiff, said Tuesday next that the officer's salary was already paid from the county general fund. Judge Adams during the day notified County Auditor John C. Crosthwait that $217 paid the former Ranger could not be charged to the present jury:

> I have never made nor heard of such an appointment, and no purpose, however noble or popular can be substituted for the statutes governing the case. You cannot "play like" an individual is a bailiff and then use public funds to pay him.

Judge Williams countered Adams' statement:

Two grand juries suggested the appointment of Captain Hamer and members of one volunteered to pay his salary and expenses from their own pockets. Each time I advised against the move.

When I appointed Captain Hamer I believed that the law abiding people of Dallas County wanted a man of his caliber; I believed they wanted to rid this community of a hoodlum like Raymond Hamilton.

Captain Hamer had proved himself to be efficient when called upon to catch Hamilton's fellow criminal Clyde Barrow. This story is familiar to everyone.

It is unfortunate for the public that those charged with enforcing the law throw stumbling blocks in the way of others, which is one of the reasons that various criminals escape punishment as long as they do.

Identification of John Bratcher, twenty-eight, Lisbon area steel welder, as the man who aided Raymond and Floyd Hamilton in the robbery of the First National Bank at Carthage was made March 12 at a hearing before Commissioner Lee R. Smith. Bond for Bratcher, previously charged with the hijacking, was raised from $10,000 to $20,000. He was ordered bound over for trial at the next criminal term at Tyler federal court.

Jack Cook, bookkeeper for the bank, identified Bratcher as one of the three men who participated in the robbery. Bratcher also was identified by Charles Hudson, Beckville, a customer in the bank at the time of the stickup. Both said Bratcher kept guard in the bank lobby while Floyd and Raymond Hamilton covered bank officials and customers with pistols and scooped up several thousand dollars in currency and silver.

An uproar was created in the courtroom when Bratcher loudly cursed both Cook and Hudson.

"They're both goddamned liars!" he shouted.

He was quieted when Commissioner Smith threatened to hold him in contempt of court.

Threads of the constant search for Hamilton, an attempted hijacking of a liquor consignment for a Dallas nightclub, and the statewide raids of night clubs by Rangers were tangled on Highway No. 1 between Arlington and Grand Prairie Sunday afternoon, March 17. Driving toward his home at Gilmer, Ranger I. T. Reckley saw bullet holes in the back of a small, fast car that passed him.

"It's Hamilton," he thought, and stepped on the accelerator. The chased driver also speeded up. Reckley emptied his automatic pistol at the fleeing car before, after a two-mile chase, he crowded it into a ditch and forced the driver to stop. An unarmed black man got out. He had sixty gallons of whiskey in the car.

"I thought you was some more of them heisters," the man told Reckley. "They jumped me just this side of Arlington and shot up the back of the car but I got away." He said he was taking the whiskey to a nightclub in Dallas.

Reckley first took the man to the Arlington jail, but later took him to Dallas. The arrest was made in Dallas County, and the automobile and liquor were turned over to federal officers.

Raymond Hamilton was hidden again Tuesday, March 19, after telling his story. To tell his side, Hamilton on Monday night had kidnapped Harry McCormick, *Houston Press* reporter, talked for two hours, then bound and gagged the reporter and left him by a roadside. McCormick was discovered and released Tuesday by a farmer. With Hamilton was Ralph Fults, who lured the reporter from his home by an anonymous telephone call and forced him at pistol point to keep a rendezvous with Hamilton. Before leaving McCormick, the outlaw placed his fingerprints on the reporter's automobile, saying, "I'm going to leave my fingerprints on your car so everybody will know I kept my word about seeing you." Hamilton had promised McCormick at the time of his conviction for slaying Major Crowson that he would escape from the state penitentiary and "some day give you a good story." The fingerprints were later identified by police identification expert Henry Keller of the Houston Police Department and fingerprint expert Fred Nash.

"Those prints are so plain that we can tell without photographing them and comparing them with our cards at the police station that they are those of Hamilton," Nash said.

Hamilton, facing death in the electric chair as well as sentencing totaling 362 years, made the following statements:

1. He had never killed a man, but would never give up.
2. He believed there were a good many people who believed in him.
3. His southern accent compelled him to remain in the South.
4. He still was in love.
5. He was wounded recently in a Dallas battle with police.
6. He didn't know what his eventual fate would be.

"I want the people of Texas to know my side of this thing," Hamilton told McCormick. "I've never killed anyone. All I'm trying to do now is protect my life—I am doing no more than any preacher would do. No man wants to die.

"I believe there are a good many people on my side—I believe some of them realize I've never killed anyone."

"Why do you stay in Texas?" asked McCormick.

"It's worse away than it is here," was the answer. "You start talking in the North or West or Midwest and they hear that southern accent, see your car covered with dust and the first thing they say from here to China is 'That's Ray Hamilton.'"

McCormick said Hamilton suddenly demanded: "Put something in your paper about my girl. Her name is Katie. I want you to say for me that if she has turned on me and put me on the spot, that I am ready to die, but I can't believe it's true."

He asked McCormick to feel a bullet that was lodged beneath the skin of his neck, near his Adam's apple.

"I got that in a Dallas ambuscade," he explained.

"I don't know what will happen to me," he concluded. "It'll have to go on like this until I am killed or until I finally get away."

He knocked on wood.

Misfortune of being mistaken for Raymond Hamilton netted L. M. McNeal, the bootlegger captured between Arlington and Grand Prairie, a sixty-day jail sentence in federal court in Dallas on March 21.

On Friday, March 22, the Department of Justice in Washington, D.C. said that additional special agents had been assigned in the hope of capturing the three leading public enemies who had evaded J. Edgar Hoover's investigators for several months. Chief targets for the hunters were Raymond Hamilton; Thomas H. Robinson, Jr., accused of collecting $50,000 ransom for the kidnapping of Alice Stoll of Louisville, Kentucky, the previous October; and Alvin Karpis, lone fugitive of the Barker-Karpis mob indicted for the $200,000 Edward G. Bremer kidnapping at St. Paul, Minnesota.

Mississippi called out its National Guard Thursday night, March 28, in a warlike hunt for a man believed to be Raymond Hamilton, and another bandit who blazed a trail of terror and banditry through Southern Mississippi during the day. The two bandits roared through several counties in stolen automobiles, wounded two persons, engaged in several gun battles, disarmed a posse of fifteen, and kidnapped at least six persons in their mad flight after robbing a bank of $1,100 at Prentiss, Mississippi, in the morning. The men, with one hostage, were last seen turning off onto a gravel road three miles west of Georgetown, Mississippi, Copiah County, twenty-five miles from the scene of the bank holdup.

Guns barked repeatedly in a fifty-mile radius of Prentiss during the day as the two men zigzagged from one highway to another at breakneck speed. Officers from practically all southern Mississippi counties joined in the chase, and the highway department blocked off a quadrangular area in which the men were believed trapped. Armed posses patrolled every road in the section. One of the bandits, a youthful blond, was reported peppered in the face with squirrel shot by a farmer, J. T. Polk, who resisted an attempt the robbers made to commandeer his car. The bandits, however, returned the fire, and Polk's daughter-in-law, Mrs. Rodney Polk, was wounded in the left arm. Deputy Sheriff W. J. Lee of Jefferson Davis County said Sheriff Ennis Crawford of Covington County was creased in the head by a bullet during a gun battle. The deputy sheriff said one of the bandits was identified tentatively from pictures as Hamilton.

In their swift change from one automobile to another, the men kidnapped farm folk, officers, and a sheriff, who later escaped after a gun battle. Militiamen at several points were mobilized for the hunt, and 150 troops at Jackson, Mississippi, prepared to leave in taxicabs to surround the area by dawn. The bandits surprised Sheriff Crawford, W. O. Thomas, cashier of the Bank of Collins, and E. L. Dent, Collins' attorney, late Thursday, forced them to ride on the side of the car as shields, and overpowered and disarmed the posse twelve miles north of Prentiss. The outlaws later ran into another group and started firing again. The possemen were forced to retreat because they were afraid of wounding the hostages. Thomas and Dent escaped during the excitement.

Three women were arrested in connection with the bank robbery, one of whom was reported to have accompanied the two men during the holdup. Authorities would not say where they were held.

After the posse was disarmed, Jefferson Davis County asked Governor Sennet Conner to mobilize militiamen. The governor instructed Adj. Gen. Thomas Grayson to call out the troops immediately. Guardsmen were quickly assembled and stationed at points along the Pearl River, the route the bandits were expected to take northward. The bandits also held up George Shivers' filling station at New Hebron, Lawrence County, during their escapade. It was difficult to check on the number of persons kidnapped in the fight, but officers said the men changed automobiles at gunpoint at least six times during the day.

Raymond Hamilton and Ralph Fults eluded officers Friday, March 29, after abandoning their last two hostages in the heart of Memphis, Tennessee. Armed with two machine guns, several rifles, and a number of pistols, the desperadoes apparently headed out of Memphis immediately after leaving their hostages locked in the rear of a coupe. However, Memphis detectives and federal officers staged a series of raids on rooming houses and small hotels during the afternoon on the possibility that the bandit pair might be seeking rest after thirty-six hours of crime and flight. The men abandoned in Memphis were M. E. Smith, Jefferson Davis County farm agent, and Ralph Bayliss, Prentiss merchant. They had been abducted Thursday.

Smith and Bayliss were members of a posse formed to scour the section around Prentiss following the bank holdup. At the police station in Memphis, Smith and Bayliss positively identified photographs of Hamilton from among photographs of several criminals. After talking with Will T. Griffin, inspector of Memphis detectives, the men were taken to the Federal Building and questioned by Department of Justice agents. Smith told Griffin that Hamilton's companion was shot in one cheek, the right hand, in the back, and in one leg, and was in a weakened condition.

"Hamilton had his machine gun on me, and I was forced to do most of the driving toward Memphis," Smith told police. Between Hernando and Memphis the gunmen stopped the car and made Bayliss change clothes with the wounded man. Bayliss had on the bullet-riddled clothing when he arrived in Memphis.

While Smith drove, Bayliss was locked in the rear of the car, and after Bayliss changed clothes with Hamilton's companion he was forced to enter the rear compartment also.

"Stay in there now, and don't cause any trouble and we'll let you out when we get to Memphis," the men said Hamilton told them. When the car came to a stop in Memphis, Hamilton told the men to be quiet and said, "We'll be back as soon as we steal another car."

Police said Hamilton and his companion might have headed into Arkansas en route to Texas. The appearance of the pair in Memphis became known while an army of peace officers, National Guardsmen, and armed citizens were searching for them in Mississippi, believing the fugitives bottled up between Columbia and Prentiss.

Two of the three women held for questioning, who said they were Estelle and Dorothy Davis of Houston, asserted that they were forced to accompany Hamilton in the holdup and were left behind at Prentiss for revenge. They were captured late Thursday as they fled across a field near Prentiss with the third woman, listed as Mrs. Vergie Johnson of Carson, Mississippi. The sisters were removed to the Hinds County jail at Jackson, where they were held incommunicado. They were to be charged, officers said, under a federal statute in connection with the bank robbery. I. F. Benedict, a New Orleans private detective present when the women were questioned, refused to discuss any of the details of the purported statements but said they told a harrowing story which, if true, convinced him they were innocent kidnap victims.

With banks guarded like fortresses against the chance that Raymond Hamilton might backtrack to Memphis for another robbery, officers pursued some two score groundless tips in a futile attempt to hunt him down on March 30. The county jail in Memphis also was closely guarded against any possible effort by Hamilton to rescue the three women held in connection with his Mississippi foray.

While federal operatives and police throughout the South tried to follow the cold trail left by the desperado and a badly wounded confederate, Estelle and Dorothy Davis were arraigned at Jackson, Mississippi, on charges of conspiring to harbor and conceal Hamilton. The sisters from Dallas were placed under $10,000 bond and a hearing was set for Wednesday, April 3. The women had been questioned throughout the day by state and federal officers. They were allowed to call their mother in Dallas by telephone Saturday afternoon, and it was understood they arranged for retaining counsel. One official said he understood a Dallas attorney would be retained. The charges against the women were contained in an affidavit signed by Dwight Brantley, special agent of the Federal Bureau of Investigation, who arrived in Memphis by plane from Dallas on March 29. Memphis police believed the desperado pair had headed for Arkansas Saturday morning, possibly hoping to reach the rough Arkansas–Oklahoma hill country without further brushes with the law. It was not disclosed whether the questioning of the two women held on charges of conspiring to harbor Hamilton had furnished any information of value, and Department of Justice officers were silent about their movements.

"We have nothing to give out as yet," A. Rosen, one of the officers, said, declining to comment on whether he had learned anything of Hamilton's possible hideouts. Another woman held for investigation in connection with the bank robbery, booked as Mrs. Virgie Johnson of near Prentiss, was brought to the Hinds County jail Saturday for questioning by federal operatives.

M. E. Smith and Ralph Bayliss, who had been left in the rear compartment of Smith's auto, were back home Saturday. Officers had no intimation, they said, of how Hamilton and his companion escaped after leaving the men locked up. Smith and Bayliss managed to extricate themselves with the aid of a tire tool.

Sheriff Campbell described Hamilton's 200-mile run across Mississippi "an amazing stroke of luck."

Two things had officers puzzled: When Hamilton and his confederate reached Memphis, they apparently had had no sleep in forty-eight hours or more. Hamilton's usual policy, the officers said, was to steal a car for his escapes. No reports of recent car thefts had been made to police in Memphis. Police checked crossroads, bus companies, and taxicab operators in an effort to learn whether the men purchased transportation to Arkansas or some other state. Raids continued Saturday on downtown rooming houses and small hotels on the possibility the desperadoes sought sleep in Memphis. Belief that Raymond had found refuge in the badlands along the Oklahoma–Arkansas border was expressed March 31 by federal and police officers in Memphis as they renewed their search. Bayliss and Smith said Hamilton and his companion hid all the silver taken in the Prentiss bank robbery somewhere near Prentiss and later divided the currency on a side road near Terry, Mississippi, counting out something like $500 between them.

Heavily armed sheriff's deputies for the third time in two days sped out of Denton Monday afternoon, April 1, 1935, to seek a car occupied by two men, one of whom the officers positively identified as Raymond Hamilton. The day before, the chase went through Denton and southeast of Denton after the man they identified as Hamilton, armed with a machine gun, picked up a hitchhiker at the edge of Denton and released him on the Fort Worth highway. It was intensified a short time later when officers saw a car which contained the slippery fugitive cross a main street in Denton. Monday afternoon's hunt started after a car answering the description of the one sought was reported in a country lane off the Sherman highway six miles north of Denton. On the officers' arrival they found it had turned around and sped toward the highway again before they reached the spot.

The Denton hunt, during the course of which deputies said they were passed by Hamilton downtown, started at noon on Sunday, when Luther Harris, sixteen, of Canton, was picked up as he sought a ride to Fort Worth. Harris said a black car halted and the driver offered him a ride. Another man was hunched far back in the rear seat and when the youth turned around, at some remark, he saw the man, wearing dark goggles, had a machine gun between his knees and several pistols on the seat beside him, Harris said. Three miles from Denton, Harris was let out as the car turned up a lane after the man identified as Hamilton asked the driver, whom he called Sam, if he could find his way across the country to Lake Dallas. Harris said the car soon returned, the two men furious because the lane had proved to be only a drive into a farm home. The car turned toward

Denton and the frightened youth fled across fields to a farmhouse, from where the alarm was telephoned to Sheriff M. S. Webster. An armed carload of deputies picked up Harris and took him to Denton. As they drove across the square, east of the courthouse, and parked in the middle of the block, a black car shot by.

"That's the one!" the youth exclaimed.

While the boy struggled with the car door to spring out, fearing a shooting, the other machine turned a corner and disappeared. The deputies said they got a good look at the rear seat occupant and were positive it was Hamilton, who was known by local officers since he was tried in Denton for the robbery of the Lewisville State Bank.

A hunt over the city and southeastern parts of the county by Dallas and Fort Worth officers and Texas Rangers failed. Late Sunday afternoon came the report that the car carrying two heavily armed men had been sighted in southeast Denton County, between Corinth and Lake Dallas. However, a prolonged search failed to locate the machine.

While all available police and federal officers were scouring Memphis for them, Raymond Hamilton and a wounded companion rented a room at a small hotel Friday morning, March 29, donned fresh clothing, and calmly left, it was revealed Monday, April 1. Will T. Griffin, inspector of detectives, said police learned of Hamilton's movements after his cast-off clothing was found. A maid at the hotel identified a photograph of the Texas fugitive as that of one of two guests of the hostelry.

On Monday, April 1, the three women held in connection with the Prentiss robbery were charged with bank robbery with a deadly weapon by the state in Jackson, Mississippi, a charge carrying the maximum penalty of death. Warrants charging the Davis sisters and Virgie Johnson were served on the trio in the Hinds County jail by Sheriff W. H. Mathison of Jefferson Davis County. The Davis women had been arrested on several occasions in Louisiana and once served prison terms at Shreveport, where Mrs. Johnson met them and invited them to visit her.

Joe Palmer moved nearer the electric chair on April 3, when the Court of Criminal Appeals in Austin denied a rehearing on his appeal. The court had recently affirmed Palmer's death sentence. Mandate was to be issued in the case April 5, and District Judge S. W. Dean of Navasota County was expected to sentence Palmer to be electrocuted early in May. Palmer's appeal claimed the murder indictment was defective because it stated that he previously had been convicted of robbery, whereas the conviction was for robbery with firearms, but the court ruled the indictment was sufficient.

"As set out in the record of his appeal, the evidence doubtless was such as to impress the jury with the conviction that the appellant was guilty of the murder of Crowson under conditions which presented no extenuating circumstances," Presiding Judge W. C. Morrow held.

CHAPTER XVII

A Capture in Cowtown

Without the firing of a shot, Raymond Hamilton was captured at Fort Worth shortly after 7:00 P.M. Friday, April 5, 1935, as he lay sprawled in a railroad yard near the highway to Grapevine. The nine-month search for the bank robber and murderer, in which officers of half a dozen states and federal forces had joined hands, ended when Chief Deputy Bill Decker of Dallas County covered him with a gun.

"Hoist 'em, Ray," Decker commanded.

The dirty, overall-clad West Dallas hoodlum, haggard and tired from constant flight from the law, immediately shot his hands to the sky, despite recent assertions that he would shoot it out the next time officers trapped him. In the capturing party were Dallas County Sheriff Smoot Schmid, whose astute work earlier in the day had made it possible to set the trap; Ed Caster, Bryan Peck, and Ted Hinton, Schmid's deputies; and City Detective Chester Reagan and Deputy Sheriff Carl Harmon of Fort Worth.

Hamilton was seized in the railroad yards at the East Belknap overpass. Captured with Hamilton was Glen Allen, twenty-nine, of Springfield, Illinois, who was held for questioning. Hamilton had two .45-caliber pistols and three extra clips, all loaded, when arrested. He had only a few dollars. His greasy overalls were quite in contrast to his proclivity for foppish attire. He was ready, however, to change into something more presentable if the occasion offered, a small black suitcase he was carrying revealed. In it were a new suit, shoes, pajamas, safety razor, and soap.

Tired and haggard, the desperado seemed somewhat relieved at the temporary lifting of the tension. He had not dyed his hair. The only attempt he had made to disguise himself, evidently, was a pair of eyeglasses found in his pocket.

The stage for Raymond's capture was set in Dallas during the afternoon when Deputies Caster and Peck arrested Nolan Alred, nineteen, of Tupelo, Mississippi, as they saw him riding a taxicab in West Dallas. In Alred's pocket was found a note scrawled on the back of an envelope, addressed to a man known to the deputies in West Dallas.

"Listen," it said, "this is Ray. This boy is O.K."

They discovered that the note was from Raymond Hamilton. The note was addressed to a local man, instructing him that Hamilton wanted an automobile stolen and delivered to him in Fort Worth, Sheriff Schmid said. Alred told the deputies where the outlaw was hiding. They took Alred to Fort Worth and notified Detective Reagan and Deputy Harmon, who joined Sheriff Schmid and the other four deputies.

"We went to the railroad yards and got about six blocks from where we thought Ray was," Sheriff Schmid said. "Alred walked on ahead. Decker trailed him. The rest of us deployed in a circle. Ray was sprawled on the tracks with six or seven bums, all just standing around. Bill walked up and put his gun on Ray. Ray didn't make a move to get his two guns; he knew it would be suicide. We all had pistols trained on him. When we arrested Ray and Allen the bums ran."

The blond hoodlum was as meek when he looked into Deputy Decker's gun as he had been on a previous occasion when officers overtook him at Howe. Erroneous reports that Ray's capture had been effected at Grapevine developed when Sheriff Schmid stopped there to telephone his office that he had caught the desperado. Grapevine citizens, mistaken in the belief their town had been the scene of the capture, telephoned the incorrect information to Dallas.

Capture of the dapper bandit gave Sheriff Schmid and his deputies a clean sweep in mopping up the once rampant West Dallas Barrow-Parker-Hamilton gang. In spite of the meek surrender, Hamilton had all the cool bravado which marked his criminal career.

"Well, Sheriff," he said, "I'll let you have all the surplus ammunition I've got with me. Do you want to hold my coat while I empty my pockets?"

Manager Lee Simmons and Warden W. W. Waid left Huntsville for Dallas soon after receiving news of Hamilton's capture to make arrangements to have him returned to the death cell. Simmons advised

Sheriff Schmid that he would leave it up to him to decide when the desperado should be returned to Huntsville.

"I'm ready to turn him over whenever Lee wants him," Sheriff Schmid said.

Warden Waid arrived in Dallas at 1:10 A.M. Saturday, April 6, and congratulated Sheriff Schmid on the capture. Indications that Hamilton would not be taken to Huntsville immediately were seen when Arch Holmes, deputy United States marshal, called Sheriff Schmid and said that he would serve a warrant on Hamilton Saturday for bank robbery. It was believed that this move was part of an effort to bring a number of persons to trial on charges of harboring Hamilton. Governor Allred expressed deep gratification when informed by Sheriff Schmid that Raymond had been captured. The governor reported that Schmid said over the phone, "I've got Raymond Hamilton and I want to claim that five hundred dollars."

"I congratulated Sheriff Schmid," Governor Allred said. "And I expressed my gratification again, not only over the fact that he was captured, but the fact he was taken without bloodshed."

The governor said he supposed Schmid would communicate with penitentiary authorities about placing Hamilton back in the death house.

"The government is ready for trial in the Raymond Hamilton cases," U.S. Attorney Clyde O. Eastus said in Fort Worth following Hamilton's arrest. Hamilton already was under death sentence in the state courts, but if there was any hitch the federal government stood ready to seek the death penalty on a bank robbery charge when the criminal docket opened in Amarillo on April 29, 1935, Eastus said. The prosecutor already had tried five cases under a new statute giving federal courts jurisdiction when a national bank or a bank of the Federal Reserve System was held up, long prison terms resulting in each instance.

Faced with almost certain death in the electric chair, Raymond said Friday night that he failed to shoot when accosted by officers because he still hoped for a break.

"I knew I didn't have a chance then, and I might have a chance some other time," he said as he answered countless questions in the county jail. "You can never tell what will happen."

The desperado revealed his true character as he faced a curious crowd. On his face was a sheepish grin, reminding onlookers of that of a truant schoolboy caught fishing. When people stepped forward to shake his hand, he proffered it eagerly. Assembled officers who had not been in at the capture, but who had known the desperado since he was a boy, clapped him on the back as he went through the crowd in custody of Sheriff Schmid. He replied to their pleasantries with a nod. Only when the two great affections of his life were mentioned did he become sullen.

"Yes, I love Katie Jenkins," he said. "I love her more than anyone else in the world except my mother."

Beyond this he would not comment except that he considered many plans for punishing those he felt were responsible for putting his mother in jail.

"I was almost crazy," he said. "I wanted to do something, but I didn't know what to do. I wanted to shoot somebody for the first time in my life.

"One thing about it," he added, "I may go to the electric chair, but I'll sure go to heaven, because I've never killed anybody.

"They told me Katie paced her cell while she was in the Dallas city jail every time she heard an extra on the streets, and I knew she was thinking of me and that she loved me. I have never ceased to love her for that. She will be loyal to the last."

Katie Jenkins was in San Diego, California, where she had gone the week before with her sister, Gladys, by bus in an effort to find work and start a new life after her association with Hamilton. The other woman in Hamilton's life, Mary O'Dare, was serving a year and a day sentence in the federal penitentiary.

Hamilton said it was true that he had kidnapped a reporter in Houston and that the story published by the newspaperman was true to the last detail.

"I wanted the public to know my part of it," he said.

He denied ever having been in Mississippi and any complicity in the Prentiss bank robbery.

"Nothing to say," he replied when asked about the affair.

Hamilton admitted he did not escape from the many traps laid for him by superhuman craftiness or extreme bravery. He explained:

> I never knew where the officers would be nor when they would start shooting at me. I never would have been there if I had known.
>
> I just always tried to be as ready as I could to move faster than they could. After all, you know an automobile can cover a lot of ground.
>
> Everytime anything would happen I would just shoot at the men who bobbed up and started shooting at me, or I would run for it. Sure, I was scared, and I probably showed it by running every chance I had.
>
> You know when a man is sure he is going to be sent to the hot

spot if he's caught there is nothing much else to do when the fire-
works start.

When they jumped me in Dallas I had no idea they were
there, but I started shooting and the policemen who came out of
the house ran back in or somewhere. I didn't see exactly where.

It was the same way at McKinney. The officers jumped up
and started shooting and I drove on as fast as I could and Ralph
started shooting out the back window and they all dropped down.

Asked how he felt to be hunted from morning to night every
day, he said:

Well, you can get used to anything after a while. I knew I was
either going to get mine or get caught before it was over and that it
was just a question of time. I couldn't stay by myself all of the
time and I felt like it was safer to have someone around. That's
what got me in bad so many times.

He said he thought at least ninety percent of peace officers were
stupid and that he would be a better officer than most of them. "I
guess that's what made me a little too cocky," he said.

Then: "No, I'm not ready to die. Who is? I've been in tight
spots before and I've gotten out of them. This is the tightest one. I'll
admit that, but, oh well, who knows?"

More than 500 curiosity seekers milled about the Dallas County
courthouse in hopes of getting a glimpse of Hamilton. Some of the
visitors lingered until midnight. Parents brought their babes in arms
and youngsters sucking lollipops rubbed elbows with women in formal dress and men in overalls.

With the capture of Raymond Hamilton, Sheriff Smoot Schmid
revealed that Gilbert Sanderson, twenty-three, who earlier had
attacked Assistant County Jailer Dick Warren, forty, in an attempted
jail delivery, was being held as an accomplice of Hamilton in the robbery of the Texas National Guard Armory at Beaumont. Sanderson,
who also was accused of taking part in the shotgun robbery of the
Mayfair Parking Station, was arrested a few days after the armory
robbery. In a lengthy written statement to Sheriff Schmid, Sanderson
admitted he had been much in the company of Raymond Hamilton
and was said to have named the woman who was with them at the
time of the armory robbery. The woman was reported to be under
arrest at the time. Another man, alleged to have been associated with
Hamilton during his days in hiding, whose identity was not disclosed,
also was being held. Several people faced arrest on charges of harbor-

ing a federal fugitive as a result of information obtained from the
two men, Sheriff Schmid said.

The grisly tale of Raymond burying a dead partner in crime
"where his body could not be found" was recited April 5 in the Dallas County jail by Nolan Alred.

"He told me this afternoon," said Alred, "that after a bank robbery last week the guy that was with him died of wounds. Just before
he knocked off he said 'Plant me where nobody'll find.' Hamilton
said he did."

The youth, who could neither read nor write, said Hamilton
told him of the incident in Fort Worth Friday afternoon just before
he started to Dallas with the note which proved the desperado's
undoing. Officers who brought Alred back from the scene of
Hamilton's capture said that he gave the name of Ralph Fults as the
man. Questioned, Hamilton bitterly denied the tale.

"Don't say nothin' about that please," he said. "Ralph is just as
alive as I am."

But Alred stuck to his story. He said Hamilton told it to him in
an effort to intimidate him just to be sure that Alred would not cause
suspicions that his traveling companion was a famous outlaw. Alred
said he met Hamilton in Memphis Sunday, March 31, in a railroad
yard. The ace bandit was shabbily dressed, he said, and asked him
what time the Rock Island freight left for the west. Alred told him it
left at 4:00 P.M., and Hamilton said, "How about us catching it?"
Alred said it was all right with him. He described what followed:

> We rode the freight to Haiti, Missouri. When we got there
> this guy flashed some money, a lot of money and said, "Let's go to
> St. Louis."
>
> I didn't know who he was then. I never did know who he was
> until this afternoon when he told me about buryin' that other guy
> in Mississippi, or wherever it was. Then I began to get suspicious,
> but I wasn't goin' to say anything, 'cause I was afraid he would
> slug me.
>
> Anyway, at Haiti he flashed all this money and said: "What
> about goin' to St. Louis?" and I said, "All right." So he bought us
> some tickets on a train and we rode over in style.
>
> When we got there he bought himself a new suit and a new
> hat and some new underclothes and socks. He bought me a few
> things, too, so I thought he was a great guy and didn't think
> nothin' else.
>
> We had plenty of money to spend and we fiddled around and
> went to a moving picture show and had a good time.
>
> Then he decided he wanted to go to Tulsa, so he bought us

some more tickets on a train and we came down there. That was Tuesday, April 2.

Then he said: "Let's go to Bristow and get a car," and we did. From there we drove to Oklahoma City and stayed around awhile, him spendin' his money all of the time, and then went to Eldorado.

We left the car there and took a train into Fort Worth. We got there at ten o'clock Thursday morning.

We didn't do anything yesterday, just sat around, and then he told me to take a note over to Dallas. I came over here on the bus and got a taxicab and delivered the note and took an answer back to him. Then he wanted me to take another note back and I didn't want to and that is when he told me about burying his pal over in Mississippi.

I took the bus again and came over here and was in a cab takin' the note out to deliver it when the officers stopped me.

I was scared to say anything at first, but when they told me they would protect me and wouldn't let anything happen to me, I told them what I thought. They said the note was signed by Hamilton but was not in his handwriting. I guess this other guy, the one that was with Hamilton when the officers got there, must have written it. We met him in Fort Worth.

I couldn't read the note because I can't read, so I didn't know what was in it, and still don't.

While Raymond was still in Dallas, his mother was allowed to visit him. He kissed the tears from her cheeks as they embraced and assured her everything would be all right.

To most Texans Ray Hamilton may have been just a small-time punk gone slightly tough, but to New Yorkers he was an important character. Some forty-five minutes after his capture, a call came to dispatcher W. S. Brogdon at Dallas Police headquarters from a New York newspaper. Unable to give them full details, Brogdon referred them to Sheriff Smoot Schmid.

With Hamilton near the obvious end of his criminal trail, the United States government on April 6, 1935, moved to punish those who had aided and harbored the outlaw during his nine-month flight from the law. Local federal officials and Sheriff Schmid had information on many who had aided Hamilton.

"Nearly forty persons will be indicted on charges of conspiring to harbor and conceal Hamilton," U.S. Attorney Clyde O. Eastus said at Fort Worth.

Speedy eradication of the social misfit loomed as law enforcement officials, "incensed" at his depredations, sought rapid delivery of the death sentence he had evaded.

"We will have Hamilton sentenced by Judge S. W. Dean of the Twelfth District Court at Huntsville early next week," said Max Rogers, Walker County district attorney, in Dallas on April 6, before he left with the armed party which returned the bandit to the penitentiary. Rogers pointed out the only legal action needed to start the desperado on the way to his last walk was formal sentencing by Judge Dean.

"This will be done early next week. I don't know the exact day yet. Thirty days after he is sentenced the execution may be carried out," Rogers said.

While a huge crowd milled about the front of the Dallas County jail, a heavily armed party slipped Hamilton out through a rear alley, handcuffed him to the inside of an automobile, and sped away. In the escorting party, which made the trip in three automobiles, were Ted Hinton, Ed Caster, and Bryan Peck, who were with Sheriff Schmid and Chief Deputy Bill Decker when Raymond was captured; Lee Simmons; Warden W. W. Waid; Rogers; T. T. Easley, night prison warden; and Texas Rangers Fred McDaniel and W. H. Kirby. Raymond rode in the middle car.

The bank robber's bravado seemed to desert him as he was led through the gates of the eighty-year-old penitentiary. He was quickly dressed and placed on death row. There he met Joe Palmer. The sight of Palmer perked Raymond up somewhat.

"Well, Joe, you're looking good," Hamilton grinned.

"Why shouldn't I?" Palmer answered. "There's nothing to do here but lie around, nothing to worry about, and lots of Negroes to wait on you."

Palmer's carefree air was shattered a few hours later when he was taken to Anderson, Grimes County, to hear Judge Dean formally sentence him to die May 10, 1935.

When Hamilton resumed his clanking march he came to the cell of Charlie Frazier. Raymond nodded to Frazier.

"Know him?" Simmons asked Frazier.

"No," Frazier replied, "just saw him a couple of times in the pen yard."

Hamilton's first prison act was to take a bath. It was taken in a tub in which doomed felons were prepared for the electric chair.

Raymond's attempts at bravado were evidently forced. Most of the time he seemed sober and downcast, with the realization that Manager Simmons meant business when he remarked, "You won't get away from us again."

Joe Palmer made an impassioned plea for mercy for Raymond

Hamilton and loosed a tirade against District Attorney Max Rogers before he was sentenced April 6, 1935, to be electrocuted May 10, 1935, for the murder of Major Crowson. Palmer said he and not Hamilton was guilty of the slaying of the guard. He said Rogers obtained conviction of Hamilton on perjured testimony.

"Fate will overtake you sometime for the injustice you have done in these cases," Palmer told the prosecutor.

The desperado began his harangue after Judge Dean asked if he had anything to say about why sentence should not be passed. Palmer asked that if Hamilton's sentence was not commuted they be electrocuted on the same night. Hamilton was to be sentenced Monday or Tuesday at Huntsville, and the indications were that his death date would be fixed May 10 or soon afterward. After Palmer had finished, Judge Dean lectured him.

"Joe," the court said, "you've had a fair trial. The jury didn't know you. You were properly represented by your lawyers.

"It is not up to you to say whether Hamilton is guilty or not guilty. It doesn't matter which one of you killed Major Crowson. You were both shooting at him and therefore were equally guilty."

Governor James V. Allred on April 6 said he wanted each officer who figured in the capture of Raymond Hamilton to write about the part he played in the capture so that the governor could determine who should receive the $500 reward.

As Raymond was lodged in the death cell at Huntsville, a Dallas psychiatrist reviewed the emotional disturbances and social mal-adjustments which had brought the youthful bank robber to his sorry pass, and voiced a warning that "all children are potential Raymond Hamiltons." For professional reasons the psychiatrist asked that his name not be revealed. His warning was specific:

> This man who now faces death is distinguishable from a huge mass of delinquents only by the degree to which he has gone and the publicity which he has received.
>
> In his effort to overcome a feeling of inferiority, probably generated by his physical smallness he has overcompensated, he has tried to make himself the most feared man in the Southwest.
>
> That is illustrated by two things. The first is that he has steadfastly maintained a spirit of braggadochio. The second is that he has continuously, in the face of tremendous odds, and showing lack of judgement, come back to the vicinity of Dallas where he could strut in front of those who knew of his supposed prowess, and who gave him a type of hero worship.
>
> He is typical of the overcompensation cases, too, because his

efforts have been more childish than adult. He has never shown the calm, scheming brain of the really clever criminal. He has simply blundered his way through his various engagements, employing the most simple means of attack and defense.

He was lonely only in the way that his extreme egocentricity demanded adulation. That is why he was never by himself. He always had a companion, and the more stupid the companion the better he liked it.

I say all children are potential Raymond Hamiltons. That is true. Every child, no matter how well balanced, if subject to certain exterior influences will become distinctly unsocial.

Most common are those incidents of a broken or unhappy home and the location of a normal house in a delinquency area. The broken home does not necessarily mean a divorced mother and father. Sometimes the mother is at work, the home is in charge of an outside individual with whom the child can not get along.

Another very common exterior cause of delinquency is maladjustment at school. Beware of having a child in an improper grade, either too high or too low. Others are inadequate recreational facilities, delinquency or social maladjustment of other members of the family or close friends, and general moral trends of associates.

Those are exterior influences on the normal child which in many cases make them delinquent. Not mentally defective but unable to accustom themselves with the laws of their communities.

In normal homes there are many delinquent children and the great majority show early symptoms which, with proper treatment, may be eradicated.

Watch the child who habitually does not conform to parental discipline and shows a definite desire to associate with persons known to be undesirable.

Be careful of irregular hours, for it is one of the early symptoms. Truancy from school and school failure should not be passed off with the remark that "boys will be boys."

If a child has no definite fixation of intent, no consecutiveness of goal, no apparent series of actions which lead toward a given point, that child probably needs attention. For it shows a poorly organized personality, a poorly integrated make-up, which is apt to allow itself to slip from a definite resentment of authority to worse and worse things until it finally becomes involved in the web of events which lead to death at the hands of society.

An interesting legal question still intervened to postpone Hamilton's execution in Texas. This was the determination of the constitutionality of Texas' law affecting escape, pending appeal. The Texas statutes provided that where a convicted person who had appealed his case escaped from and remained without the custody of the law for a period longer than thirty days, the appeal could not be prosecuted. Hamilton became the first death-house escapee denied the ordinary course of appeal and would almost certainly become a test case. The constitutional point on which the state defended its statute was that the defendant was denied no legal right that he had not willfully discarded without coercion from court or people. Had he been unlawfully convicted, the courts were open to him for remedy. By failure to appear on his own appeal, he had withdrawn it. There was nothing illogical in the law, which provided an automatic penalty for the man who climaxed habitual defiance of it by escape.

CHAPTER XVIII

A Date With Ol' Sparky

Raymond Hamilton, standing before District Judge S. W. Dean on Monday, April 8, in Huntsville, was sentenced to die in the electric chair in the early hours of May 10, 1935, for the slaying of Major Crowson. The district courtroom was crowded at 3:00 P.M. when Hamilton was taken to court to receive his sentence. Judge Dean first took cognizance of a story published that morning in a Houston paper which said Hamilton had been convicted of being an accomplice in the killing of the prison guard at the Eastham farm at the time Raymond and Palmer escaped. This story also said Hamilton was not technically guilty.

"I do not know which one of the escaping prisoners shot Major Crowson," Judge Dean said. "Palmer and Hamilton were both shooting, and one is as guilty as the other."

Judge Dean then informed the defendant that he must die in the electric chair in the early morning hours of May 10 and asked him if he had anything to say. Hamilton addressed the court at some length.

"I first want to say, Judge, that I did not kill Major Crowson," he said. "I have never killed anyone. I have had plenty of opportunities to kill people but I would not do it and I would not let others do it if I could help it. Some people might be able to get a fair trial in your court in Huntsville, but I don't think I could or that I did.

"The District Attorney, Max Rogers, the prison system manager, Lee Simmons, and the court stenographer, P. H. Singletary, had made up their minds that it would be a feather in their caps to give

208

me the death penalty in that trial and they were determined to do it at all odds. I was convicted on perjured testimony. Well, if they can now get any pleasure out of this they are welcome to it. I want to say, too, that I am the only convict who was ever given the death penalty for killing a prison guard."

When told that the date set for his execution was the same as that set previously for the electrocution of Joe Palmer, Hamilton expressed gratitude. He concluded his statement to the court by saying that if he had to die he could die like a man and that he was not afraid.

Neither Nolan Alred or Glen Allen were to be charged, Sheriff Smoot Schmid said on April 8. Both were soon to be released, he said. Sheriff Schmid's deputies, who knew Hamilton's West Dallas pals and haunts like a book, had information in their possession showing that a number of persons aided the outlaw in his long flight from the law.

State Senator Tarver McIntosh of Collins, Mississippi, broke a return trip from West Texas on April 9 to congratulate Sheriff Schmid upon his capture of Raymond Hamilton and to tell him how big Hamilton's guns looked when he disarmed a Mississippi posse after the Prentiss robbery. Senator McIntosh was a member of the posse so disarmed, having joined in the hunt just to be able to tell his fellow legislators how it felt to be on the firing line. He said that, at almost any time during the proceedings, possemen could have killed Hamilton and his companion, Ralph Fults, but that it would have meant taking innocent lives. The Texas bandit, he said, was cool throughout the entire affair and impressed the trapped men as being deadly and determined. Fults was wounded, but not at all seriously, and McIntosh doubted the report of the desperado's subsequent death. Schmid, he added, could have a sheriffship in Mississippi anytime he wanted it.

Ralph Fults paid an informal visit to his hometown of McKinney Tuesday night, and shortly thereafter all surrounding roads were bustling with firearms as officers scurried out from all sides in search of him. Fults was traveling in a khaki-topped roadster of popular make, officers said, and was accompanied by a man and perhaps two women. The fugitive was sighted as he drove through the town, and officers immediately started in pursuit. He left McKinney in the direction of Dallas, but may have changed his course shortly as he quickly outdistanced pursuers. His visit to McKinney was verified by relatives, who said he had paid them a visit.

Early Wednesday, April 10, officers were centering their search in the vicinity of Weston, northwest of McKinney, where it was thought he might try to visit some of his relatives. His flight from McKinney was immediately telephoned to Dallas and the description was broadcast. Several squads of city and county officers patrolled roads north of Dallas, some officers carrying the search to Lake Dallas in Denton County, which country was said to be well known to the fugitive.

Fults had separated from Hamilton at Memphis, according to reports reaching Dallas investigators. They were wondering what caused the separation. Senator McIntosh said Fults kept a rifle pointed at the posse of twenty men while Hamilton took their guns from them.

In a letter received April 10, Sheriff C. G. Maxwell of Atoka, Oklahoma, asked Sheriff Schmid for aid in his efforts to witness the execution of Raymond Hamilton on May 10.

"You will recall," wrote Sheriff Maxwell, "that I was crippled and my undersheriff was killed by Clyde Barrow and Raymond Hamilton in a battle August 5, 1932."

This sentence was pointed out by Sheriff Schmid as one of several contradictions he had encountered to the claims of Hamilton that he had never killed anyone. Prison Manager Lee Simmons said so many officers who had brushes with Hamilton had asked for the privilege of seeing him die that it might be necessary to allow only prison officials to witness the electrocution.

After a day of headlong flight during which he overturned and lost one automobile, kidnapped a farm youth, and stole a new car in which he dodged through a small army of heavily armed officers, Fults, known to Texas officers as the number-one chump of the Southwest, remained uncaught Friday night, April 12. The title of number-one chump was fastened on Fults when, with one of ex-Governor Miriam A. Ferguson's conditional pardons in his pocket, he joined forces with Raymond Hamilton. The latest pursuit of Fults began early Friday morning, when Collin County officers sighted him near McKinney and gave chase. He outdistanced them, but overturned his car by driving too fast. The officers reached the wrecked machine in time to see him disappearing over a hill at the far side of a pasture. In the car they found ammunition and two suitcases in which were clothes with the initials "R. F." sewn on several garments.

He next appeared on foot at the home of Vick Howell, ten miles west of McKinney, where he gave a fictitious name and said he was trying to return to his home after being released by kidnappers. He induced Howell's son, Cecil Howell, twenty-three, to drive him to Dallas. After getting away from the farm he revealed his identity, took the youth captive, and forced him to drive to Renner. There he saw a new car in Dr. O. T. Mitchell's yard and forced young Howell to go and see if the ignition keys were in it. Finding they were, Fults took Dr. Mitchell's car and drove off, leaving young Howell.

Fults related a long story to young Howell of his escapades with Raymond Hamilton, the youth said. He told of his taking part in the bank robbery at Prentiss and of escaping the barrage of rifle fire in the McKinney ambuscade. He told young Howell that he faced a death penalty for the Mississippi bank robbery and declared that he would not be taken alive. According to his story to Howell, Fults did not know what caused Hamilton to leave him on their safe arrival in Memphis. He said he bought two railroad tickets, but that Hamilton failed to meet him. He said he was low in funds, but that money meant nothing to him.

Sheriff Schmid led five deputies from Dallas to join in the chase, when McKinney officers telephoned him shortly after Fults was jumped.

Another effort to capture Ralph Fults went awry Saturday night. Sheriff Schmid and Texas Ranger Sgt. Sid Kelso led the search but declined to say where they went. It was generally believed they went to search hideouts in the vicinity of Lake Dallas.

Application for the $500 the State of Texas offered for the capture of Raymond Hamilton was filed Saturday, April 13, with Governor Allred by Nolan Alred. His telegram read: "I respectfully claim the reward for furnishing information leading to the apprehension and arrest of Raymond Hamilton."

After sawing their way through three steel barriers, three prisoners in the Dallas County jail (one an alleged pal and another an alleged enemy of Raymond Hamilton — and all regarded by peace officers as desperate criminals), escaped from the sixth floor of the jail building shortly after 3:00 A.M. Sunday, April 14. Escaping were John P. Bratcher, twenty-eight, held by federal authorities for participation in the Carthage bank robbery; Olen Ray Tyler, twenty-six, convicted in Freestone County on a murder charge, held for failure to make appeal bond, said to have been at one time gunning for Hamilton in a quarrel over the affections of Katie Jenkins; and Tommie English Bryant, twenty-four, recently given twenty-five years for robbery of the City Milk Company in January, and who threatened to blow up officers with nitroglycerine when arrested at a Fairmount address.

Ralph Fults was captured by Denton County officers Wednesday morning, April 17, and was held overnight in the Dallas County jail Wednesday on the way to Huntsville. Fults was brought to the Dallas jail at midnight by Rangers Sid Kelso and Fred McDaniel, where they planned to question him further before taking him to Huntsville. Misdeeds of former years caused Fults to become the unwilling accomplice of Hamilton, he said after his arrival in Dallas.

"Hamilton found out I was out of the pen," said Fults, "and he looked me up. I knew him while I was down there, you know. I went out with him intending to just go for a short ride. I told him I couldn't help him because I was cool. I told him that if I was hot I wouldn't mind. Then we drove into that ambush close to McKinney and had to do some shooting. I figured I was in for it then and had just as well stay with him. Hamilton is a fine kid." Their separation in Memphis was accidental, he declared.

District Attorney Max Rogers, reviewing the case of Raymond Hamilton, told the Texas Board of Pardons and Paroles that no reason could be shown why the death verdict against Hamilton should be set aside. The case review, sent to the board April 25, 1935, was made public the next day at Huntsville. Rogers cited that Hamilton was convicted under the law of principals and that neither he nor Joe Palmer would take the stand in their own defense. These points were stressed to refute Hamilton's claim that he had never killed anyone and that he was convicted on perjured evidence.

"It was the state's theory," Rogers said, "that Major Crowson, the slain guard, was killed in the furtherance of a conspiracy organized by Hamilton and made possible by his relatives, Floyd Hamilton and Lillie McBride, and his friends and former associates, Clyde Barrow and Bonnie Parker, the conspiracy being to assault their guards and effect an escape from the Eastham prison farm, and, in carrying out the common design, that both Hamilton and Palmer were armed and shooting and that each shot at Crowson, and, under the law of principals, it was immaterial which actually fired the shot that killed Crowson. The conspiracy was originated wholly by Hamilton and not Palmer."

Regarding Hamilton's claim that he had never killed anyone, Rogers said: "Twenty-four citizens of Texas, twelve at Hillsboro and twelve at Huntsville, by their verdicts as jurors, have said that he has been proved a murderer beyond a reasonable doubt. To impeach their verdicts, under the most solemn oath known to man, stands alone the unsworn statement of a convicted robber and thief and a proven gangster and murderer."

The Board of Pardons and Paroles in Austin on April 29 reported adversely to Governor Allred the applications of Raymond Hamilton and Joe Palmer for commutation of their death sentences to life imprisonment. The governor said that before he acted on the report he would give it and the records in the Hamilton and Palmer cases careful study. The board recommended that "all applications for clemency in any shape or form in behalf of Hamilton and Palmer be denied." The report, signed by all three members, continued:

> Many citizens have written us in behalf of Raymond Hamilton because of his youth, but a youth who can terrorize the citizens throughout Texas and nearby states, rob banks with firearms and rob and kidnap citizens certainly is old enough to be restrained and to be given the same punishment that should be administered to a well-matured man.
>
> While we have a deep feeling of sorrow for the mother of Ray Hamilton and the other near relatives of both parties, yet we also have a deep feeling of sorrow for the mother of Major Crowson who, while in the morning of his life and obeying the laws of his country and offering his body as a bulwark to protect the law-abiding citizens against those hijackers, was murdered in cold blood by the guns that Raymond Hamilton had smuggled into the penitentiary and used by him and Joe Palmer in effecting their escape.
>
> In view of the fact that both Hamilton and Palmer are shown by the records to be the very worst class of criminals in the penitentiary and that the evidence shows beyond a reasonable doubt that both were guilty in the killing of Major Crowson, we do not believe it best for society that their sentences be commuted to life terms in the penitentiary because their criminal record shows that no sooner would a commutation be granted than they would at once begin to study some kind of a scheme and some kind of a conspiracy to set themselves free regardless of how many men they killed in doing so.
>
> Since the evidence in the case amply justified the highest penalty known to the law and since the claims that Ray Hamilton fired only one shot, which killed no one, is not borne out by a scintilla of evidence, but he is shown beyond a reasonable doubt to have been guilty of firing several shots at Crowson and since there is not a single extenuating circumstance in behalf of either Joe Palmer or Raymond Hamilton, we recommend that all applications for clemency in any shape or form in their behalf be denied.

Raymond's mother spent fifteen minutes with the condemned desperado in his death cell at the state penitentiary Tuesday, April 30. She came to Huntsville from Austin with the Rev. Eddie Clayton, Dallas minister, after she had pleaded in Austin with Governor Allred to spare Hamilton's life.

"I don't remember all that Ray had to say," she said after the visit. "He said he was feeling fine and that he still had hopes of escaping the chair."

Mrs. Davis was admitted to the death cell as Raymond was preparing to eat his evening meal.

Judge O. S. Lattimore said Monday, May 6, in Austin that the Court of Criminal Appeals had refused to admit a petition for a writ of habeas corpus for Raymond Hamilton. Judge Lattimore said he and Judge F. L. Hawkins refused to admit a petition presented the week before by a man giving the name of Taylor. He said the petition, in which the principal allegation was that Hamilton did not have a fair trial, did not justify a writ.

Alice Hamilton Davis continued her fight Wednesday, May 8, to save her son from the electric chair. She appeared at state prison with an application for a writ of habeas corpus, which was signed by Hamilton in his death cell.

The writ, directed to the Court of Criminal Appeals in Austin, apparently dealt with reversible errors in his Walker County trial for the slaying of Crowson. Mrs. Davis, accompanied by Katie Jenkins, was admitted to Raymond's cell after a half-hour wait. The women left for Dallas after the visit, and Mrs. Davis said she was taking the application for the approval of attorney Albert Baskett. It was to be filed at Austin Thursday, May 9.

CHAPTER XIX

The Final Walk

On Friday, May 10, 1935, Raymond Hamilton was placed in the electric chair at 12:19 A.M. He followed Joe Palmer by only a few minutes. Palmer had been placed in the chair at 12:04 A.M. and pronounced dead at 12:08 A.M. Hamilton's face was ashen as he walked the few steps to the chair from the floor of the death cell, but his step was comparatively firm. He was accompanied by three Catholic priests.

"Do you have anything to say?" Warden W. W. Waid asked.

"I got the information — I think it was from the secretary to the governor — that they wanted me to confess that Hillsboro murder," Raymond said. "I didn't commit that murder. The man that did it is dead. If he wasn't, I wouldn't say anything, anyway."

As he was strapped into the chair, he turned to Father Hugh Finnegan, Catholic chaplain of the prison who was leaving in two weeks for a trip to Ireland. Hamilton said, "I hope you have a nice trip, Father."

Just before the current was applied, Raymond turned momentarily to the assembled witnesses and said, "Well, goodbye all."

Epilogue

The electrocution was witnessed by several peace officers, including Sheriff Smoot Schmid of Dallas and Sheriff C. G. Maxwell of Atoka, Oklahoma. Also present were newspapermen, the official witnesses, several legislators headed by Speaker Coke Stevenson of the House of Representatives, and Pat Moreland, secretary to Governor Allred. Hamilton's body was sent to Dallas, where his mother had arranged for burial. Palmer's body was sent to San Antonio on funds furnished by fellow convicts.

Private funeral services for Raymond Elzie Hamilton were held in the McKamy-Campbell Funeral Chapel at 3:00 P.M. Saturday, May 11, 1935. Burial was in Elmwood Memorial Park on Scyene Road. Songs played during the services were "Shall We Gather at the River," "Life Is Only a Dream," and "Beautiful Isle of Somewhere."

Bibliography

Books

Crimes and Punishment. BPC Publishing Ltd., 1974.

Gordon, Frost H. *I'm Frank Hamer.* Pemberton Press, 1968.

Hamilton, Floyd. *Public Enemy Number 1.* Dallas: Acclaimed Books, 1978.

Hinton, Ted, and Larry Grove. *Ambush.* Austin: Shoal Creek Publishers, 1979.

Hoekstra, Ray. *God's Prison Gang.* Dallas: Fleming H. Revell Company, 1977.

Maddox, Web. *Black Sheep.* Austin: Nortex Press, 1975.

Parker, Emma, and Nell Barrow Cowan. *The True Story of Bonnie and Clyde.* New York: Signet Books, 1968.

Simmons, Lee. *Assignment Huntsville.*

Magazines

Biffle, Kent. "The Men Behind the Star." *Dallas Life Magazine*, August 28, 1983.

Chambers, Jim. "Scoop!" *D Magazine*, April 1983.

Crumbaker, Marge. "How Crime Pays." *Tempo Magazine*, January 19, 1969.

Maguire, Jack. "The Real Bonnie and Clyde." *Southwest Airlines Magazine*, May 1979.

Phillips, John Neal, and Ralph Fults. "Partners in Crime." *Dallas Life Magazine*, June 10, 1984.

Articles

"Help for the Cons — A Texas in Profile." Associated Press: April 18, 1966.

"Lancaster: A History, 1845–1945." Lancaster Historical Society.

Newspapers

The Dallas Morning News (January 1, 1931–May 11, 1935)
Hillsboro Mirror
The Leader–Courier (November 26, 1981)
The New York Times (July 23, 1934)
Prentiss Headlight (April 4, 1935)

Interviews

Alspaugh, Othen, Florence Hill, friend of Raymond Hamilton's step-relatives.

Alspaugh, Weldon, Florence Hill, friend of Raymond Hamilton's step-relatives.

Brewster, Harold, Stringtown, Oklahoma, resident during the Stringtown shootout.

Cannady, Turk, Cedar Hill, resident during the two Cedar Hill robberies.

Crawford, Maude, Grand Prairie, bookkeeper of the Grand Prairie State Bank during the robbery.

Fouts, Roy, Cedar Hill, employee of Strauss Brothers Store when Raymond Hamilton came in before robbing the Cedar Hill bank.

Goldman, Alta, Florence Hill, Raymond Hamilton's step-aunt.

Goldman, Roxie, Florence Hill, Raymond Hamilton's step-aunt.

Goldman, Stanley, Florence Hill, Raymond Hamilton's step-cousin.

Goldman, Weldon (Can), Florence Hill, Raymond Hamilton's step-cousin.

Hamilton, Floyd, West Dallas, Raymond Hamilton's brother.

Hamilton, Mildred, West Dallas, Raymond Hamilton's sister-in-law.

Holveck, Charlie, Florence Hill, resident of southwest Dallas County during Raymond Hamilton's crime career.

Holveck, R. C., Florence Hill, schoolmate of Raymond Hamilton.

Hood, Shorty, Cedar Hill, resident and eyewitness during one of the Cedar Hill robberies.

Hughes, Essie, Stringtown, Oklahoma, resident during the Stringtown shootout.

Hyder, Tom Bullock, Lewisville, state representative and pursuer of Raymond Hamilton following the Lewisville robbery.

Jones, Penn, Midlothian, newspaperman and authority on southwest Dallas County and Ellis County history.

McGlothlin, Ray, Dallas, eyewitness to the Continental Oil Company robbery.

McManus, Jerry, Dallas, psychiatrist who offered insight into Raymond Hamilton's criminal behavior.

Shellito, Jake, Florence Hill, neighbor and friend of Raymond Hamilton's step-relatives.

Sidell, Mildred, Florence Hill, Raymond Hamilton's step-cousin.

Rev. L. B. (Pete) Trone, Cedar Hill, in bank during the second Cedar Hill robbery.

Vincent, Garland, Cedar Hill, longtime postmaster and resident during the Cedar Hill robberies.

Wolfskill, Dr. George, Arlington, professor of history at the University of Texas at Arlington.

Correspondence and/or records were received from the Bay City, Michigan, Police Department, Collin County, Dallas County, Ellis County, Fayette County, Federal Bureau of Investigation, Grayson County, Hill County, Kaufman County, McLennan County, State of Michigan, Tarrant County, State of Texas, Texas Department of Corrections, Texas Department of Public Safety, and Wharton County.

DESPERADO ARSENAL — *The weaponry and other material shown were taken from Raymond Hamilton's car following his capture at Howe, Texas, following the Lewisville, Texas, bank robbery April 25, 1934. According to firearms experts Rick Cartledge and Tom Swearengen, Hamilton's cache included (from left) a Remington Model 31 riot gun, a sawed-off Browning 12-gauge automatic shotgun with homemade shoulder strap, internal parts from a cut down Browning, two Winchester auto-loader rifles, and a factory Winchester Model 1897 riot gun. Other items in the photo include gas grenades, stolen license tags, ammunition boxes and ammunition, an iron, and a field surgery kit.* — Photo courtesy Dallas Public Library

Index

221

www.ingramcontent.com/pod-product-compliance
Lightning Source LLC
Chambersburg PA
CBHW061253110426
42742CB00012BA/1906